ACCESS
THROUGH
INNOVATION

ACCESS THROUGH INNOVATION

New Colleges for New Students

James W. Hall

nucea

National University Continuing Education Association

American Council on Education   **DXI**   Macmillan Publishing Company

NEW YORK

Collier Macmillan Canada

TORONTO

Maxwell Macmillan International

NEW YORK   OXFORD   SINGAPORE   SYDNEY

Macmillan Publishing Company
866 Third Avenue, New York, N.Y. 10022

Collier Macmillan Canada, Inc.
1200 Eglinton Avenue East, Suite 200
Don Mills, Ontario, M3C 3N1

Library of Congress Catalog Card Number: 90–42638

Printed in the United States of America

printing number
1 2 3 4 5 6 7 8 9 10

Library of Congress Cataloging-in-Publication Data

Hall, James W.
   Access through innovation : new colleges for new students / James
W. Hall.
      p. cm. — (American Council on Education/Macmillan series in
higher education)
   Includes bibliographical references and index.
   ISBN 0-02-897177-9
   1. Educational innovations—United States. 2. Education, Higher—
United States. I. National University Continuing Education
Association (U.S.) II. American Council on Education.   III. Title.
IV. Series.
LB1027.3.H35   1991
378.73—dc20   90–42638
                                                          CIP

*This volume is dedicated
to all those men and women
who have pushed open
the doors to educational opportunity.*

Contents

Foreword

Ours has been called the "knowledge society," and rightfully so. Today, knowledge is a key tool for the vast majority of Americans—especially those in service-related employment, including education, government, health, recreation, finance, and communication. Manufacturing has acquiesced to service, ushering in a post-industrial era where work is increasingly the product of brainpower rather than muscle or machine.

Consequently, ongoing higher education has become more critical than ever, not only in maintaining and improving our lives here at home, but in competing effectively in an expanding global market. Where in the past we focused our educational efforts almost exclusively on the young, we have now widened our embrace to include the growing number of men and women who are middle-aged and elderly.

We must make higher education accessible to *everyone who needs it*— from the high school graduate to the senior citizen, and, of course, with no barriers founded on race, religion, or creed.

As we approach the century's end, the U.S. population as a whole is aging—while the growth of the work force is slowing. What the trends will mean for our young people a decade from now is a dual responsibility: generating productivity and supporting an aging population. What that will mean for our older people, in many cases, will be the challenge of prolonging careers and continuing to participate actively in the work force past the time we have long identified with the beginning of retirement. The challenge it will present to us as a society is clear: to provide Americans with ongoing training and continuous education.

Lifelong education, then, is certainly one of the most critical areas of higher education in the United States today. If higher education is to remain true to its original charge, then we must address ourselves to the needs and aspirations of certain groups—groups I would call the "educationally neglected." Who are these people? Who are the groups not being served as effectively as possible by our overall system of higher education? Let's look at just a few.

First, there are still many homemakers and mothers, who, in addition to carrying out their traditional responsibilities, wish to return to the job market or to participate more fully in society. To accomplish these goals requires career updating as well as additional general education.

Certainly, higher education has acknowledged the special needs of women—special because of their many roles in our society—both in intellectual development and personal self-fulfillment. But many young women still receive partial or full college educations and are never given an opportunity to realize their potential.

Then there is the mid-career worker on the assembly line in Detroit or Buffalo who has gradually become aware that life is more than a turn of the wrench, over and over, day after day. Or he suddenly finds that foreign competition or takeovers have led to a job loss and a new position requires a different level of educational attainment.

The problems of the uneducated or low-skilled in our society have been made more difficult by technological progress. The demand for unskilled labor, even for the manipulative and craft skills, is declining. The demand for service, technical, managerial, and professional ones are on the rise. Today, higher education often offers the most direct path to personal economic security and to social acceptance for the adult as well as the youth.

Society now places so great a premium on education and training that to be without current skills is to be excluded from many benefits and rewards. We cannot afford to treat any human being as if he or she were unneeded material to be casually discarded. We have been slow in responding to this particular challenge. The problem confronts us in all sectors of society, and nowhere is the challenge greater than in the central cities and in declining rural communities.

The third neglected group is the elderly. Examine the retiree's dilemma when he or she discovers that, because of medical breakthroughs and improved health care, he or she may have as much as twenty additional years of retirement. Yet, society often treats this person as wholly unproductive, banishing him or her to some retirement village in Arizona or Florida, to waste away what might be very useful years. Can we really afford to ignore this precious labor power resource? Here are human beings with energy, knowledge, wisdom, and—most importantly—time. With a minimum of retraining, they might make their retirement years more rewarding from their own perspective as well as society's. Does our system of higher education not have an important role to play in learning how to respond and develop the potential of these citizens as well?

The last of my "neglected" figures is the individual who seeks adaptability. Here is an opportunity for society to provide cultural and intellectual armor so that a person can withstand rapid change. In addition to the "retooling" and "catch-up" functions, there will be growing needs and demands by our citizens for assistance in coping with a world and society undergoing rapid and explosive changes. It is more than expanding and deepening personal pleasure, or providing the material ability to exist. It is a form of personal and psychological armament for enhancing survival as rational beings.

Adaptability embodies more than technical training. It recognizes a much broader range of needs—the need to learn about the whole human community: the people who inhabit it, the physical and social environments in which we dwell and work, the sciences, the humanities, the arts. And—perhaps most important—how people live with each other.

We live in a paradoxical world—growing in numbers, shrinking in space. We live in a world which is becoming increasingly interdependent. We live in a world where change is often so rapid and massive that the individual feels on the brink of psychological gridlock. Average citizens feel the all-pervasive pressures of the world around them, changing at an awesome pace. For them, additional, carefully developed and continuously updated education may be the key to coping with a dynamic world in flux.

My own interest in lifelong education dates back to the early 1970s, when I was president of Michigan State University. There I chaired an institution-wide Task Force on Lifelong Education—the findings of which were eventually incorporated in *Patterns in Lifelong Learning*, co-edited by Paul Miller, Father Theodore Hesburgh, and me. And during the course of that study, my colleagues and I encountered what was then one of the few institutions where lifelong education was a fundamental mission: Empire State College.

Created in 1971, Empire State College was one of the first "universities-without-walls"—a pioneer in decentralized, nonresidential, and often highly innovative higher education. Its programs offered educational access to students of all ages. Its classes ran not only during the day but also evenings and weekends to accommodate the schedules of working men and women. Its curriculum was highly individualized, responsive to the needs and circumstances of people from a wide range of backgrounds and with an even broader spectrum of interest, priorities, and ambitions.

A few years later I moved to the State University of New York system, of which Empire State College was a part. There I met Jim Hall, its president. And for a good part of the 10 years I spent as SUNY's chancellor, one of my recurrent pleasures was my association with what he, his fellow administrators, and Empire State College's faculty of "mentors" were accomplishing. Through creativity, dedication, and a firm belief in the value of what it was created to achieve, Empire State College has taken one giant step after another toward a truly pluralistic model of higher education. And through continuing innovation, Empire State College is still moving in the same direction.

I personally find encouragement in the pages of this book. Although he casts an unflinching and critical eye on both the past and the present systems in America, Jim Hall does not do so with defeatism or contempt. His is a spirit of learning from past mistakes, recognizing the strengths we have, and building upon them to create something new and vital. The future Jim Hall envisions is crowded with demanding challenges, but it is a future built on hope.

Read on: listen, absorb, think. Jim Hall's ideas can be the building blocks of change, if we have the energy and vision to put them into action.

CLIFTON R. WHARTON, JR.

Acknowledgments

This book rests upon the work of many who have gone before. But especially I want to acknowledge the colleagueship of John H. Jacobson, Loren Baritz, Arthur W. Chickering, and Morris T. Keeton, from whom I learned much. Without the work of David Riesman, Frederick Rudolf, Laurence Veysey, and Peter Drucker, the patterns of change and reform would have been less clearly understandable. I am indebted to Robert Hassenger, Lee Herman, Peter Princep, Daniel Granger, Henry Spille, Corinne Jacker, and Ann Weissman for many good suggestions. The Rockefeller Foundation and its Study Centre in Bellagio, Italy gave me the time, venue, and retreat essential to complete much of the first and most difficult draft. Milton R. Stern's keen reading and advice greatly sharpened the book and helped me to avoid many errors. Wilma B. Hall's perceptive questioning strengthened clarity and structure. I was assisted in preparation of the manuscript by Teri McCarthy and Susan Bayer. I am grateful to all for their generous and critical assistance.

JWH

Introduction

The United States is experiencing a sea change in the ways it conducts its national life. Assumptions about how business is run, how labor is defined, and how and to whom information is transmitted are being sharply challenged by changing circumstances. New technologies and intensified international competition using practices which challenge established American trading patterns are just two instances of such pressure for change. Rapidly changing demography, especially in the South, the West, and in the great cities, is another factor for change. In the face of such challenges, the basic assumptions and institutions which undergird American life have lost much of their capacity as guides and guarantors of national success.

In the past, at such times of rapid change, America has turned to higher education as a repository of wisdom to provide a locus for debate and a place where the nation, in its multiple dimensions, might examine logically and dispassionately its problems and opportunities. After World War I the nation turned to higher education for new ways of looking at world cultures. Following World War II the G.I. Bill and the community college offered solutions to new problems. Similarly the nation turned to the university for responses to Sputnik in the 1950s, and for approaches to equal opportunity in the 1960s.

But the university today, along with most of America's institutions, seems bent in upon itself, contemplating internal icons while neglecting the external values that our history verifies as important. Each new assault on the university turns the academic community ever more inward, away from reality, away from the future. Recently the voices for such reactionary withdrawal have been especially strident. They speak of a closed, rather than open, curriculum. They urge limits on the range and diversity of students who might gain access to higher learning. And they offer to shape all of these through assessment tools that would ensure greater compliance and uniformity. Although these voices propose to improve the "quality" of education, they do not speak out of the extraordinary and successful history of reform in the American college and university.

This is a book about innovation, invention. Its thesis is that, contrary to public perceptions about the university and internal attempts at separation and purification, higher education has, from its earliest days, repeatedly introduced far-reaching innovations, responsive to the economic, social, and political needs of an expanding nation. Access and extension—reaching

1

out to serve new populations—are in fact the most persistently accurate descriptors of American higher education.

The university, as an institution in the American pluralistic tradition, is immensely varied. From Yale to Bob Jones, Whatcom Community to Chico State, each bears its own history, carries its own problems, pursues its unique agenda, and is governed and led by its own board and administration. As a consequence, the university follows a broken trail in the manner and swiftness with which it responds to national need. Nonetheless, at important junctures in the past, higher education has ultimately responded vigorously and productively to urgent social, political, and economic challenges.

Extraordinary new challenges to American and, indeed, world society require creative interaction by the university with business, labor, government, and many other social institutions in the period immediately ahead. But in these years of social change, turbulence, and ambiguity, many academic institutions have resisted change. In so doing, they take paths that do not traverse the kind of institutional change that brought about the extraordinary past success of American higher education.

Some individual colleges or universities respond in kneejerk style to transient needs, creating new programs with little academic preparation or content, often without the support of the teaching faculty. They hope that such "responses" may bring a rapid infusion of tuition funds to meet urgent budget requirements. Still other institutions, facing similar pressures on enrollment and resources, turn inward, away from the American people. These colleges streamline programs, tinker with the curriculum, tighten budgets for faculty and library, expand spending for advertising and recruitment, improve management controls, and pray for better times.

Both responses, perhaps marginally helpful in the short run, have occurred increasingly since about 1975, a pivotal point in the life of most colleges and universities. About that time, many undergraduate colleges began to see a decline in the number of applicants from secondary schools. About the same time, escalating inflation began to distort established patterns of resource allocation. Colleges tended to interpret these conditions as "enrollment" or "deficit" problems. But what higher education really confronts is a sea change which bears down on this nation with tsunamic proportion and speed.

For the past two decades, higher education has sought to solve its enrollment and fiscal problems by emulating practices prevalent in the 1960s in American industry and government. Just as business once sought capital concentration through corporate conglomerates, so higher education created new statewide public educational systems and private regional consortia. Federally sponsored statewide planning commissions shaped and controlled growth, or at least attempted to make certain that decline would be equitable and orderly. Master plans and detailed strategic plans, state level academic review, and collection of masses of data for number crunchers supported centralized decision making, in the hope that efficiency and rationality might be achieved. By now the language of these strategies is familiar: *cost-effective*, *cost containment, program budgeting, statistical analysis, bottom-line assessment*. Nameless and faceless management groups, both on the individual campus and in the geographic aggregate, are expected to produce the academic, economic, and political solutions to every problem. Michel Foucault might call such efforts "insanity in the age of reason." The prevalence and power of committees would astonish the earlier leaders of American education, just as, in the business arena, it would amaze John D. Rockefeller, Andrew Carnegie, or Henry Ford.

But if such bureaucratic strategies have demonstrably helped to address some of education's short-term problems, they are not likely to address the kinds of relentless change that now face higher education in America. Nor do they, as this book will attempt to show, reflect a pattern of strategic response in keeping with the conditions and values that have distinguished American education in the past.

The capacity of the university to weather this new stormsurge will require a new style of leadership and entrepreneurial management—and at the local campus level. Our history shows that the college and university is neither frozen in structure nor role. For over three centuries, it has responded to needs for advanced learning through repeated metamorphosis in response to the changing conditions and requirements of American society. Given leadership in the face of impending disjunctive changes in the way our society acquires, transmits, and comprehends information, the next twenty-five years could witness one of the historic periods of innovation in American higher education.

Educational innovation and entrepreneurs are entwined in the national experience. No nation has created such an extensive and responsive educational system for so many people as has the United States. Its institutions, truly the jewels in the American crown, are the legacy of inventive and visionary leaders. Yet commentators repeatedly decry the lack of such leaders today, suggesting that the times and conditions inhibit their emergence.[1] Perhaps this is more a case of misdirection than an absence of leadership. Too often innovative leadership has been confused with opportunism. Planting new off-campus ventures, for example, across the countryside to make a quick profit for the institution's balance sheet is not leadership. Nor is it a valid university response to the need for access. Such opportunism seldom seeds an academic program with a well-conceived curriculum or capable instruction, nor does it bring new flowers into blossom.

Successful academic leadership begins with a rich knowledge, a respect for learning, and confidence in the capacity of students. Leadership benefits from a sound understanding of the values and conditions that sustain and motivate Americans, and of the ways colleges and universities have responded in the past to the needs of the American people. As one who has spent a good part of his life in trying to find new solutions to student access, I hope I can help administrators and faculty to navigate outside the idea-inhibiting traps of committees, procedural master plans, and progress reports. If we are to develop a surer sense of how colleges can respond to national necessity, we must all work with a richer appreciation for the past, while grasping the implications of rapidly changing social conditions in the present.

The university's basic achievement in America, unique in the world, is broadly based, available and accessible education. Dorothy Canfield Fisher, in her inaugural address as President of AAAE in 1927, said, "In the back of my mind I always have the idea of educating everybody." This is the course through which the university in America can guide and tame the enormous forces for change it now confronts.

Today is a time of exciting possibilities. The opportunity for innovation that can improve, even transform our institutions of higher learning, is as real as at any time in our history. Institutional decline, needless bureaucratization, and academic demoralization need not describe the future of colleges. New and needy students, fascinating and undeveloped technologies, and improved knowledge about teaching and learning itself are the raw materials that will help to shape the future.

Part One of this volume examines the American environment for collegial innovation and provides an historic perspective, showing how social and environmental values have actually stimulated both process and product. In Part Two the emergence in recent years of a number of highly innovative institutions or programmatic approaches is considered in light of these historic perspectives. Finally, Part Three projects possible paths and opportunities for innovation in higher education's future and offers some practical examples and suggestions for educational leadership.

NOTE

1. See Warren Bennis, *Why Leaders Can't Lead* (San Francisco: Jossey-Bass, 1989).

PART ONE

INNOVATION IN THE AMERICAN PAST

Innovation and improvisation were essential to successful adaptation of the university on American soil. American colonial colleges, although fashioned after the familiar models of England, incorporated new elements from the very beginning. These new patterns were amplified and extended in successive responses to the American environment. The unintended result was a structure of higher education radically different from the English, Scottish, or German prototypes in the experience of most of their founders. Part One introduces the environmental context and values that have shaped American higher education. It then examines some of the key educational innovations in the American past that set the stage for the experimental efforts of the present time.

Chapter 1

Introduction:
The Environment for
Innovation in America

Innovative is the most consistent descriptor of American higher education. Driven before the winds of a dynamic society and navigated by academic entrepreneurs, the whole enterprise can be characterized from its earliest beginnings by reference to improvisation and reform. From the founding of Harvard, the first English-speaking colonial college in 1636, the American environment required that higher education become substantively different from its English and European models. Since that time, it has continued to embody the fluid, improvisational, and innovative character of American society itself.

Innovation is not synonymous with change. Change is merely a shift from one practice to another. By contrast, innovation is *purposeful* change, directed change, which self-consciously attempts to improve, reform, make new. Innovation is an attempt to improve quality and service: the quality of a product must be better than before; a service must be improved for the same consumers or must serve more and different people.

Such innovation is not the exclusive license of particular institutions of higher education. Private or public, traditional or non-traditional, liberal arts or community—none has a particular claim on innovation. In fact, the very presence of such diverse institutions is itself a force for change, especially in the absence of centralized coordination. Often enough colleges reputed to be "innovative" may be so only with respect to their past experimental reputation or a pronounced existing difference from other institutions; in the present they may not be responding to changing needs at all. So-called "innovative" or "non-traditional" colleges, once leaders in educational reform, may become so hidebound and sterile in the present as to preclude further significant change. In such organizations, where rapid change once took place, the pull toward stability is a powerful balancing force. Conversely, some of the more exciting innovations today occur in the programs of highly stable, conservative institutions. Unlike colleges so innovative that they may be organizationally unstable, traditional institutions may be better positioned to carry out successful change. Innovation is found widely in higher education.

Of course innovation, in rhythm with the ebb and flow of social movements, is more successful at some times and places than others. American society has, after all, experienced its periods of optimism and pessimism, its spells of hell-bent economic expansion interspersed with seasons of financial panic and ruin. Sometimes new inventions, such as the cotton gin, the steam engine, the electric motor, and airplane, to name but a few, unlock tremendous energy and stimulate dynamic innovation and growth. Such societal breakthroughs often trigger expansive episodes in higher education as well. At other times, society's preoccupation with the status quo has led to periods of retrenchment, panic, and depression. Ripples from these waves of social dynamism wash upon the beachheads of the college campus. But the sloughs of social despond leave their residue as well.

It is common enough today to think of education, higher education in particular, as a consciously conserving establishment, resistant to change. Hence the attribution of innovativeness as a *central* facet of American academe may strike some as perverse. To be sure, some of education's organizations are among the most lethargic and inscrutable of all our institutions. School curricula may lag some ten to twenty years behind state-of-the-discipline information. Changing the length of the school curriculum from twelve to eleven years or the baccalaureate curriculum from four to three years has proven impossible. Student evaluation seems designed only to exclude those less agile rather than to make learning accessible. Seemingly endless debates rage around the canon of the liberal arts curriculum, without discernible improvements in student learning. And the lifetime employment embodied in the idea of tenure may guarantee that tradition, or worse, "middlescence," becomes the controlling ethos of education.

The university is, by its purpose, structure, and governance, indeed a highly conservative organization. Like all organizations, the university seeks stability and treasures security and certainty. But during its three-century-long American quest, whenever the university has imagined itself to have found an inner stability, it has been prodded, frustrated, sometimes energized, and almost always eventually changed by the shifting demands of the American social environment.

The university is thus of two minds: one is intensely protective of its traditions and practices, openly resisting change and public intrusion; the second consciously seeks new knowledge, new audiences, and new structures in interaction with the leading edge of society. American society itself expects and requires both approaches. The resulting conflict of expectations between preservation and innovation creates a kind of schizophrenia for higher education and thereby generates inner tension and external misunderstanding. As a result, universities receive a healthy share of public criticism and, by their very character, indulge themselves in recurrent bouts of self-criticism. This tension between preservation and innovation is not a phenomenon reserved for the recent past but a tension which has been present from the university's earliest development on this continent.

As the young nation expanded westward, colleges were created behind each new frontier as an expression of community stability and maturity, as a way of retaining or establishing links with the Eastern past, of ensuring an educated clergy in the wilderness. But even while they instinctively sought stability, these moving and changing people, in a new geography within a radicalizing economic and political environment, demanded innovation. Even as each new group created its own college as a symbol of stability and a link with the past, people imposed new demands upon the college.

All of this underscores the obvious: that colleges and universities are inescapably the product of American society. Like American society, they aim to "strike a balance between the tendencies of the ivory tower, the community of learning, and the service station."[1] Thus, the university is an echo chamber of its social milieu. Like the body of a violin, it can enhance, clarify, and project the tones it is given, often with great beauty. But the impulse comes from without, from those who play upon its strings.

Innovation and reform in academe are almost never the result of planned internal change, but occur as negotiated responses to external cultural, economic, and political forces.[2] By examining the historical and rational background of higher education and by placing the experimental and reformist efforts of recent years within this context, one can think constructively, if speculatively, about how higher education is likely to develop in the promising decades ahead. It is no accident that educational experimentation and innovation has occurred with such frequency and with such remarkable success in this country.

Innovations in American higher education, since the earliest days, have been imperfectly directed toward three discernible social goals or values. The first is *egalitarianism*, fostering equality through inclusiveness and opportunity for all people. The second is *individualism*, providing for personal choice, freedom to learn, and recognition of personal merit. The third is *pluralism*, promoting diversity by increasing institutional breadth and outreach. These three values are often contradictory and produce conflict. But Americans have expected their institutions to pursue them all. Innovation in response to these values has been a continuing necessity for survival and success in the American system.[3]

EGALITARIANISM

The egalitarian value appears when individuals or groups find that they cannot obtain access to required goods, services, or structures. Their needs are translated into social demands. When institutions are able to respond freely, or at least with a minimum of regulation, to such social demands or needs, a fertile climate exists for improvisation and innovation. The demand as well as the opportunity for higher education in America has varied at different times and in different places. In colonial America, the need for new generations of educated clergy and civic leaders was sufficient to spawn nine colleges before the War for Independence, and hundreds of others in the nineteenth century. But no others, save clergy and a few gentlemen, perceived a need for a college education until quite late in the nineteenth century, when an increasingly industrialized society required graduates with knowledge of science and technology, and a growing leisure class sought an acculturating experience for its young. In the twentieth century, the perceived need for higher education increased further with the political enfranchisement of numerous immigrants, African-Americans, and women. In the United States, equality is expressed as opportunity, and it is propelled by powerful economic, social, and political muscles. The demand for equality, expressed through empowered individuals or groups, is a fundamental value driving innovation.

INDIVIDUALISM

Individualism tends to run against egalitarianism, for it allows the individual, as a unique entity, to exercise personal choice, to move freely, to stand out from the group, and to be recognized for personal merit. For example, the idea of *excellence* in America carries an especially individual meaning. Although the New England Puritans railed against the temptation that good works could increase an individual's merit before an omnipotent God, they also believed that such personal achievements were likely indicators of one's merit. Though such religious "election" by God early threatened to become a form of social elitism, the rapidly changing social environment made exclusionary religious or social practices difficult to maintain. By the middle of the eighteenth century, Benjamin Franklin verbalized what many already understood—a credo of personal reward based upon meritorious accomplishment. The idea that an individual should rise through hard work and personal competence became a widely accepted value. At first schooling and later higher education became the vehicle allowing one to rise to capacity. Graduate and professional schools, the university commitment to research, and experiments in support of improved teaching and learning are all innovative responses to the demand to allow the individual to display merit. Although this value has proven especially difficult to meet in the past, competitive pressures in the world today impel the university to renew its drive for excellence.

An important aspect of individualism is *mobility*: the freedom to move from one place to another and the possibility to move from one status to another. A widespread belief has been that through personal initiative, individuals might rise in the world. For those who were not native born, the motivation to leave their place of origin, whether through pressure, initiative or speculation, was especially strong. For those who reached the American shores, the opportunities were such, with a land of abundance and a need for skilled and unskilled labor, that stories about social and financial success found resonance and affirmation. Mobility became an operating myth, a characterological belief of Americans. Although this reality was not experienced by every person, it was an article of popular faith and, as such, a real condition. For most of the eighteenth and nineteenth centuries, mobility was accountably real in the tales of those who trekked to the West, those who forsook the certainty of the present for the dream of land and fortune. By the end of the nineteenth century, even though Frederick Jackson Turner tells us that the frontier was closed, the dream of social mobility had supplanted the physical reality, giving new credibility to the myth. An important part of that reinterpretation of mobility was the belief that education, and, increasingly, a *college* education, was an essential means to upward social movement.

PLURALISM

Pluralism describes conditions which allow for multiple or optional responses to social demand. Although it has taken various forms in the past, today *multiculturalism* is the most pressing emerging expression of pluralism. It is a powerful force for change, compelling new demands on curricula, on college academic organization, and on student life. But we must also consider pluralism more broadly.

Pluralism is the logical consequence of a strong tradition of separatism and of the possibility for physical and social mobility. *Separatism* is the tendency to create another option if the existing choice doesn't suit. Historically, separatism describes practices among the earliest of American colonists to reject the established church and create a purified new one—a kind of innovation. In America, separatism became a way of thinking, and both individualism and pluralism are among its practical consequences. Pluralism does not thrive in societies where control is vested in a single power structure. Nor does it flourish when mercantile, monopolistic, or centrally planned systems control the economic and commercial enterprise.

Pluralism gained an early start in the American colonies, founded as separate governing units, under different sponsorship and laws. From early on, these colonies reserved many powers to themselves, an important issue in the struggles with England in the second half of the eighteenth century. Without central control, special interest groups created structures which allowed them to interact and to compete on an equal footing. For those temporarily on top, a tolerance for pluralism had to be extended to others in order to retain that privilege.

In higher education, pluralism led to the founding of widely diverse institutions under independent leadership, policies, and governance and to the possibility of choice for students.[4] New colleges and universities with significantly varied purposes have since come to be, and these institutions have themselves often reached beyond their physical campus, either through branches, colonization, extension, or most recently, distance education. Pluralism also encouraged increasing independence of colleges and universities in matters of curriculum, finance, and accreditation. And, most importantly, it accorded, to an extent unknown elsewhere, relatively greater influence to the individual student.

Pluralism, in all its dimensions, is a value which exposes wide and multiple channels to institutional improvisation. In the United States there has been nothing comparable to an establishment university. Had the social elites become identified with a single institution, perhaps such an established, and therefore controlling institution, might have developed. But there have always been too many options, too many places, so that even the elites did not have just one obvious choice. That condition has invariably exposed colleges and universities to the kind of market competition more obviously experienced today by airlines, truckers, the post office, and the communications industry. The opportunity for the consumer to choose rather than be forced to accept the given, the leftover, or the pre-determined has significantly strengthened the hand of the consumer in determining the shape and substance of the college experience.[5]

Colleges, however, have not passively accepted the dominance of the consumer. They have inspired collaborative efforts (such as voluntary regional accreditation) which have had, as their major purpose, the presentation of a united collegial front for the regulation of admissions practices, the designation of leading scholars, and the definition and improvement of standards. But such efforts are a kind of restraint of trade, a practice which has never worked for very long in the American environment. Certainly, in their efforts at regulation, colleges have not succeeded very well. Students who receive a degree in business administration from a regional institution rather than from the University of Pennsylvania's Wharton School do not gain the same easy entree into the corporate world, but they do hold a marketable degree which will in many cases serve them in finding an interesting, challenging, and well-paying job. The job marketplace has usually needed more educated and trained persons than could be produced by the most acclaimed universities alone, and this fact has conferred value upon the degrees of many less prestigious institutions. The cash value of the degree, distinct from its intellectual value, is finally determined not by the college which issues the diploma, but by the marketplace and its estimate of the performance of individual graduates.

Egalitarianism, individualism, and pluralism are mutually reinforcing.[6] Aspects of each act upon aspects of the other, and it is difficult to disentangle these complex values entirely. It is even more difficult to show the process by which these values cause change to occur. Their mere presence does not produce innovation in American universities. But clearly, in periods when colleges and universities have responded positively to these values, significant public acceptance and, *ipso facto*, institutional progress has occurred. Conversely, during periods when colleges have ignored or resisted these external values, institutional stasis and, in some cases, paralysis and decline have occurred.

The linkage between external pressure and internal change is made through individual leaders. People with special talents and entrepreneurial skills perceive the implications of prevailing social conditions and translate them into initiatives which bring about change. Such individuals, sparked by these three peculiarly American values, have been essential to the success of higher education in the past and to the important innovations of recent times. Creative leaders and innovative managers, responding sensitively to the underlying liberalism of American social values, will be at the heart of future innovation. For them, the American university, in spite of the innate conservatism of an educational structure, can offer the rare venue to "get something done" in an otherwise frustratingly bureaucratic society.

NOTES

1. Amy Gutmann, *Democratic Education* (Princeton NJ: Princeton University Press, 1987), p. 189.
2. See also Martin Kaplan, "The Wrong Solution to the Right Problem," in James W. Hall (ed.), with Barbara L. Kevles, *In Opposition to Core Curriculum: Alternative Models for Undergraduate Education* (Westport, CT: Greenwood Press 1982), pp. 3–12.
3. Others have attributed the peculiar innovativeness of American higher education to slightly different values. Derek Bok, looking from the internal perspective of the university, sees autonomy, competition, and responsiveness as central (*Higher Learning*, Cambridge, MA: Harvard University Press, 1986, p.10). Burton Clark, in positing a transnational framework for analysis, sees universities motivated by justice, competence, liberty, and loyalty (*The Higher Education System*, Berkeley, Cal., University of California Press, 1983), Chapter 7.
4. Burton Clark, *Higher Education*, p. 143, shows that in nations where tightly centralized planning and control is exercised by government, universities tend to uniformity—are less open to organic change except through external direction.
5. David Riesman develops this theme extensively in *On Higher Education: The Academic Enterprise in an Era of Rising Student Consumerism* (San Francisco: Jossey-Bass, 1980).
6. For a fuller treatment of the characterological qualities of Americans, see James W. Hall (ed.), *Forging the American Character* (New York: Holt, Rinehart & Winston, 1971).

Chapter 2

Creating An American Tradition Through Innovation

From the seventeenth century, innovation in American higher education has waxed and waned as it has responded to or exempted itself from the prevalent conditions and values of the larger society. Dynamic and structurally innovative in the Colonial era, higher education stagnated between the War for Independence and the Civil War, unable to meet social needs. Although again expansive with the growth of the nation in the late nineteenth and early twentieth century, the university in more recent times required a social revolution to reawaken its inventive spirit. As these innovative phases alternated with periods of stasis and consolidation, the university nonetheless shaped solutions to educational problems created by changing social conditions and values. By the beginning of the twentieth century, the process had created a distinctly American college and university tradition.

Harvard College, founded so consciously and purposefully almost as soon as colonists could think beyond their urgent needs for subsistence and security, was affected from the very beginning by the new environment. Harvard, then hardly to be compared with the modern college, was the creation of its time and place and embodied the Puritan commitment not only to creating "a city on a hill," but more importantly, "to a learned clergy and a lettered people."[1] Separated from the green of Emmanuel College of Cambridge by one ocean and barely sixteen years, in 1636 Harvard was already being shaped by the necessities of the Massachusetts Bay Colony. "The founders of Harvard College were educational conservatives. They were not attempting to create new forms of education. Yet in fact they did. And the pattern they extemporized proved to be permanent, and a model for American institutions of higher education."[2] Colonists could not rely on sufficient assistance from the old country. American colonial life required homespun improvisation.

In particular, three new structural patterns, initiated at Harvard but widely imitated thereafter, laid the foundations for important future developments. First was the authority of the undergraduate college, rather than the university, to award the baccalaureate degree. This deviant pattern led to increased academic autonomy and to the centrality of the liberal arts college within

American institutions. Second was the change in means of institutional support. Harvard, without the endowments provided in England by land rents, had to rely upon community generosity in the form of private gifts and public fees or taxes. This undermined the kind of administration and, indeed, curricular philosophy that owed to the financial autonomy characteristic of the English university. Finally, both of these patterns encouraged the practice of college governance by an independent corporate board of overseers or trustees, introducing an external factor into the making of institutional policy. These structures, each conditioned by the new environment, increased the necessity of higher education to respond to growing egalitarian, pluralistic, and individualistic values.

Consider first the matter of access. Access is implicit in the question of how to provide education for "a learned clergy and a lettered people." Although information about the personal requirements for admission, other than the academic expectations of certain levels of competency in Latin and Greek languages, is difficult to gain, it seems clear that the issue of religious qualification was debated from the outset. Whether Samuel Eliot Morison's assertion, that Harvard's founders intended an education "suitable either for a general education or as a basis for professional training in divinity, law, and medicine,"[3] is an accurate description of reality, Bernard Bailyn points out that the liberal Unitarians who came to power at Harvard after 1805 noted "the absolute refusal, from the start, to impose exclusionary oaths on its members."[4]

Among the early alumni, about 50 percent were preachers. By the end of the seventeenth century, nearly all of the ministers in Massachusetts and Connecticut were graduates of Harvard College. The necessity for a knowledgeable, locally grown clergy was thus fully met.[5] But concern was not limited to the education of clergy, for laws passed after 1647, which urgently ordered towns to maintain teaching institutions, reflected a deep fear of the "imminent loss of cultural standards." Many believed that unless education was extended, civilization would be "buried in the grave of our fathers."[6] Education began to take on new shapes, "a pattern woven of the necessities of life in the colonies, and...repeated...in every region as the threat of the environment to inherited culture made itself felt."[7] Cotton Mather saw "creolean degeneracy," or intellectual decline in succeeding generations, as a real and present danger. So, although religious in its context or orientation, the curriculum was secular in many aspects,[8] serving students, including a few American Indians, other than those preparing for the ministry. These liberal, inclusive patterns became more pronounced in the eighteenth century colleges.

Certainly the issue of access to education had its parallel in the more general issue of participation in church governance. In the Bay Colony, arriving Colonists and non-church members were excluded from the privilege of participation in Puritan church governance. Many baptised worshippers could not vote in church matters because, by virtue (or the lack thereof) of not having yet affirmed their conversions before the congregation, they were not yet known as "Saints" and so could not become voting church members. Non-members, prohibited from exercising this franchise in church matters, pressed for admission to church governance. In this way, the so-called Half-Way Covenant, which permitted such church goers to become members,[9] was devised. Although this change seems modest to a contemporary reader, it provoked vigorous conflict at the time. Insofar as this innovation represented a first limited step toward a more egalitarian response by the dissenting or separatist tradition brought to the New World by the first colonists, the Half-Way Covenant, while hardly establishing broad democratic governance, helped progressively to open the way for wider participation. The same social forces affected admissions at most of the colonial colleges.

Of course easier access had its early detractors. Efforts to restrict access and maintain exclusivity provided a counterforce that surfaced periodically, both in the public at large and within higher education. A South Carolina newspaper editorial of 1770 expressed opposition to a college in South Carolina because "learning would become cheap and too common, and every man would be for giving his son an education."[10] But by the late eighteenth century, strong voices were raised in support of new institutions that would allow more students to gain an education while remaining closer to home. The Charleston *Gazette* argued in 1769 that "boys now sent to college at Philadelphia ought to be kept home, both to save money and to attach them to their native province"; a published reply said, "From want of a college among us, youth of moderate fortunes are reduced to the necessity of a common confined education... many of whom would, otherwise, have been an honour and a credit to their country and friends."[11] Although the issue of access versus exclusivity has continued to occupy educators to the present time, the push for access and opportunity from the earliest days, not just for "a learned clergy" but also "a lettered people," caused new institutions to be founded, gradually wedging open the doors of academe.

This impulse to found new colleges was an early response not only to the egalitarian impulse but also to pluralism. After all, Harvard alone might have sufficed to serve the limited population of the American colonies, and this might actually have strengthened the role and influence of that institution. But the history of higher education in America would read very differently, and innovation would not likely have been a salient characteristic. The early imprint of Congregational polity, with its principle of local congregational control, established a pattern soon applied to the control of colleges. From the first, Puritans affirmed congregational principles of individual church control as the true scriptural form of organization. Although most colonial American colleges were chartered by the Crown, their founding was not, strictly speaking, by the English government establishment but rather by different governmental units or dissenting religious parties. Harvard was controlled by the Puritans, the ascendent religious and political group in England in the early to mid-seventeenth century. William and Mary (Virginia,

1693) reflected a somewhat more secular, civic-spirited response to the need for trained public servants, as well as an educated clergy. As Harvard began to succumb to the more liberal themes of the early eighteenth century, Yale was founded (Connecticut, 1701) by the more conservative, orthodox wing of Puritanism. The College of Philadelphia (University of Pennsylvania, 1755),[12] located in a colony with a strong tradition of Quaker toleration and in a city which, with 40,000 residents by 1775, was the largest city in America or England save for London, was officially affiliated with no church. From the beginning, then, the governing and policy-making structure of the college was largely accountable to its own public board rather than to the authority of a single superior university, or to an established government ministry.

By the time of the War for Independence, nine colleges had been founded. Unlike their European counterparts or even universities founded in the Americas by other European powers, they were created independently of one another, with no superior university, as at Oxford and Cambridge. The Spanish in America founded the University of Mexico in 1553, the University of San Marcos in 1572, and others long before the Puritans established Harvard in 1636. Like the English-speaking colleges, they faced the new environment as well. But these Spanish universities did not emerge in a separatist and pluralistic cultural setting and were controlled by the centralized Spanish empire. The possibilities for innovation through pluralistic development were thus limited.

The physical environment influenced governance as well. In England schools were traditionally supported by private endowments of land and so maintained considerable internal autonomy for the faculty. Although this practice was attempted in America, land tenants simply would not stay and work a landlord's property, so additional financial help in the form of private gifts and public taxes was needed periodically by the colleges.[13] This had the effect of injecting a public, external factor into college control, a form of governance thoroughly unknown in Europe and Britain—a major American innovation. The control of these colonial colleges, under the conditions of pluralism and enlightened tolerance, passed gradually from the clergy to church laymen, and finally to secular trustees.

Nor was corporate ownership vested in "the youthful, transient hands of the teachers,"[14] as in the guild tradition of Europe. The college, through its own public board, became "an artifact of the community as a whole,[15] responsive neither to its own inner needs nor to the government but to wider community values. This pattern of governance was uniquely American, and it established a necessary condition for institutional innovation. The practical result was that the college president's authority as the executive officer of the trustees or corporation increased. College presidents had unusual authority to employ and release faculty and staff and to determine the curriculum and academic standards. Such leaders could exercise considerable initiative in innovation, even while teaching, preaching, administering discipline, counselling godliness, and raising money.[16]

Public financial control might have led to a controlling role by government in this early period, for with the power of the purse often comes the power to make policy. Colonial colleges did receive some financial support from their colonial governments. The issue was a matter of considerable debate during the Revolutionary period, and was not fully settled until the Dartmouth College court decision (1819) confirmed the right of private boards to "control what they had created," even against the state itself.[17] But competition among colleges with different sponsors gradually set practical limits on the degree of external control or intervention which might be exercised by the public's financial support. To a lesser but nonetheless real degree, the same spirit inhibited church denominations from creating narrowly sectarian colleges. It discouraged governing boards from enacting admissions practices which discriminated on the basis of religious preference. No doubt in reaction to the prevailing exclusive practices at Oxford and Cambridge and in keeping with the enlightened practices of the mid-eighteenth century, many American colleges practiced increasing religious pluralism.

Plans for a single national or federal university did emerge from time to time. George Washington proposed such an institution and left an endowment for it in his will. Enlightened gentlemen and organizations, like Benjamin Rush, Joel Barlow, and the American Philosophical Society, sponsored proposals which would have created, had they succeeded, a secular, centralized national higher education system. But such plans failed to gain adoption, unresponsive as they were to the separatist, pluralistic requirements of the people and their individual states. These early colleges, although modeled on the English college, established from the very beginning new patterns which were responsive to the American environment. As in other areas of national life, innovation was not to be in the founding of large centralized institutions but in the spawning of many small, decentralized colleges.

Bailyn says, in summing up the impact of the new environment, "the [English] pattern of education was destroyed: the elements survived, but their meaning had changed and their functions had been altered. By 1800 education in America was a radically different process from what anyone in the early seventeenth century would have expected."[18]

Colleges which emerged in the early nineteenth century faced new demands. Although higher education responded rapidly to the expanding conditions of pluralism and the high mobility of people, the kind of curriculum offered rapidly fell out of phase with the needs of American development. Society required something different than a bachelor's degree organized around classical languages, but colleges were unwilling to consider other, more utilitarian curricula. Although many new colleges were founded based upon a classical curriculum, there was occasional transient experimentation by hopeful and creative leaders. But none could counter the declining use of higher education by a rapidly growing population. The rise and fall between 1817 and 1827 of Transylvania University, Kentucky's "Harvard of the West," is a good example[19] of what happened to many antebellum colleges. Rejecting the need for advanced but practical higher education, colleges either quickly failed or else, like Transylvania, catered to a very small student demand.

Although the term "college" was used loosely as new towns and religious denominations competed to found colleges in order to establish their "respectability," nonetheless, explosive college-founding followed the War of 1812. Moving closely behind the first wave of trans-Appalachian migration, these infant colleges reflected the ideals of individual leaders, usually clergymen.

In such an environment, an educational leader, on the basis of his personal capability, could try out ideas and see them succeed or fail. These early patterns encouraged the extraordinary spread of new colleges during the nineteenth century. Although Presbyterians and Congregationalists were most vigorous in promoting the need for colleges and an educated clergy in the early decades, by the 1830s both Methodists and Baptists had joined those denominations which sponsored colleges. Moreover, Baptists were the most insistent in their demands for total separation of church and state,[20] a persuasion that was a powerful deterrent to state control of the many new colleges which Baptist evangelism founded across the middle and southern states. Roman Catholic orders also insisted on such separatism in founding forty-one autonomous colleges before 1850.

Most of these colleges enrolled a few students for a time, then passed quietly out of existence.[21] One study of sixteen states shows 412 college closings and only 104 survivors, leading Frederick Rudolph to estimate that as many as 700 colleges were founded and had failed before 1861.[22] Just as unusual opportunity existed for entrepreneurs to risk founding a new business enterprise in this era, so there was little to restrain an individual educator from attempting to institutionalize his ideas in the form of a new college. Potential support for such initiatives came from the plethora of towns and church synods which sprang into being. But failure was also easy.

The 1820s and 1830s were a period of great opportunity for Americans with ideas and entrepreneurial spunk. Numerous educational leaders were on hand, trying out their ideas for change and reform. Some of these individuals dared to introduce new ideas into the college curriculum, ideas which, had they been widely implemented, might have made the college more responsive to the student and so more successful as an institution during this period of American life. These leaders were often charismatic and persuasive, but, as Rudolph shows, unable to bring about innovations which would stay the course.[23]

The failures of these innovators may help us to understand better the conditions that yield success. One such academic leader was George Ticknor, the first American to do advanced scholarly work at a German university. Asking basic questions of traditional Harvard practices, he queried the appropriate length of the academic calendar, suggested classifying students by talent and achievement, decried the lack of course offerings which might be directly useful to young men, and criticized the prevailing mode of learning by recitation. Another, James Marsh, upon his appointment as president of the University of Vermont in 1826, advocated division of that college into departments and encouraged the introduction of discussion into the classroom. Jacob Abbott, while a professor at Amherst in the 1820s, proposed that colleges should provide a curriculum which might support more adequately society's needs for modern languages, engineering, practical physics, and history. Phillip Lindsley, who became president of the University of Nashville in 1824, urged the creation of a European style university which presented the full humanist tradition while offering curricula responsive to the practical needs of a highly diverse Tennessee population. One of the most creative and liberal educators of the period was the Reverend Horace Holley, who became president of Transylvania in 1818. But his innovations were either too advanced for his contemporaries, or he lacked the management skills to implement them. Although a graduate of conservative Yale, he was reported to be "holding up to ridicule the doctrine of human depravity" and the "real personality of the devil," not to mention the creation of the world. The Presbyterians of the Kentucky synod secured a charter for the more properly orthodox Centre College in 1823, and, a few years later, reacting Transylvania trustees forced Holley to resign.[24]

Perhaps most striking of all were Thomas Jefferson's plans for the University of Virginia, adopted by the Board of Visitors in 1824. His plan called for eight schools, covering both classical and contemporary subjects. Students were free to elect studies in whichever school they wished. He also planned schools of commerce, manufacturing, and diplomacy![25] Moreover, Jefferson's proposed innovations included "the substitution of the elective system for a prescribed course of study, the dissolution of the ties between church and academy, the switch from a predominantly classical curriculum to one embracing technical and utilitarian branches," and "the importance of moral and political education under our American system of government."[26]

Significantly, however, the plans of each of these farsighted leaders, even of one so eminent as Jefferson, either failed quickly or were unable to be replicated in other places. Following this early period of experimentation and entrepreneurial leadership, the status quo, expressed perhaps most fully by the regressive Yale Report of 1828,[27] was so widely accepted that, says Rudolph, "the reformers were so successfully routed that for almost fifty years the American college was necessarily put beyond the sympathy and understanding of the American people."[28]

And so while there were few limits to the possibility for individuals to create academic institutions, there was also little demand for the college product. Without that demand, colleges, even those led by the most visionary, could not flourish. The need for a collegiate education, save by certain clergy, simply did not exist before the Civil War. Although pluralism tolerated the creation of new colleges, demand for access was low. No general need for higher education existed. The ability of the individual to experience upward social mobility did not yet require even a secondary school education. A young person could succeed quite handsomely without a diploma or degree. As a result of that social and economic reality, until quite late in the nineteenth century, even secondary schools were generally unavailable to the population-at-large, and wide differences existed from community to community in the availability of grammar schools.[29]

Moreover, the leveling character of egalitarianism supported resentment of elitist, classical higher education. A strong undercurrent of anti-intellectualism persisted. Richard Hofstadter described this as resentment of "a kind of excellence, as a claim to distinction, as a challenge to egalitarianism, as a quality which . . . deprives a man or woman of the common touch."[30] People were generally suspicious of the liberalism or privilege of the college campus. Jacksonian America championed the aggressive, untutored but talented self-made man. For such individuals, the classical college offered little that was deemed necessary or useful. Perhaps public schools served the people, but colleges served the rich. Better to make a living, and a good one at that, than waste precious time attending a college at pursuits which were "unworldly, unmasculine, and impractical."

From such a creative and fast-moving society as Jacksonian America, colleges might have become vehicles of national importance. Imagine if higher education had responded to the widespread interest and need for practical and general education. But, in spite of the efforts of some reformers, colleges continued to define their mission narrowly to serve early to mid-teen students who, prepared in classical languages, pursued a tightly defined classical curriculum. Because colleges typically did not attempt to provide practical academic subjects which might have been useful and attractive to a largely rural, small manufacturing economy, a broad-based need was not established for their services. As late as 1839 only eleven colleges had more than 150 enrollees; the average college enrollment was far smaller. Hardly anyone went to college.

Gradually a few innovations did occur which began to make a difference. Fraternities in the form of Greek letter societies began at Union College as early as 1825, clearly an effort to improve college life for the residential student; these organizations soon spread to other colleges. Harvard offered the Bachelor of Science degree starting in 1851 as a way to open the curriculum to the newer subjects. In a similar vein, Yale offered the Bachelor of Philosophy degree after 1852.[31] A kind of cooperative farm-work system was tried for a time in an attempt to help farm boys to enroll in college and manage their finances as well. A variety of ingenious, if sometimes demeaning, strategies were tried to gain financial support for failing colleges.[32] A few institutions founded in this era are noted for their innovative character. Oberlin College, for example, founded in 1833, thrived under its president, the famous evangelist Charles Grandison Finney. Oberlin admitted an African-

American student as early as 1834 and in 1837 became the first college to admit women.[33] Although founded by the Congregational Church, Oberlin's admissions were consciously non-sectarian.[34]

But most colleges were not as innovative as Oberlin. Especially in the South they remained quietly irrelevant to the major changes which were then reshaping American society, their curricula almost entirely limited to the classical. The great economic, political, agricultural, and moral issues of the period were simply not to be found in the accepted courses of study. Moreover, in many colleges those teachers who tried to lecture on such issues were often denied further employment. Textbooks from the North were assailed as well.[35] Unlike the colonial college, which responded well to the more limited but urgent needs of its time, the nineteenth-century college was unable to define a market which could meet the necessities of that time. The notion of providing any form of education for workers or adults, though urgently needed by an industrializing nation, was a totally foreign idea (see Chapter 6). Although many were eventually to survive and prosper, the college was, at that time, a failing institution.

President Francis Wayland's often-quoted 1850 Report to the Brown Corporation captures fully the failure of the college to respond to its environment. "We have produced an article for which the demand is diminishing. We sell it at less than cost, and the deficiency is made up by charity. We give it away, and still the demand diminishes. Is it not time to inquire whether we cannot furnish an article for which the demand will be, at least, somewhat more remunerative?"[36] Ironically, then, the extraordinarily dynamic first half of the nineteenth century, during which an astounding number of new colleges appeared across the breadth of the American landscape, proved quite inhospitable to higher education.

Even as the college declined, new leaders began to respond to the rapidly changing conditions of post-bellum America and created or remade institutions which would later become highly successful, unlike anything the Western world had yet seen. The vast social energy released after the Civil War, in combination with immigration, westward movement, and industrialization, opened an expansive period of innovation in higher education. Ralph Waldo Emerson, in his "Essay On Politics," observed that "everyone of [the state's institutions]...was once the act of a single man."[37] He described an institution as "the lengthened shadow of one man." Such singular leaders now created institutions which changed American higher education.

Perhaps the first leader of stature to attempt to create a real American university was President Henry Tappan of the University of Michigan. As early as the 1850s he championed the model of the German university, urging both a scholarly faculty and, in a uniquely American compromise, a comprehensive response to broad public needs. But Tappan was dismissed from his post in 1863, partly because his ideas were too far ahead of those of the Michigan public. President Wayland's *Report* urged that there be "radical change...

[in] the system of collegiate instruction."[38] He sought flexibility for students to determine their courseload, free course election, and new courses in applied and technical subjects. He gained early support for his proposals, but by 1856 innovation had so stirred faculty and trustees into resistance that Wayland was replaced. But both Tappan and Wayland had pointed the way for the university to respond to an industrializing nation's needs for more broadly defined curricula, with technical and elective subjects.

Charles Eliot, president of Harvard from 1869 to 1909, was not to fail. His success in introducing into the Harvard curriculum the elective system, which allowed students to select courses based upon individual need and interest, needs no elaboration here. That innovation, which made possible the introduction of the sciences into the main curriculum at Harvard,[39] finally transformed the American undergraduate experience. By 1900, most colleges had embraced some variation of the elective principle. Eliot was perhaps the first leader whose understanding of the values and conditions of the American environment enabled him to introduce successfully and to manage innovation over a period spanning forty years. "The individual traits of different minds have not been sufficiently attended to," he said.[40] He understood that a relationship existed between motivation for learning and excellence. Giving rein to individual preferences not only anticipated some of the findings of later learning theorists but was responsive to the prevailing conditions of individualism and pluralism, which supported student choice. In the process, Eliot enabled the Harvard curriculum to become modern. Moreover, by introducing those changes gradually, taking care to enlist the support of others, he avoided effective resistance to his proposals, and innovation was institutionalized.

The elective principle was far-reaching and contributed to most of the practices which have come down to the present as "traditional," but which were quite innovative at the time. Among these are the grouping of requirements into concentration and distribution, the major concentration, and departmentalization of academic knowledge and the gradual professionalization of expert scholars by discipline. Academic rank was to grow from the competition for scholars among contending universities and departments. Most of all, the elective principle made it possible for the curriculum to respond to student interests and needs, as well as to recognize the emerging needs of industrial America.

Such curricula were found most fully in the rapidly developing state universities of the Midwest and West. Either founded by or enhanced by the financial provisions of the Morrill Act of 1862, many of these universities advanced the notion that higher education should be furnished to all citizens, a principle unheard in Europe at the time. Led by such presidents as James B. Angell of Michigan, Daniel Coit Gilman while in California, and later, although differently, William Rainey Harper at Chicago, the idea that the university in America would offer a comprehensive program of services to a diverse range of students became well established over much of the nation. Soon universities, in order to strengthen the ability of students to pursue a university education, introduced such innovations as the certification of public high schools, more flexible admissions requirements, and the admission of women students. Increasingly, too, the university attracted the interest of some of the great fortunes of America: Rockefeller, Carnegie, Mellon, Stanford. These donors did not act entirely out of altruism, for they shared the belief that individual merit, demonstrated through performance at the university, would benefit industry and government. The number of top business executives with some college education began to climb.[41] Although success was still easily achieved by the "self-made" individual, the college degree began to represent a desirable credential.

Cornell, following its founder's assertion that he would found "an institution where any person can find instruction in any study,"[42] became, in1869, the most aggressive of the new universities in offering a full range of vocational, professional, and applied science courses. Its first president, Andrew D. White, institutionalized this approach by bringing to it both scholarly credibility and financial backing. Only three years after its founding, Cornell could claim, at better than 250 students, the largest entering class in American collegiate history.

With these innovations, colleges and universities became, for a time, so diverse that it is difficult to define a single model. Small colleges continued to be established by Protestant religious denominations and Catholic orders, but they were usually financially tenuous and very small. The pluralistic demands of the population generated as many plans and variations as had been contemplated but unrealized by the clerical founders of the early nineteenth-century church college. Many other innovations were to follow in this period of diversity and incipient success: the graduate school, schools of business, other professional and vocational schools for an ever-widening range of careers, fellowships for students, the separation of student behavior issues from academic performance, and the beginnings of university extension. Testing and grading also made its debut about this time. Unlike the European practice of evaluating students wholly on their performance in year-end or comprehensive examinations, the American practice put heavy emphasis on lecture attendance and frequent tests. "In America the power of the university to force the fleeting attention of the students upon their academic obligations had to be demonstrated, not once a year or only before the bestowal of a degree, but again and again and again."[43] The small college traditions required that American students be monitored closely and nurtured.

Even so, through much of the century, many parents openly resisted sending their sons to college. For the great masses of immigrant children, whose families tended to work as unskilled laborers, the reality of social opportunity and personal improvement was gained through hard saving and sacrifice in order to purchase property. Education, even at the lower levels, was usually forgone for these children. Not until the grandchildren of immigrants came of age, when the family had acquired property, security, and modest social status, was the university a possible option, and even then for a very few.[44] Only late in the century did the parents of farm boys come to understand that state universities might offer advantages to the farmer through "scientific agriculture."[45] "The hope of the colleges that they would serve the people as social, economic, and political elevators was not yet shared in a substantial way by the people themselves."[46]

As a consequence, the stable existence of many colleges and universities was not ensured until the population at large began to find a real need for their services. Such a trend began late in the century. In 1880, 115,817 students, only 2.7 percent of the 18–21 age group were enrolled; a decade later it was 156,756, or 3.0 percent. By the beginning of the twentieth century, about 4 percent of the typical age group were attending college, and, from that time forward, demand for a university education increased markedly. In 1910, 4.8 percent of the cohort enrolled and by 1920 over 8 percent.

Ironically, this increased growth rate and success brought a decline in academic and organizational experimentation. As the great private and state universities responded competitively to their new-found status, institutional conformity resulted. By the late nineteenth century "every institution," in the words of Rudolph, "knew that it had to do something, even, if necessary, defend its right to stand still."[47] Standing still, however, was not really a possible choice in such a rapidly changing environment. Laurence Veysey describes in detail the decline of diversity and experimentation at the end of the nineteenth century in his important volume, *The Emergence of the American University*. From the close of the Civil War until the end of the nineteenth century, new colleges and universities—constructed around the needs of the state, the ideas of an educational leader, or the ideals of a denomination—were founded at a rapid pace. By the close of the century, however, the accepted structure and values of these institutions tended to become increasingly uniform across the nation, and the extraordinary climate which had stimulated so much innovation and reform had changed. Veysey sees the significant innovations as the creative output of one late nineteenth-century generation of educational leaders.[48] Their visions and reforms, combined with increased student demand, supported extensive innovation. But after that initial flourish, Veysey argues, increased competition rather than stimulating institutional differences in this period produced, after the turn of the century, universities that were "more standardized, less original, less fluid."[49] More and more, Americans looked for institutions which featured well-defined academic departments and offered the full complement of academic and professional subjects. Seeking to demonstrate such features, colleges and universities could no longer afford to seem different, unusual, or idiosyncratic. Before 1890, Veysey says, there were many possible choices for institutions to become different; but afterwards, homogenization was common. The American university structure was in place by 1910, and significant variation in the model, except in the early forms of extension

(Chapter 6), was not possible later.[50] This period of stability and uniformity coincided with the "success" of the university, and for a time the thrust toward innovation flagged. Perhaps the university reflected the new-found consensus of the American public, which expressed self-satisfaction and complacency in many areas of national life. After the 1890s, "the American academic establishment lost its freedom"; competition "dictated the avoidance of pronounced eccentricities."[51] Innovation, pursued in response to American conditions, had by the close of the nineteenth century produced an institution uniquely complex, diffuse in purpose, and American. But the earlier multiplicity of responses to an increasingly pluralistic nation diminished.

Thus the American university brought standardization of organization and practice into the twentieth century. The reputation of a university now rested not on its creativity and range of services, but on its quality as perceived in the reputation and accomplishments of its compartmentalized faculty, in the number of ornamental buildings which decorated the campus, and in the burgeoning numbers of books reposing in the library. The modern model of the distinguished residential university was cast, and for a time it seemed resistant to further experimentation.

That residential model was constructed around the older European tradition of a community of scholars. Students joined that community for a period of time, reading with professors, utilizing the library, and doing examinations to certify that they had indeed measured up to the expectations of the university. Such a model required that all of the resources which a student might ever need—the faculty of scholars, the books, and the community supports of residence (health care, social life, and sports)—be assembled in one place for all time, available to the student as needed.

The pressures for standardization swept through education. Professional schools wanted an assured college product, and the Carnegie unit, which defined an interchangeable academic unit, came along in 1906, anticipating the American industrial assembly line. Itself an important technical and lasting innovation, that unit defined time served, not academic content. On balance it probably made college-going less mysterious, more accessible. By 1919, the American Council on Education and the National Conference Committee had defined the college itself in similar quantitative terms: standardized student admissions requirements, 120 units of credit for the degree, specified numbers of faculty, library books, and teaching loads. And the departmental major was standard everywhere. After nearly three centuries of innovation and change in response to the American environment, the American university was a success. An American residential model was established.

Such a residential model perfectly fitted the needs of the bulk of college attenders, primarily white children of upper- and middle-class parents, through much of the first half of the twentieth century. These students sought to maintain or improve upon the social status of their parents. Although the "lesser breeds without the law" might occasionally get in, this pattern was especially prevalent at the most highly regarded institutions, whose practices

met the needs of their students quite admirably. Although the professionalization of academic life and scholarship developed rapidly throughout this
period, the rigor of academic demands on the students varied widely in intensity. Veysey, with a touch of caricature, says, "the most important function
of the American professor lay in posing requirements sufficiently difficult to
give college graduates a sense of pride, yet not so demanding as to deny
the degree to anyone who pledged four years of his parents' resources and
his own time in residence at an academic institution."[52] This generation
produced the stereotypes of American collegiate life, with its colorful fraternities, the football weekend, and the idea of a transitional period of life
during which a young person might hopefully pass to maturity and subsequent social responsibility. Veysey sees in the university of this period "an
agency for social control" and a place which had as its "primary responsibility...the custodianship of popular values."[53] Even today this model is the
popular image, if not the reality, of the university.

Yet in many respects that pattern has been increasingly unable to meet all
of the needs of the egalitarian, pluralistic, individualistic, and mobile society.
In the 1920s and 1930s, as the needs of an increasingly diverse population were felt on the university campus, the innovative spirit was renewed.
Widespread innovation in higher education reappeared when rapid change
and an unprecedented cultural clash brought increased appreciation of the
potential importance of higher education in supporting upward social mobility. And even for established American families, Laurence Veysey speculates,
the gaining of a college degree became "an insurance policy against down-
ward mobility" in competition with the rising mass of immigrants.[54] As 5
million people who saw some form of service in World War I returned to
civilian life, normal life in America was never again to be the same. Fully
one half of the population was now urban, only 27 percent was agricultural.
For many Americans caught in the conflict between rural conservatism and
urbanization, education looked like a way out. The enrollment in higher
education kept increasing. By 1930 it had reached 1,100,000 and by 1950,
in the midst of the G.I. enrollment surge, it reached 2,659,000. By 1980 it
would exceed 12 million.

New educational leaders, schooled in the liberal Progressive tradition,
came to positions of influence. As in the past, the truly successful ideas as
well as the social pressures for change originated outside the academy. If
Herbert Croly could call the "promise of American life" one of "comfort and
prosperity for an ever increasing majority of good Americans," his vehicle
for attaining that promise, for all of his doubts about the "subsidized word,"
was education.[55] The work of the philosopher John Dewey was percolating
in the minds of educators as well. A growing public interest in higher education and the emergence of new and empowered leaders brought higher
education into an extraordinary period of reform and innovation. So even
though the traditional university grew stronger, with the coalescence of the
world's most distinguished graduate and research departments, undergradu-

ate higher education entered a time of vigorous experimentation. University extension and the idea of continuing education began to be recognized as an alternative for older and part-time students. Even as the great universities solidified the structures of the academic departments and the scholarly guilds, new academic approaches and organizational ideas were hatched. Their description and analysis forms the subject of Part Two.

NOTES

1. Frederick Rudolph, *The American College and University* (New York: Alfred Knopf, 1968), p. 6, as cited from Samuel Eliot Morison, *The Founding of Harvard College* (Cambridge, MA: Harvard University Press, 1935), p. 45.
2. Bernard Bailyn et al., *Glimpses of the Harvard Past* (Cambridge, MA: Harvard University Press, 1986), p. 10.
3. Samuel Eliot Morison, *Founding*, p. 250.
4. Bailyn, *Glimpses*, p. 5.
5. William Warren Sweet, *The Story of Religion in America* (New York: Harper and Row, Rev. 1950), p. 54.
6. Bernard Bailyn, *Education in the Forming of American Society* (Chapel Hill, NC: University of North Carolina Press, 1960), p. 27.
7. Bailyn, *Education*, p. 29.
8. Bailyn, *Glimpses*, p. 8.
9. Sweet, *Story of Religion*, 1950, p. 58.
10. Rudolph, p. 20, citing from James Howard Easterby, *A History of the College of Charleston Founded 1770* (Charleston, 1935), p. 10.
11. Carl Bridenbaugh, *Cities in Revolt* (New York: Capricorn, 1955, 1964), p. 379.
12. Bridenbaugh, *Cities in Revolt*, pp. 216–17. The University of Pennyslvania dates its origins to the Academy in 1740, although Bridenbaugh (p. 178) dates the Academy from 1751.
13. Bailyn, *Education*, pp. 44–45.
14. Bailyn, *Glimpses*, p. 15.
15. Bailyn, *Glimpses*, p. 18.
16. See Russel Blaine Nye, *The Cultural Life of the New Nation: 1776–1830* (New York, Harper & Row, 1960), pp. 172–173, 182–183.
17. Bailyn, *Education*, p. 47.
18. Bailyn, *Education*, pp. 14–15.
19. See Richard C. Wade, *The Urban Frontier* (Chicago: University of Chicago Press, 1959), pp. 233–243.
20. President Manning of the Baptist Rhode Island College (Brown) was among the most vigorous advocates for strict separation of church and state in the formative Revolutionary period. Sweet, p. 189.
21. Donald G. Tewksbury, *The Founding of American Colleges and Universities Before the Civil War* (New York: Teachers College, 1932), p. 28.
22. Rudolph, p. 47.
23. Rudolph, pp. 116–122.
24. Sweet, p. 213.

25. Rudolph, p. 125–126.
26. Merrill D. Peterson, *The Jefferson Image in the American Mind* (New York: Oxford University Press, 1962), p. 242, with reference to Henry Baxter Adams, *Thomas Jefferson and the University of Virginia* (Washington DC: United States Bureau of Education, 1888).
27. An edited version of the *Yale Report of 1828* can be found in Arthur Levine, *Handbook of Undergraduate Curriculum* (San Francisco: Jossey-Bass, 1978), pp. 544—556.
28. Rudolph, p. 130.
29. Although in some areas, such as rural western new York State, there was a remarkably high level of elementary and secondary school attendance. See Whitney R. Cross, *The Burned-Over District: The Social and Intellectual History of Enthusiastic Religion in Western New York, 1800–1850* (Ithaca, NY: Cornell University Press, 1950).
30. Richard Hofstadter, *Anti-Intellectualism in American Life* (New York: Vintage, 1962), p. 51.
31. Rudolph, p. 232.
32. Rudolph, pp. 177–200.
33. Although women were "kept in their place." Women students "laundered and mended the mens' clothing, cooked and served meals." See Nancy Cassidy Dunlap, "Out of the Fairytale: Women and the Curriculum of the 1990s," in *Symposium: Adults in Higher Education* (Mt. Pleasant, MI: Central Michigan University, 1989).
34. See Timothy L. Smith, *Revivalism and Social Reform* (Nashville, TN: Abingdon Press, 1957), pp. 103–113.
35. Clement Eaton, *The Freedom of Thought Struggle in the Old South* (Durham, NC: Duke University Press, 1940; Revised 1964), Chapter IX: "Academic Freedom Below the Potomac," pp. 216–237. See also Albea Godbold, *The Church College of the Old South* (Durham, NC: 1944); Winthrop S. Hudson, *Religion in America* (New York: Scribners, 1965), p. 155 *n.*
36. As cited in Rudolph, pp. 220.
37. From Ralph Waldo Emerson, "Politics," in *The Portable Emerson*, Mark Van Doren (ed.), (New York: Viking Press, 1946), p. 189.
38. Rudolph, pp. 238–239.
39. Several well-known institutes, such as RPI (1824) and the two military academies had provided most of the available formal scientific or technical training.
40. Rudolph, p. 292.
41. Mabel Newcomer, *The Big Business Executive* (New York, 1955).
42. From Ezra Cornell's Charter Day Address, as excerpted in Levine, p. 561.
43. Laurence R. Veysey, *The Emergence of the American University* (Chicago: University of Chicago Press, 1965), p. 299.
44. Stephan Thernstrom, *Poverty and Progress: Social Mobility in a Nineteenth Century City* (Cambridge, MA: Harvard University Press, 1964; Atheneum, 1969–75).
45. Rudolph, p. 261.
46. Rudolph, p. 216.
47. Rudolph, p. 330.
48. Veysey, p. 330.

49. Veysey, p. 330.
50. Veysey, p. 338.
51. Veysey, p. 340.
52. Veysey, p. 440.
53. Veysey, p. 440.
54. Veysey, p. 266.
55. Herbert Croly, *The Promise of American Life* (New York: Macmillan, 1909), p. 10, pp. 400–404.

PART TWO

INNOVATION IN THE PRESENT

What has become of innovation in recent academic generations? For over three hundred years, American higher education has responded reflexively to the prods of society, sometimes reacting positively, more often hesitantly, to the values of the social environment. The traditional university undergraduate residential college was generally adequate to the demands of its students. It had successfully survived the ravages of several wars, the withering effects of financial depression, and occasional but daunting incursions upon academic freedom from the external world, particularly during the immediate post-World War II years. By mid-century, higher education functioned particularly well for the professoriate itself, who made significant gains as professionals during the postwar period.[1] For unusually talented students, the university offered the honors program, the integrated or interdisciplinary program, or a wide range of unique colleges which accomodated pluralistic individual choice.

For a time, counter pressures for increased access to educational opportunity and for curricular options were deflected away from what was perceived to be the main road. For the commuting student, the community college and some urban commuter universities offered opportunities, even if these options were often considered second rate by the profession. For the adult student, extension programs offered access, and a few such programs eventually could yield a degree. Moreover, the campus made numerous modifications, with federal prodding and support, to accomodate physically handicapped students. And the distant or non-resident student, unable to come to a campus at all, had, in addition to correspondence study, the beginnings of study by television broadcast.

But surging residential enrollments and an almost universal desire on the part of the faculty to teach "better" students led to increased admissions requirements and to general neglect of what were often considered to be the peripheral students served through extension, evening school, and correspondence. Off-campus, adult programs, which began to flourish in

31

the 1930s and 1940s, were now relegated to the academic basement. And the community college accomodated the less academically prepared, who might otherwise have pressured the university for admission.

All-in-all, by the mid-twentieth century, the distinctive American pattern of the university was a great success. Nearly half of all school graduates now went to college, attending classes or seminars taught by departmentally based scholars. Mass higher education was a reality. For most members of the faculty, innovation centered on one's own research and the teaching of new courses with new academic content. But beyond these ongoing and critical micro-innovations, programmatic or institutional novelty in response to changing social needs was found only at the periphery of most universities.

Yet even while the traditional residential model occupied center stage as the popular version of "college," in a highly mobile and pluralistic society there were other unmet needs which required attention. And so around the edges of the traditional, individuals experimented with innovations, some of which have since become important new models.

Signaled by the political shift of 1960, major changes in society brought increased pressures upon higher education. By the mid-1960s the need for new responses could not be ignored. Americans had not often experienced violent radical activism among its college students. It was not merely the fact of the student riots and protests of the 1960s that electrified the press and populace but that they occurred on university campuses. In the late 1960s a number of students entered higher education as a way to avoid being drafted and sent to fight in Vietnam. The strategy worked, but students were in school perhaps for the wrong reasons, raising the potential for conflict between the purposes of the institution and those of the student. Suddenly student voices made themselves heard on the campus and beyond, and voices beyond the campus demanded change. Because many writers have chronicled the complex campus conditions of this period, I will not repeat them here.

The significance is that the sharp confrontation between campus tradition and external social and political values made conditions ripe for substantial educational innovation. *Egalitarianism* now meant equal educational opportunity for new and previously underserved students. Equality and social mobility united as values in common, a formidable force promoting a vision of education as the gateway to social acceptance and economic achievement by whole new groups of potential students. *Pluralism* affected the university in several dimensions. The United States was rapidly becoming a multi-cultural society. Students of a much wider diversity of backgrounds and circumstances than ever before began to trickle into college in greater numbers. These students required a much wider variety of curricula and instructional modes. They also demanded new efforts to extend the boundaries of the campus through educational extension and out-reach. And, perhaps less happily, *individualism* was expressed through an intense, sometimes narcissistic emphasis on personal choice and idiosyncratic consumerism.

The 1960s were the catalyst for questioning and reform, but it was the remarkable confluence of events in winter 1970–1971 that allowed educational ferment to erupt upon the national scene. Suddenly innovation was highly visible on all fronts. Adult degree programs were well under way at Syracuse and Oklahoma, the New York Regents Degree emerged from an existing college testing program (CPEP), opportunity programs which provided a transitional year into college for underprepared students were widely available, and Alan Pifer at the Carnegie Corporation asked if it was time for an "external degree." New, non-traditional institutions appeared with each passing month, including Empire State College, Minnesota Metropolitan, Evergreen State, the Institute for Personal and Career Development at Central Michigan University, the University-Without-Walls, and the California Consortium. In 1971 a Commission on Non-Traditional Study began to review new approaches to higher learning and issued its report with 57 recommendations in 1973. By then the Carnegie Commission on Higher Education, under the leadership of Clark Kerr, had issued a succession of important volumes which called for significant reforms in American colleges and universities.[2] So pervasive was the call for reform that many of the professional educational organizations, including the American Council on Education, the American Association for Community and Junior Colleges, the Council of Graduate Schools, the National University Continuing Education Association, the Federation of Regional Accrediting Commissions in Higher Education, the regional accrediting associations, and many of the scholarly associations initiated their own studies.

The federal government, motivated largely by its expanding commitment to student financial aid, especially for minorities, women, and vocational students, issued the critical *Report on Higher Education*, the "Newman Report," in 1971. This report soon led to the adoption by the Ninety-Second Congress of the Educational Amendments of 1972 to the Higher Education Act of 1965, which explicitly endorsed reform, innovation, and improvement of what was now called "postsecondary education." A new federal agency, the Fund for the Improvement of Postsecondary Education (FIPSE), was authorized to advance these goals through a program of specific grants. "Improvement" included founding new institutions, new programs for career and professional training, the encouragement of experiential learning, the use of educational technologies, a focus on individual educational needs, and improvement of graduate education. Gerald Grant and David Riesman have described the most remarkable outcome of the whole turmoil of the 1960s as "a considerably greater degree of autonomy for students," which led, they argue, toward "an over-optioned life."[3]

But we can also recognize something more fundamental at work here. The many innovative responses of the university from the 1960s to the present can also be understood as consistent with the historic pattern of responsiveness to the American environment. Since the 1960s, new academic programs, new institutions, and new approaches to teaching and learning have come into being at an unprecedented rate, reflecting the underlying tendency of American higher education, even after a half century of relative academic and structural uniformity, to improvise, innovate, and reform.

Of course in a volume of this size, not every important development can be considered.[4] This is not an account of all that is fresh and new in American higher education. Countless important innovations, discovered by each professor in the process of creating a new course or even a single lecture, although quite central to the reform of *content* in higher learning, cannot be considered here. Likewise, neither the pursuit of research, a uniquely innovative process of the university, nor the many important programs for the support of research with business, industry, and government are discussed. I will not attempt to analyze the extraordinary elaboration, process of specialization, and division which has characterized the academic disciplines in this century. Continuing professional education, research, and graduate study, while important areas for change and reform, are not treated.

No single volume could treat every instance of innovation, and other recent volumes have dealt with related themes. For example, innovations which spur closer links with secondary schools hold much promise for addressing a number of pressing articulation problems, but this is a key recommendation in Ernest Boyer's recent book, *College*.[5] Others, such as the development and improvements in core or general education, are widely discussed by other writers. Moreover, while general education reforms tinker with the curriculum, they are not particularly innovative beyond the normal and expected revision of curriculum which necessarily attends the business of a college.

The focus in this volume is largely on *undergraduate, for-credit education*. In Part One, I attempted to show the operation in history of consistently important American values as forces for change and to provide an intellectual and practical context for understanding how higher education responds to social priorities. Allan Bloom, for instance, has argued that American higher education must return to an earlier pattern of classical study. But Bloom is wrong about the American pattern and social context. Change, not classical constancy, has been the pattern. The mainstream of development in higher education, over three centuries, has not been exclusionary and elitist, but inclusive and encompassing. For purposes of illustrating these points in some detail, Part Two examines six extraordinarily rich and complex areas of innovation, measuring their impact upon the emergence of an American paradigm: new approaches in the liberal arts curriculum, access for new students, innovation and multiculturalism, adult continuing higher education, external degrees, and experiential degrees.

NOTES

1. See Christopher Jancks and David Riesman, *The Academic Revolution* (Chicago: University of Chicago Press, 1968).
2. For example, Carnegie Commission on Higher Education, *Less Time/More Options: Education Beyond the High School* (New York: McGraw-Hill, 1971).
3. Gerald Grant and David Riesman, *The Perpetual Dream: Reform and Experiment in the American College* (Chicago: University of Chicago Press, 1978), pp. 188, 190.
4. For a succinct summary of many of the non-traditional academic programs of the 1970s, see James W. Hall and Robert Hassenger, "Nontraditional Higher Education Programs," in Harold E. Mitzel (editor in chief), *Encyclopedia of Educational Research*, 5th ed. (New York: The Free Press, 1982), vol. 3, pp. 1336–1342.
5. Ernest L. Boyer, *College: The Undergraduate Experience in America* (New York: Harper & Row, 1987).

Chapter 3

Innovation and Curriculum

When one speaks of innovation in higher education, innovation in the undergraduate curriculum comes first to mind. Many of the historic innovations described in Part One are curricular in nature. Such developments are at the core of the academic and intellectual process, and even a cursory discussion of all their varieties would be beyond the purpose of this volume. However, there are several traditions of curricular and structural innovation which are important to the themes I have attempted here. One tradition is the integrated, or interdisciplinary, curriculum. A second uses human development as a key to organization. A third utilizes the structure of the cluster college to promote curricular coherence. Collectively these approaches represent what is for some observers the very center of educational innovation, while for others they represent a much too limited concept of the "innovative" in higher education. Some of these innovations are, in the words of Gerald Grant and David Riesman, "telic"—reforms which attempt to redefine or change the meaning or purposes of the baccalaureate,[1] even, some would argue, to give it meaning where none currently exists. These curricular areas of reform have, indeed, a long, distinguished, and continuing impact.

But the purpose for reviewing these innovations in some detail here is to show how they have tended to lead higher education *away* from responsiveness to American values. Although widely studied and written about, the overall effectiveness of these reforms seems less than might have been expected. In fact, most have failed, at least in the sense that they are now either terminated or substantially diluted from the ideals and objectives of their founders. Outside of their important place in the institutional memory of the higher education fraternity itself, the limited success of these innovations is best explained because they were *internally* generated university reforms which responded only in the most modest way to external egalitarian, individualistic, and pluralistic values. In some aspects they may be considered elitist, limited, occasionally precious. But they need to be described to show how differently conceived are the innovations described in subsequent chapters.

These curricular innovations can be said to have begun with the general education, or "liberal culture," movements of the early 1920s. The general education movement was a significant exception to the academic uniformity that set in after the turn of the century. Laurence Veysey sees the advocacy of liberal culture as a reaction on the part of humanists and its advocates against the growing hegemony of research and the German scholarly tradition. The strongest base of support for general, liberal education was in the small colleges, where philosophy, religion, literature, and history were centerpieces of the curriculum. Unable to compete for the major scholars of the day or to afford truly advanced instruction in science and the professions, these colleges espoused instead a concept of the baccalaureate which emphasized the summative, integrative aspects of all learning. Such learning, they advised, might be applied to the understanding of human social, moral, and aesthetic problems. Moreover, these advocates of liberal culture identified the holder of the B.A. degree with mastery of the genteel tradition's gentlemanly graciousness and moral code, characteristics of the "well-rounded man."[2]

Some of these idealists were responsive to the progressive impulse which sought to broaden the understanding and sensibilities of the American public, thereby bringing about improvements in government and society. Others were more elitist in their purposes, thinking education the means to separate men from the rude masses. On a practical level, the advocates of culture tended to lobby against free electives, against vocationalism, and, in some cases, against science. Development of the intellect and "qualities of the mind," they thought, should be the central objectives of an undergraduate education.

Veysey calls the Progressive era "the nadir of the small college in America."[3] Certainly many thought that most small colleges would close their doors or select a vastly transformed mission. But by choosing to stress liberal culture, aesthetic and moral values, these colleges now began to establish a new place for themselves, a firm and, for some, a distinguished niche in American higher education. By 1910 a widespread reaction to the elective principle led to restoration of course prescription and coherence to the curriculum of many colleges. Although widely varied in application, the idea of a more integrated "curriculum" had highly vocal advocates on every campus. For those faculty who might have espoused Christian piety in an earlier generation, the study of civilization and the humanities was, in effect, the new religion—an academic religion. Perhaps this helps to explain the particular attachment of the more secular of the old denominational colleges to the new ideal.

From this impulse came the first Western Civilization courses for undergraduates, an important and far-reaching curricular innovation. These cultural topics had their political implications, and so the development of such approaches soon interested faculty in the larger institutions as well. Columbia College's post-World War I general education course in Contemporary Civilization, and somewhat later in Humanities, are examples. Most importantly, these courses were designed to fill the educational gap for American students whose secondary education lacked the integration of the European lycée or gymnasium.[4]

Alexander Meiklejohn's experimental college at Wisconsin (1927–1932) became, with its Athens-America "great books" approach, the protoype and inspiration for many of the general education innovations that followed. But long before either his presidency at Amherst or his Wisconsin experiment, Meiklejohn expressed his view that the purposes of a liberal arts college should "broaden and deepen the insight into life itself,...open up the riches of human experience...arouse an understanding and appreciation of these, so that life may be fuller and richer in content...."[5] From such ideas descends a remarkable network of disciples who spread the general education concept. In particular the seed traveled with Robert Maynard Hutchins to Chicago, where the "Chicago Plan" sprouted.

Developed in the 1940s, some might call the Chicago Plan the most innovative expression of general education. Its key features freed the student from course enrollment by requiring year-end examinations supervised by an Office of University Examiner. Completely non-departmental in concept, the program enrolled many of its students after only two years of high school. The teaching faculty was quite independent of the graduate research faculty, and since student evaluation was externally conducted, these teachers could function as senior intellectual coaches, helping students to gain the competencies needed for success. The model, which did serve large numbers of students, did not fail. But following Hutchins's retirement it was terminated in 1953 by action of the University Senate.

The fact that such an intellectually rigorous program at a major university could end so suddenly is indicative of the difficulty inherent in bringing about lasting change. Many of the research faculty resented the autonomy of the College. Other divisions of the University resented the competition for students and faculty positions. Many resisted the underlying interdisciplinary baccalaureate concept, which denied student majors to departments. But most significantly, leadership failed. Robert Hutchins was one of the last American university leaders who could say confidently, "It's going to be this way because I want it to be this way." With his departure, a sound educational idea, left to the inevitable compromises of competing departmental politics, could not endure.[6]

But there is another way to view Hutchins's college. Hutchins's idealism linked the Chicago program to his belief that liberal education was critical to maintaining a free society and democratic institutions. As "American" as this idea sounds, it is not well rooted in American values. Its Platonic approach envisioned the creation of intellectually elite leaders, a concept quite foreign to the values of individualism, pluralism, and egalitarianism.

Over the years intricately ingenious changes have been played over a common ground, and the experiments of this period are richly described in the literature. What is most important for the purposes of this volume, however, is not the large numbers of such experiments or even their almost inevitable transience. What is important is whether and to what extent these programs were reforms that helped the university to respond to the dominant values of American society, especially as expressed through contemporary political and social leaders.

THE INTEGRATED OR INTERDISCIPLINARY CURRICULUM

St. John's College in Annapolis, and later Santa Fe as well, is the purest example of the wholly prescribed integrated curriculum. Even today it is a small successful effort to define the means to a baccalaureate degree as ends in themselves, creating for students, in the words of its founding dean, Scott Buchanan, "a great conversation about the great questions."[7]

Innovation was possible at St. John's in 1937 because the college —heavily in debt, its accreditation revoked—was on the verge of closing its doors forever. Buchanan, a visionary educational leader, was literally able to announce a wholly new curriculum. Probably this kind of innovation is possible, given good leadership, only at the creation of a new institution or program, or in the depths of institutional crisis. Ten years later Buchanan wanted to create a "permanent revolutionary committee" that would bring continual change in the St. John's curriculum, but, reflecting a common reaction from those who have experienced significant change, the faculty preserved the original design, now firmly institutionalized. If Buchanan thought that some changes were in order, he was by then unable to make it happen. Even later, when the Santa Fe campus of St. John's was founded, it proved, save for the architecture, to be an exact replica of the Annapolis program.

Another example, important because it developed much later within a distinguished multiversity, was the Experimental College at Berkeley. First offering instruction to 150 students in Fall 1965, the idea was the dream of Joseph Tussman. His academic reform was a two-year integrated general education modeled after Alexander Meiklejohn's experimental college at Wisconsin. Tussman acknowledged his program as "a simple act of discipleship,"[8] a college which "offered the solution to the central problems of undergraduate education." His freshman-year plan added seventeenth-century English texts to Meiklejohn's Greek and Roman and continued the second-year emphasis on American books. Indeed, the reading list parallels many of the St. John's great books of three decades earlier.

Interestingly, Tussman "accepted" a 30 to 1 student/faculty ratio so as to "avoid the individual tutorial" method. Three years later, when very high attrition from the program had effectively reduced the ratio to 20 to 1, Tussman added *regular* individual tutorial sessions and regarded these as essential. Each student spent a thirty to forty-five minute session with a professor at least once in two weeks.

From the first, Tussman attracted the more dissident students at Berkeley, students who sought more "freedom" in the pursuit of a B.A. Unfortunately, for all but a few students, the disjunction between their expectations of a college education and the expectations of the few adventurous and creative academics who offered well-planned and integrated curricula was too great. The Experimental College was terminated by the Berkeley faculty in 1969. Student radicalism undermined many of the experiments of this period. As Harris Wofford says about the students at SUNY's Old Westbury campus, "En route to Old Westbury, somewhere in the assassinations, riots, wars, trips to the moon, television and drugs through which they had lived, established society's grip on them seemed already to have been broken and with it their grip on the world."[9]

In some cases the "honors" program attempted to bridge the liberal culture idea of the college with the research mission of the university. Its early innovators were at Reed and Swarthmore. In time this academic approach, always limited to the strongest students, was adopted by large numbers of institutions. Such programs have the advantage of providing opportunity for advanced study in an individualized way. For a few especially talented students, honors programs may accomplish many of the integrative goals sought by reformers like Meiklejohn and Buchanan. But the number of students served in these programs is necessarily small. Moreover, since students do not usually enter these programs until the second or third year of college, studies tend to be specialized within a discipline or interdisciplinary problem rather than supportive of general education.

During the last two decades, newly created colleges have made numerous efforts to implement institution-wide interdisciplinary teaching and learning. Here can only be mentioned efforts at such diverse colleges as Evergreen State (Washington), Old Westbury (New York), Oakland (Michigan), Hampshire (Massachusetts), Ramapo (New Jersey), Santa Cruz (California), Stony Brook (New York), Montieth (Michigan), and Sangamon (Illinois). In each instance, although inherently fascinating for academics and some students, subsequent patterns have shifted away from a single-curriculum vision for all students toward a more pluralistic one. And in each case, the external demands of students have been most instrumental in shaping changes more in keeping with American values than the original version.

HUMAN DEVELOPMENT AND THE CURRICULUM

Concepts of human development and learning inspired another group of colleges and curricular plans. These concepts are embodied in the theoretical work of Carl Rogers, Abraham Maslow, and others and were most fully explicated at Johnston College in 1969 (The University of Redlands, California) and at Kresge College in 1970 (University of California at Santa Cruz). Johnston developed a high reliance on T-Group, or sensitivity, approaches, while Kresge, in addition to T-Grouping, emphasized key ideas of participatory democracy, consensual decision making, and personal integrity and growth. A key learning principle was bringing faculty and students into close contact, often by diminishing the appearance of the authority of knowledge on the part of the teacher. Teacher and student were both learners. Scott

Buchanan had expressed the problem differently years earlier at St. John's; he regarded "most college teachers as mere experts who were angered by those who dared to question their authority and who desperately attempted to hold their ground with a flood of esoteric information when the challenge persisted."[10]

Kresge's Provost, Robert Edgar, was a Cal Tech microbiologist who came under the influence of Carl Rogers. Following one year to plan, in fall 1970 Edgar enrolled forty students in a credit course entitled "Creating Kresge College," a planning year that had become standard practice for many of the new colleges then in the nursery. Edgar wished to "create a community with an egalitarian mood. Students must have control and responsibility." In fall 1971, 275 students and 118 faculty initiated the first full year of instruction. With an evangelical, "born again" rhetoric, the college drew students who sought to find themselves. Emphasis was on the living/learning link. "We hope," said Edgar, "the close sharing relationship... will be typical of the way students and faculty relate to one another. In this 'home' situation where one is accepted and loved, personal problems can be worked out...."[11]

But the intensity and purity of such a communal innovation, like that of the utopian communities of the early nineteenth century, were difficult to maintain. Dissension and dropout brought deterioration. Although 590 students enrolled in 1973, only half of these were in residence, posing a distinct problem for a college organized around community. By the mid-1970s the original Kresge College was contained in "The Corner of the College," a subgroup which remained small enough to preserve the founding ethos. The history of Johnston College is not dissimilar. Although the purest application of the human development model declined sharply after the mid-1970s, in the pluralistic tradition, dozens of highly idiosyncratic postsecondary institutions were subsequently founded, many of them in the state of California.

One of the most successful is the Fielding Institute, founded in 1974, which offers the doctorate to mid-career professionals in clinical psychology and human and organizational development. The academic program is rooted in contemporary learning and human development theory, and it employs a "contract learning" approach, experimental use of a computer communication network among its dispersed faculty, students, and alumni, and a commitment to organizational evolution through a shared social vision and consensual decision making process. This program, although numbering less than 600 students, appears presently to be a successful curricular innovation using human development principles. Whether or not such a model can succeed for undergraduates, for a very large constituency, or for less well-prepared and self-directed students will be worth knowing. William Maehl, an experienced administrator in adult continuing education from Oklahoma, has succeeded Fielding's first president, Frederic Hudson.[12]

One reason the state of California has engendered large numbers of educational innovations may be that its regulatory environment is more loosely controlled than in many other places. California also attracted during the 1960s a considerable number of entrepreneurial and creative persons whose organizational efforts led to the creation of new institutions. As with the Fielding Institute in Santa Barbara, many of these are small programs with narrowly focused missions. On the other hand, the National University, founded in 1971, claimed 9,200 students by 1986 and 13,425 at seven regional campuses by 1988. Unfortunately, it may have been the very existence of many relatively informal and sometimes academically inferior programs that has inhibited a more positive response to innovation from the dominant public universities. For some years the California legislature, under the instigation of such assemblymen as John Vasconcellos, has urged, without success, the creation of a "fourth sector" of postsecondary education as a way to provide increased access for bypassed students.

CLUSTERS FOR CURRICULUM REFORM

In a number of instances, new organizational structures were created to stimulate interdisciplinary liberal education. Although many unique organizational patterns have appeared from time to time, most are little more than tinkering with academic organization or administrative offices. But the cluster college looked like a major groundbreaking innovation in American higher education. For one thing, it seemed a way to stimulate curricular innovation within a multicollege structure.

The Five College Consortium in the Connecticut Valley, with its Hampshire College (1965) progeny, is a cluster. While other long-established consortia, less favored by geography, have sought to gain the advantages of becoming large scale while maintaining separate identities, the Massachusetts model actively cross enrolls students, provides an efficient bus service between campuses, and follows a common calendar. The Claremont Colleges are another example of clustering, if not cooperating institutions.[13] In the mid-1960s, the cluster concept spread nationwide, from the University of California at Santa Cruz to Michigan's Grand Valley State Colleges. Many of the newly planned institutions of this period, such as the State University of New York at Old Westbury and New Jersey's Ramapo College, featured a cluster plan, but budget limitations or limited enrollments have since hampered these developments.

In a sense, the cluster concept of multiple colleges under a centralized authority is a return to the old English pattern rejected by the American colonies in the seventeenth century. Santa Cruz is called by Grant and Riesman "a significant innovation in the organizational structure of a university," a blend of Berkeley and Swarthmore.[14] A graduate of Swarthmore, Clark Kerr, as chancellor of Berkeley, had tried unsuccessfully to create a college environment. When he became president of the University of California system, he had the opportunity to try again. In contemplating the new Santa Cruz campus, he invited his planning officer, Dean McHenry, "to find some way to make it small as it grows large."[15] The response was a cluster of special colleges. Cowell College opened in 1965, and a new college followed annually, creating what Grant and Riesman have called at Santa Cruz a "vibrant pluralism" and "genuine attention to educational issues."[16] Kresge College at Santa Cruz, opened in 1970, has already been described.

The cluster concept migrated with Martin Meyerson, new president of the expanding University of Buffalo, acquired by the State University in 1962. Meyerson, who had been the acting chancellor at Berkeley at the time several of the California experiments were approved, prodded Buffalo to become a highly competitive center with talented and widely diverse students. In attempting to respond to their needs in a period of increasing student dissent, in fall 1966 Meyerson proposed, as part of his academic reorganization, a system of residential colleges. Students should "have the opportunity to associate with or live in a college which will include residential and dining facilities, study and recreation space.... Some faculty...will live in them. ...Each of the colleges may be expected to develop a character of its own ...we must be aware of the great diversity of life styles and life ideals we must satisfy."[17] The first six colleges were broadly interdisciplinary and, following an open invitation in 1969 for proposals for additional colleges, ten additional colleges were approved. But Meyerson's absences and subsequent departure for the University of Pennsylvania, combined with a heavy dose of student and faculty radicalism, permitted weeds to prosper side by side with flowers. Some of the colleges generated vigorous controversy at the University and in the city of Buffalo. The colleges, as Arthur Levine points out,[18] were never created in place of the regular academic departments, but were supplementary, voluntary, and so peripheral. When criticism came, as it almost always does in the early years of an innovation, it was no surprise that the University required that each college be reviewed and in 1975 "rechartered." Moreover, when budgets were reduced later that year by a statewide expenditure ceiling, the colleges, in competition with the academic departments, came up short. Unlike UC Santa Cruz where the colleges *are* the university, at Buffalo the half-way innovation could not flourish.

These cluster colleges emerged in the midst of a turbulent, politically charged era, especially so at the large, prestigious universities. Educational and political leaders of widely different persuasions were able personally to initiate whole colleges during this epoch. Given the chaotic climate, radical experimentation was possible, but in many cases such experiments were educationally marginal and later terminated. As a consequence of both turbulent beginnings and subsequent financial difficulties, a full appreciation of the effect of the cluster concept on American higher education is not yet possible. But the cluster college does appear to be able to respond to large numbers of students in pluralistic ways within a high-quality educational setting. Moreover it shows the potential to bridge both American pluralistic and individualistic values while meeting serious academic expectations.

It is useful to review these extraordinarily creative and complex liberal education programs from the perspective of this volume's themes. Virtually all of these curricular innovations deliberately limited access because they were based on the belief that small size was critical to an effective program for students. Intense interaction with tutors and the need for substantial give-and-take in seminars demands either small numbers of students or very large cadres of teachers. But it has proven close to impossible to identify, attract, and retain over time sufficient numbers of faculty who are willing to give over their careers to such demanding, intense, and single-minded modes of teaching and learning. Tussman cites the need for enough committed faculty as his principal problem. But the problem was often even deeper. Small groups of idealistic and motivated teachers—working in highly scrutinized, glass-bottomed, pressure cooker environments—also exposed sharp and sometimes irresolvable philosophic and personal conflicts. Harris Wofford said, "One of the troubles with experimental colleges is that they attract too many experimental people."[19] The intensity of such tensions was called "traumatic" at Berkeley, and Tussman's experience was repeated everywhere.

Curiously, faculty and staff of these new experimental colleges were also almost totally opposed to the massive enrollment growth which had given them birth in the first place. Almost all of the experimental programs were initiated as sidebars to the growing massiveness of the modern university. These faculty and staff members opposed the pluralism of the multiversity, interpreting the conflict in higher education, as Tussman put it, not as between students and administration, faculty and administration, or faculty and students but as between the university and the college. The college, Tussman argued before the Berkeley faculty, does not "extend the frontiers of knowledge; it cultivates human understanding."

In the final analysis, these curriculum reformers not only rejected the university structure, they opposed the egalitarian and pluralistic values which the larger university claimed to support. And they also promoted a particularly narrow personalism rather than the broader value of individualism. They rejected, for example, recognition of individual merit through performance, subordinating this to a commitment to non-punitive evaluation practices and a leveling of the teacher's role. "Let us have the market if we must," said Tussman, "but let us not confuse it with the college. Free men are not produced in stores." His curriculum, therefore, sought to reverse the "competitive individualism" which characterized, he charged, both students and faculty in the American academic enterprise. Tussman, for example, speaks for all of these reformers in asking "whether the lower division belongs in the university at all."[20]

The failure of these innovations to produce lasting changes, changes which have done more than give a fine education to a few thousand students and deeply engaged the attention of a handful of interested educators, is partly that they consciously rejected the American conditions essential for successful innovation. Although each of the experimental colleges of the 1960s and early 1970s met the needs of a limited number of unusual and talented students, more recently their enrollments have declined as increasingly consumerist students make other choices.

Between 1950 and 1970, nearly 700 new colleges were founded, and almost 6 million additional students enrolled in colleges. Widespread innovation through new programs and whole new institutions was possible because the rapid growth in enrollment, supported by huge increases in public appropriations, generated new instructional positions faster than they could be properly allocated and filled through normal departments. But in the mid-1970s, the first oil crisis brought high inflation; deficit budgets at colleges led to intense program review and cutbacks. Many of the new and experimental colleges were caught in a state of partial development. Critical resources and momentum were lost, in some cases, irretrievably.

Riesman and Grant believe that the widespread resonance of the student-faculty movements of the mid-1960s occurred because of the confluence of a series of conditions unlikely to occur again. They cite very rapid growth in enrollment and faculty positions, a tightening of selectivity in student admissions, increased pressure on students to perform and faculty to publish, the overall size and bureaucracy of institutions, the large number of students who chose to remain in school to avoid the Vietnam draft, and the increasing conviction on the part of some that success derived from "cumulated advantages."[21]

By the mid-1970s, administrators and professors, as some complained, seemed exhausted or "burned out." The optimism of a 1964 issue of the academic and social quarterly *Daedalus* on "The Contemporary University" had been replaced six short years later by a *Daedalus* issue entitled "The Embattled University." Instability and frustration, products of surging growth and diversity in enrollment, questioning and experimentation, and finally revolt with both physical and curricular destruction now set in motion a conservative counterpoint propelled by the collective guilt of a generation of academics. Allan Bloom expresses this guilt in his 1985 volume *The Closing of the American Mind.* Clark Kerr has called this a "climacteric period," a great turning point in the history of higher education. By 1975 the era of unbridled acceptance of change had ended, and the search for new stability had begun. Highly touted experiments at Brown, Stanford, Old Westbury, or Buffalo, to name but a few, were terminated or "brought under control" in that year. For all the well-intended efforts, innovators had not yet succeeded in creating models which could respond to American egalitarianism, pluralism, and individualism, while also tending to the legitimate and central academic objective of improving the quality of education itself. *Daedalus* looked "Toward an Uncertain Future." More longlasting, socially responsive and integral reforms would need to be rooted in these values, and they were not long in coming.

In considering the shift away from an overpersonalized and occasionally narcissistic approach to curriculum, the leadership role of Ernest Boyer, currently President of the Carnegie Foundation for the Advancement of Teaching, is worth noting. Boyer has, for more than a generation, been at the forefront of innovation in American education. The reason is that he has correctly read the deeper values and conditions of American society. Thus his most recent vision of the undergraduate experience captures the essence of a new synthesis which more appropriately represents the historic balances of American higher education. "We...embrace," he says, "the notion that the aim of the undergraduate experience is not only to prepare the young for productive careers, but also to enable them to live lives of dignity and purpose; not only to generate new knowledge, but to channel that knowledge to humane ends; not merely to study government, but to help shape a citizenry that can promote the public good."[22] In the next chapters I will explore reforms which, rather than serving small, selected groups of young students, were designed to bring Boyer's goals within the reach of significant numbers of new student populations.

NOTES

1. Gerald Grant and David Riesman, *The Perpetual Dream: Reform and Experiment in the American College* (Chicago: University of Chicago Press, 1978), pp. 17–18.
2. Veysey, *Emergence*, p. 180–203.
3. Veysey, p. 237.
4. Robert L. Belknap and Richard Kuhns, *Tradition and Innovation: General Education and the Reintegration of the University* (New York: Columbia University Press, 1977), p. 50.
5. Alexander Meiklejohn, "College Education and the Moral Ideal," *Education*, vol. 28 (1908): 558. See also Alexander Meiklejohn, *The Experimental College* (New York: Harper & Bros., 1932).
6. See F. Champion Ward, "Requiem for the Hutchins' College: Recalling a Great Experiment in General Education," *Change*, vol. 21, no. 4 (July/August 1989): 25–33. See also, F. Champion Ward (ed.), *The Idea and Practice of General Education* (Chicago: University of Chicago Press, 1950).
7. Grant and Riesman, p. 19.
8. Joseph Tussman, *Experiment at Berkeley* (New York: Oxford University Press, 1969), flyleaf quotation, p. V.
9. Harris Wofford, "SUNY at Old Westbury," in Gary B. MacDonald (ed.) *Five Experimental Colleges* (New York: Harper & Row, 1973), p. 173.
10. Grant and Riesman, p. 65.
11. See Grant and Riesman, Chapter IV, pp. 77–134, for a detailed treatment.
12. *Fielding in the 1990's Project: A Vision and a Plan* (Santa Barbara, CA, March 1986).
13. The Claremont Graduate School, which draws from the faculties of each of the Claremont Colleges, is an exception to this generalization.
14. Grant and Riesman, pp. 287–288.
15. Grant and Riesman, pp. 254 and 255.
16. Grant and Riesman, p. 290.

17. Arthur Levine, *Why Innovation Fails: The Institutionalization and Termination of Innovation in Higher Education* (Albany, NY: SUNY Press, 1980), pp. 37–41.
18. Levine, *Why Innovation Fails.*
19. Wofford, pp. 159–160.
20. Tussman, *Experiment at Berkeley.*
21. Grant and Riesman, pp. 191–194.
22. Boyer, *College*, p. 297.

Chapter 4

Innovation and Access

The American egalitarian value has been and is the persistent external force stimulating educational innovation in the mid- and late twentieth century. Expressed in higher education as a quest for access and equal opportunity, response to the egalitarian value has been persistently elusive, for it comes into conflict with the university's struggle for excellence achieved through student and faculty selectivity. The battle lines are often drawn between those who see quality as antithetical to access and those who believe that quality can be achieved, even redefined, while increasing access. The debates over who should be admitted have usually focused on who can best benefit from the faculty and resources placed at a student's disposal. Before each of the major access innovations of our time—the G.I. Bill, the community college, and open admissions and Educational Opportunity Programs—these debates have occurred. The first came over the G.I. Bill.

THE G.I. BILL

Long years of depression followed by World War II had brought some colleges and universities, especially many of the small Catholic, black, and women's colleges to the brink of insolvency. Then one of the most stunning reversals in the entire history of American higher education occurred. The Servicemen's Adjustment Act of 1944 and 1945 (the "G.I. Bill") was at first conceived as providing a readjustment period for potentially unemployed returning soldiers. An urgent economic problem faced the nation; the problem cut across all strata of society and all regions of the country. It was created by an expected mass migration of people from the battlefront to the labor front. The G.I. Bill was supported by liberals and conservatives alike in the belief that "the economy and not the veteran needed adjusting."[1]

At the outset, however, it was unclear that educational leaders would respond favorably to these conditions. Old fears, such as dilution of quality and distortion of mission, not dissimilar to those which limited the responsiveness of the pre-Civil War denominational colleges, were expressed *sotto voce*. Veterans as students, it was predicted by such eminent leaders as James Conant of Harvard, Robert Hutchins of Chicago, and Francis J. Brown of the American Council on Education, would stress vocationalism over the liberal arts and would generally bring the "least capable among the war generation" into college. The War Department doubted that more than 7 to 8 percent of the veterans would take advantage of the Bill and thought that many of these would attend less than college-level schools. For a brief time, the battle between elitism and egalitarianism, exclusion and response, was heard on the Hill and echoed across the country.

Misgauging the people's pulse, *The Saturday Evening Post* of August 18, 1945 entitled a piece "G.I.'s Reject Education."[2] But 2,232,000 veterans attended college over the next five years, with over 1 million of these older students on campus in the year 1947–1948. Enrollments at many colleges were temporarily doubled. An amazing 37 percent of veterans eventually used the benefits, and every study shows that the vast majority were highly motivated, serious students whose grades and academic interests proved the early skeptics wrong. The president of Northwestern University called it "the greatest experiment in democratic education the world has ever seen."

Assessing the permanent impact of this highly innovative government act is more difficult. Keith Olson's excellent study and assessment perhaps underestimates some important results in concluding that the program left "only tangential" influences on higher education. It is probably true that "veterans demanded no changes in the basic structure or values of higher education." But his passing observations that rapid expansion and federal support had occurred without concomitant government control, that older and often married students had been admitted to the campus, and that class size had been demonstrated to be surprisingly expandable, are more significant than he suggests. At the very least, the university was now better prepared for the onslaught of students that followed the quiet decade of the 1950s. And the positive experience of educated G.I.'s in the dynamic postwar economy undoubtedly led them as parents of the "boomers" generation to stimulate the next generation's interest in going to college.

In terms of total numbers, the ability of American higher education to absorb stunning increases in student enrollments, decade after decade, is itself an unparalleled phenomenon. American higher education provides a degree of access found almost nowhere else in the world. In 1880, little more than a century ago, 115,817 students, or 2.7 percent of the 18–21 year age group, attended college. In the next sixty years enrollments increased by a factor of ten, reaching 1.1 million in 1930, and 2.6 million between the end of World War II and 1955. Then came the floodtide, enrollment surging by 1 million by 1960, another 2 million by 1965, a further 3 million by 1970, and yet 3 million more by 1975. Enrollments peaked at just under 12 million about 1979. That same year the number of instructional faculty reached a high at 830,000, the number of full-time students peaked at around 7 million, the number of women surpassed the number of men for the first time, and a cabinet-level U.S. Department of Education was created by Congress. Government and higher education had responded at every level to this national demand for the opportunity to go to college. Many innovations made this achievement possible, including teacher training, books, and equipment. No criticism of restricted access which follows should be understood to diminish the magnitude of that accomplishment.

But the question of who should be admitted to college, which appeared in the debate about the G.I. Bill, was also found in planning for major university systems. The State University of New York, created in part to meet the influx of veterans, existed as an organizational entity for only two years when its first Master Plan appeared in 1950. That plan projected the "estimated number of persons having the ability to complete various levels of college" in New York State in 1960 and 1966.[3]

	1960	1966
13th–14th grades	208,000	286,000
15th–16th grades	114,000	155,000
Above 16th grade	49,000	66,000

Although these projections were later proven to be very low estimates when compared to actual enrollments, they were actually more inclusive than the projected numbers of college-going students proposed by President Truman's Commission on Higher Education. The Commission's report in 1947, *Higher Education for American Democracy*, is best remembered today for its support for the community college. But even while projecting a need for increased enrollment capacity, the Commission's recommendation assumed that "not more than 20 percent of the pool of 18–21 year olds would be full-time students." While 49 percent of youth 18 & 19 "had the mental ability to complete grade 14, only 32 percent of youth 20 & 21 would be able to complete grade 16."[4]

That prevailing and restrictive view of the population's educational capability changed only slowly during the 1950s. But when the next SUNY plan appeared in 1960, it said, "New conditions and wholly new requirements have arisen, the nature of which emphatically suggests that each and every institution of high learning in New York State will be severely pressed simply to meet the demands of an expanding student population." The notion of "rising aspirations" was now seen as more important to college-going rates than the earlier rather limited measure of "mental capability."[5]

THE COMMUNITY COLLEGE

Although private and public senior colleges and universities expanded to meet the demand, it was the community college that increasingly permitted access into the system. Today, some 55 percent of all entering college freshmen enroll first at a community college.[6] In some states, most notably California, students who do not meet the academic qualifications for admission to one of the university campuses begin study at a community college.

The community college as an organizational innovation is as important in its way as the development of the land-grant university nearly a century earlier. The same values which supported the national commitment to serve all Americans with some form of instruction in the public schools in the 1920s and 1930s now stimulated interest in more universal undergraduate education, especially through the "fourteenth" year.

Junior colleges and private two-year colleges came into being in the 1920s, with more than 200 extant at the beginning of World War II. But these early forms, most privately supported, generally did not share the mission that would characterize the later "community" college.[7] Of the earlier institutions, some served as college preparatory schools, offering the first two years of a liberal arts curriculum. Others were more akin to finishing schools; still others were highly specialized business institutes, religious seminaries, art schools, and the like. After World War II, many veterans found their way into these specialized or preparatory colleges. The Truman Commission report is credited with the first use of the term "community college" and defining most of the guiding principles for the new institution.[8] But not until the late 1950s did the community college emerge in its present form. Hundreds of new community colleges were founded in the late 1950s and the decade of the 1960s.

Innovations were both curricular and organizational. Community colleges offered a new mixture of academic courses, incorporating both the arts and sciences transfer and college preparatory programs of the older junior colleges, with the career offerings of the specialized institute or proprietary school. With classes close to the student's home, this new hybrid institution offered something for everyone, especially access for those who could not afford a distant residential college. Organizational innovations included a new form of financial support, enlisting local tax powers, either through the school tax or special district or county appropriations. Local trustees governed policy. This meant that neither statewide officials, as in the case of public colleges, or private donors, as with the private arts and science colleges, would control these institutions. Moreover, such broad fiscal support meant that the cost to the "consumer" (the student) could not be matched.

Established four-year colleges might have initially opposed this development as unwanted competition, but in the late 1940s they were overflowing with veterans. Shortly thereafter, with the return to normalcy in the 1950s, four-year colleges and universities were mostly relieved not to have to respond to the growing pressure for vocational programs. Although credit enrollments in higher education actually declined slightly from 2.65 million in 1950 to 2.57 million in 1955, immediately thereafter the massive enrollment surge began. Within the next five years they increased by 1 million, an increase of 39 percent; in the next five years by 2 million, up 56 percent. As colleges prepared to accommodate such increases in the 1956–1960 period, the community college found support from local politicians who sought opportunity for their constituents, from corporate employers who needed trained technicians and white-collar linesmen, and from the senior colleges and universities, who were thereby excused from helping to alleviate that pressure. Christopher Jencks and David Riesman describe the community college movement as "a safety valve releasing pressures that might otherwise disrupt the dominant system."[9]

For many years the transfer arts and sciences program was the prestigious track in the community college, and, in such states as California, the student was encouraged to contemplate movement into a state college for upper-division study. But more recently, this earlier pattern has changed, with occupational programs commanding the majority of enrollments. By 1979, the number of students enrolled in community colleges surpassed, for the first time, the number of undergraduate students enrolled in senior colleges. Uncertain whether its mission is two years of postsecondary study or two years of university coursework, the community college proves a highly successful, if unstable and shifting, innovative model. The community college is thus its own prototype, an American innovation which continues to produce fascinating initiatives and variations. Most significantly, it follows the historic trajectory of the American university to reach out, to extend its services into more and more communities, and to respond to the broad educational needs of society.

OPEN ADMISSIONS AND EQUAL OPPORTUNITY PROGRAMS

Yet even the community colleges were unable to fulfill the aspirations of students who had been bypassed by the massive growth of higher education. While the 1954 *Brown v. Board of Education* Supreme Court ruling reversed the 1896 *Plessey v. Ferguson* decision, which upheld the constitutionality of providing "separate but equal" schools and universities, it was not until the end of the 1960s that empowered African-Americans were able to translate that new court interpretation into opportunity in higher education beyond historically black institutions.[10] Between 1960 and 1980, minority enrollment in higher education doubled from 600,000 to 1.2 million; but total college enrollment trebled in the same period to 12.1 million. As increasing numbers of African-Americans entered the university, their collective voices began to call for reforms which might enable the university to serve them more effectively. Often enunciated in the form of non-negotiable demands, they sought the admission of larger numbers of minority students and participation in the decision processes relating to recruitment, admissions, and the management of financial aids. And because retention of African-American students was rapidly becoming a major issue, demands also included provision for special programs to improve basic skills, the availability of African-American tutors and counsellors who might relate more sympathetically as role models to African-American students in the largely white professional staff of the university, and for some significant new offerings which incorporated the African-American experience as seen through such subjects as history, literature, and sociology into the curriculum. W. E. B. DuBois' earlier call to educate "the talented tenth"[11] now became an urgent cry for opportunity for all.

In 1969, the City University of New York (CUNY) responded to that call by announcing a major innovation in admissions practices—open admission. In a sense New York City, with its long tradition of free tuition, was the logical place for the nation's most comprehensive innovation in access to college. Although some state universities had earlier accepted all students who were high school graduates, large numbers of these applicants were routinely flushed from the system during the first term of study. By the mid-1950s CUNY's senior colleges were overcrowded, even with a stiff grade average required for admission. Moreover, minority enrollment at the senior colleges was less than 10 percent.

The New York State SEEK program (Search for Education, Elevation and Knowledge) was an early response, providing remedial courses, individual tutoring, and financial stipends to those from poverty areas who did not meet the usual criteria for admission to a senior college. EOP and HEOP (Educational Opportunity Programs) also gave special support to needy students who required transitional preparation for college-level study, and these were most heavily subscribed to by students attending the community colleges. A third special program was the EOC (Educational Opportunity Center), which, although non-collegiate, provided remediation, completion of the secondary diploma, and counselling.

But African-American and Hispanic students considered this triad of special programs as token efforts, and took political action for the admission of large numbers of additional students directly into the senior colleges. Violent demonstrations accompanied these demands at campuses across New York City during 1968 and 1969. Daily activities of the faculty and administration were interrupted, arson and vandalism were widespread, and special measures introduced to maintain security brought police and the courts into campus life. On July 9, 1969, CUNY announced that admission to the university would be open to all, beginning in September 1970.[12]

Even so, open admission did not mean that entrance to a senior college was open to any student who wished to attempt to study. Previously the criterion for admission to a senior college was graduation in the top quarter of the class and the completion of certain college-qualifying course units. Under open admission, a diploma was still required, but those in the upper half of the graduating school class with an average of at least 80 percent were now eligible. Although these new criteria were far from allowing totally open admissions, they did produce a flood of students, swamping the classrooms and other facilities of CUNY colleges.[13]

Ironically, large numbers of white students, previously ineligible for admission to a senior campus, became eligible under open admissions and so continued to represent a substantial majority of those who came. At one campus, Brooklyn College, total undergraduate enrollment climbed from 19,428 students in 1969, the year before open admissions, to 29,812 in 1975, the last year of the experiment. But the September 1975 entering class of 4,000 students was 80 percent white and mostly middle class.[14] And while 72 percent of the 1960 Brooklyn College class had earned the degree within five years of admission, less than 25 percent of all CUNY entering freshmen earned a baccalaureate degree under open admissions.

The formal end of the innovation in open admissions coincided with deep citywide budget cuts during the New York City near-bankruptcy in 1975–6. The State of New York assumed full funding from the City for the senior colleges and, for the first time, tuition was imposed equal to that of the SUNY system. Even without a change in the admissions requirements, the enrollment at Brooklyn College collapsed from 30,000 in 1975 to only 16,000 in 1979.[15]

Because open admissions was so innovative and dramatic, it stands as an important model and has been intensely researched.[16] Studies of open admissions students found little correlation between special tutorial or remedial courses and success, although such enrichments seemed to improve the "total college experience." Brooklyn College President John Kneller said, "There is no question that Open Admissions had to . . . take place. The only question is whether it should have been done in the way it was, given the realities of public funding, and given the reality of the faculty who had to do the job."[17] The statement about faculty is most significant, for it raises forcefully the issue of quality of instruction, as perceived by the faculty, and access, as perceived by the student consumer. How is it possible for highly skilled academics, trained to probe the limits of scholarship, even with undergraduates, to systematically lower the classroom expectations, to tailor the sophisticated levels of instruction for those who read and write inadequately? The disjunction between professional aspiration for the scholarly role and student need for compromise was too great.

Open admissions at CUNY was a magnificent experiment in the tradition of American egalitarianism. Its failure can be attributed to many factors, but mostly it was a program enforced too quickly by external social forces, without adequate preparation and funding. Prevailing values of the university and the student were too far apart and too abruptly forced together. Society and university were out of sync, and the innovation collapsed. Long before open admissions, CUNY understood the social problem and had established goals and timetables for implementation. But as witnessed with the G.I.Bill, the land-grants, and the community college movement, external forces can stimulate sweeping innovation; but they can also cause innovation to career out of control or, conversely, return abruptly to a more traditional equilibrium.

ACCESS AND THE FUTURE

Even with the increased opportunities of recent years for women, adults, and minorities, there are still 50 million households in the United States where no family member holds a bachelors degree, and the number increases annually.

Only 19 percent of American adults currently hold college degrees, less than one in five. The rate of growth in the U.S. labor force is slowing and will increase by only 21 million, or 18 percent, by the end of the century. More significantly, African-Americans, Hispanics, and Asians are expected to make up 57 percent of that labor force growth. Women will represent 64 percent of that growth. By the year 2000, African-Americans are likely to constitute 12 percent of a total work force of 139 million, Hispanics 10 percent, and Asians 4 percent.[18] Peaking in 1962 at 40.6 years of age, the median age of the labor force declined to a low of 34.6 in 1980 and has since been rising again. By the year 2000, the median worker age should reach 38.9, as fewer and fewer young people enter employment.[19] Even while the number of 14 to 24 year olds who are the entry-level college students and workers in the labor force is shrinking rapidly, the number of young people who are disconnecting from school, from work, from any skill development, is rising dramatically.

These projections make inescapable the need for improved service to underprepared and bypassed students, a most critical area for future innovation. Recently the trend of minority enrollment has been upward, except for African-Americans, whose enrolled members declined by 102,000 students between 1980 and 1984, even while the number of African-American high school graduates increased by nearly 400,000 to an all-time high. In 1978, 46 percent of those school graduates went to college; if that rate had been sustained in 1984, there would have been 316,480 rather than 265,000 African-American students in college. "Where," asks Solomon Arbeiter of the College Entrance Examination Board, "are the missing 51,480 students?" Arbeiter finds that the military services have enlisted many more of these high school graduates, while others have gone into proprietary schools or the labor force.[20]

By contrast, between 1976 and 1986, African-American enrollment at traditionally black colleges increased from 455,000 to 613,000 students, while holding almost level at all four-year institutions at about 215,000 students.[21] Fifty-five percent of African-American students are in two-year colleges, and few are pursuing liberal arts transfer programs at the associate degree level. In 1976, 59,000 African-Americans earned four-year college degrees, but this declined to 57,000 in 1983 even as the eligible African-American population increased sharply.

African-American social patterns appear to be changing faster than social institutions. Minority communities, which housed a diverse range of families in the 1950s and 1960s, provided, especially in the African-American ghetto, role models of two-parent families, working fathers and mothers, church and community leaders. School-going was promoted as an important opportunity, and, in the earliest period of equal opportunity, many new students enrolled in higher education. More recently, however, the more successful African-Americans have moved away from the ghetto to middle- and upper-class neighborhoods, leaving behind the homogenous poor. As they look about they see few role models for hope and improvement.[22] These young people will become adults, desperately in need of educational opportunity, yet unable, in many cases, to come to a classroom regularly. American society is accumulating a huge burden of debt to people now coming to adulthood who have been bypassed by the whole educational system. If undereducation, illiteracy, and the unacceptably high high school and college dropout rate is to be reversed, every possible method for educational outreach will be needed.

This scenario has led former U.S. Secretary of Education Terrel H. Bell to call for "a Marshall Plan" to deal with a nation-threatening problem.[23] He suggests a goal to increase the number of adults holding college degrees from the present 19 percent to 35 percent by the year 2001. To make this goal possible, universities, Bell says, will need to "restructure their modes of delivery of instruction and services. We'll need to use cooperative models, including work-study, instructional television, instruction at the work place, and faculty/computer approaches." Here is a prescription for important future innovation rooted firmly in American needs and values.

What approaches to innovation promise to improve the enrollment and success rates of African-American and Hispanic students? Few issues seem likely to be more important or command more thought from school, college, foundation, and government officers. Some foundations have committed substantial grant funds to new approaches, seeking replicable models. The Ford Foundation has for several years supported programs at community colleges, where most minority students are enrolled, trying to improve retention and encourage upward transfer to a senior college. Among the areas for promising innovation are teacher training programs which create new role models for school children, setting high expectations within a disciplined environment. Combinations of work and study seem fruitful approaches, one of the more interesting being a School and Business Alliance, headed by former Queens College President Saul Cohen and New York State Commissioner of Economic Development Vincent Tese. They have persuaded some of New York's largest employers to provide meaningful jobs for high school students while they continue to study. The model should be extended into college as well. Perhaps most important will be experimentation with alternative methodologies of teaching and learning. Working mothers need flexibility of time and place of study. African-American males, especially absent in senior colleges, might benefit from participation in small groups which generate peer interest and pressure. Two-year college students need, from the day of admission, attentive academic and career advisement which establishes personal goals and prepares them for transition to senior colleges or for work. And large numbers of older and experienced employed minorities, for whom today's opportunities did not exist, can benefit from further adult higher education. In this way they will provide necessary role models while bringing new competencies to the community.

In conclusion, by allowing the university to respond actively to the American egalitarian value, by offering previously bypassed students the opportunity to show personal merit, and by creating new pathways to social mobility, these access innovations have transformed the entire context of higher education in the late twentieth century. Yet much remains to be done if the demands for access are to be successfully met. Moreover, access is not enough; completion of a college degree and entrance into the mainstream of American life is the goal.[24] Further innovations have tried to improve this ratio of success for new and non-traditional students. In an increasingly multicultural United States, the question as to whether or not ethnic cultures benefit from ethnic identity in higher education is an important matter pondered in the next chapter.

NOTES

1. Keith W. Olson, "The G.I.Bill and Higher Education: Success and Surprise," *American Quarterly*, vol. 25, no. 5 (December 1973): 596–610.
2. Olson, p. 601.
3. State University of New York, *The Master Plan* (Albany, June 1950), p. 21.
4. The President's Commission on Higher Education, *Higher Education for American Democracy, Vol. I* (New York: Harper & Row, 1947), pp. 41–43.
5. SUNY, *The Master Plan, Revised* (Albany, 1960), pp. 12, 16.
6. Dale Parnell, *The Neglected Majority* (Washington, DC: Community College Press, 1985), p. 99.
7. In 1981, private two-year colleges counted for 25 percent of all two-year institutions but enrolled only 200,000 of the 4.5 million students.
8. Parnell, p. 84.
9. Jencks and Reisman, pp. 481–492.
10. Jencks and Riesman, pp. 406–479.
11. W. E. B. DuBois, "The Talented Tenth" (1903), as quoted in Leslie H. Fishel, Jr., and Benjamin Quarles, *The Negro American: A Documentary History* (Glenview, IL: Scott, Foresman, 1967), p. 369.
12. Murray M. Horowitz, *Brooklyn College: The First Half-Century* (New York: Brooklyn College Press, 1981), pp. 162–171.
13. Horowitz, p. 164.
14. Horowitz, p. 167.
15. Horowitz, p. 213.
16. See for example Theodore L. Gross, *Academic Turmoil* (Garden City, NY: Doubleday & Co., 1980); David E. Lavin et al., "Open Admissions and Equal Access," *Harvard Educational Review*, (February 1979).
17. Horowitz, pp. 169–170.
18. U.S. Bureau of Labor Statistics, *Monthly Labor Review*, (Washington, DC, September 1987).
19. U.S. Bureau of Labor Statistics.
20. Solomon Arbeiter, "Black Enrollments," *Change*, vol. 19, no. 3 (May/June 1987): 14–19.
21. Walter R. Allen, "Black Colleges vs. White Colleges," *Change*, vol. 19, no. 3 (May/June 1987).

22. A series of recent issues regarding African-American communities are discussed in Andrew Hacker, "American Apartheid," *The New York Review of Books*, vol. 34, no. 19 (December 3, 1987): 26–33. See also William J. Wilson, *The Truly Disadvantaged: The Inner City, the Underclass, & Public Policy* (Chicago: University of Chicago Press, 1987).

23. *To Secure the Blessings of Liberty: Report of the National Commission on the Role and Future of State Colleges and Universities*, Terrel Bell, Chair, (Washington, DC, 1986), p. 4.

24. The reader is also referred to K. Patricia Cross, *Beyond the Open Door* (San Francisco: Jossey-Bass, 1971); and Carnegie Commission on Higher Education, *New Students and New Places* (New York: McGraw-Hill, 1971).

Chapter 5

Innovation, Pluralism, and Multicultural Higher Education

The force of the American value of pluralism is far-reaching in supporting innovation. Pluralism enforces tolerance for other views and other people, even when few of the contesting groups within society would willingly tolerate another. Martin Marty, University of Chicago historian of American Religion, likens pluralism to the commercial needs of the marketplace. In school textbooks, he notes, "What Mormon...will buy a book that has a line that Mormons find unsatisfactory? What non-Mormon will allow what might look like something favorable to Mormons?...Since one cannot please, then is it not advisable simply to be silent about religion in texts?"[1] Unlike *egalitarianism*, which is demanding and political, or *individualism*, which requires personal choice and may be self-centered, usually aggressive, and occasionally narcissistic, *pluralism* is permissive, tolerant, laissez-faire.

But such toleration is itself a condition conducive to change, especially change which promotes student access. Institutional branching and mutation is encouraged by the demands of different religious or ethnic groupings. Pluralism's permissive character has allowed higher education to make learning available in many places, at many times, and in myriad useful forms. It gives the student consumer an ability to demand services and programs. Because many colleges compete vigorously to meet these demands, individual students are increasingly able to find academic programs which match their personal educational goals and learning styles.[2] Institutions of every level and widely varied purposes, and programs ranging from the most highly specialized academic area to off-campus courses for part-time students, all fit snugly, if not always comfortably, in the pluralistic bed of American higher education.

Despite the competition for students that it engenders, pluralism serves the university well. Pluralism precludes decentralized educational authority. As a result, no "flagship" university, no central "ministry" of education, and no external examining body controls the chartering of degree-granting institutions. This condition has allowed hundreds of small colleges to develop across the continental landscape. It spawned multitudes of special purpose colleges serving women, Roman Catholics, African-Americans, Baptists, Swedes, Mormons, and every other self-defined group.

Pluralism also allows for differentiation of programs and scholarship. No overarching authority establishes the curricula required for degrees or sets the examinations for graduation. These conditions provide a very positive environment for innovation in the shape and content of academic study for different groups or individuals. As American educators and public officials contemplate the possible effects of proposed statewide or national competency examinations, they would do well to have in mind this cultural value.

Slowly in recent years, sometimes grudgingly, pluralism has begun to be transformed into a more actively positive *multiculturalism*. Multicultural implies a celebration rather than mere tolerance of diversity. It recognizes differences and elicits their strengths. It avoids the mediocrity of the melting pot, conjures up the *paella* with recognizable parts of the whole, rather than the smoothly blended *vichysoisse*.

In education, multiculturalism finds expression in the value of languages other than English as bearers of culture and commerce. Multiculturalism lifts up the history and language of ethnicity, then redefines ethnicity itself. In tertiary education, multiculturalism creates both the need and political force for distinctively separate academic departments, such as "Black Studies," or "Judaic Studies," or even for whole institutions dedicated to meeting the needs of a defined population, as at Boricua or Hostos Colleges (New York). In the United States, higher education has responded at different times in its history to the multicultural drive. Historically black colleges and Catholic institutions are early responses. More recently, Latino programs and institutions are emerging. Institutions uniquely designed for Native Americans seem likely to grow and succeed. And American schools are now being purchased outright by Japanese, as they buy corporations, to create responsive places for their own nationals. Multiculturalism is very much a part of higher education in America, and it is thereby a significant force for change and for innovation. Consider several examples.

CHURCH COLLEGES

Historically interesting are the Roman Catholic colleges which have met both the aspirations of local religious teaching orders and the needs of Catholics for inexpensive, accessible, and, in some cases, religious higher education. The more than 300 Roman Catholic affiliated colleges and universities in existence by 1980[3] grew in response to the needs of Catholics for places where they could both preserve their values in a Protestant, but increasingly secular world, and gain the access to higher education denied to many by the dominant society. Catholic populations, concentrated in the cities, created urban Catholic colleges and universities. Unable to afford the

cost of living at a distant residential campus, Catholic students could com-
mute daily at a fraction of the cost. And since most of the teachers were priests
or nuns whose services were inexpensive, tuition fees were kept relatively
low. Since the children of immigrant unskilled laborers usually could not
go even to secondary school, a great many of the Catholic colleges founded
before 1920 either failed or remained very small. But as a lay demand developed for Roman Catholic undergraduate education, the response was in
the tradition of American pluralism.

Prevailing notions of Catholic hierarchy and centralism to the contrary, Catholic colleges and universities were founded and operated by autonomous teaching orders which represented every existing ethnic, language,
class, and regional division among Catholics. As each Irish, German, Polish, Italian, or Latino congregation reached social maturity, new colleges,
or transformations in the ethnic makeup of existing colleges, occurred. Roman Catholic colleges are striking examples of higher education's response
to pluralism. Although by the late 1960s the founding of new Catholic colleges tapered off, the recent rapid increase of Hispanic and Chicano populations, especially in Texas, Florida, and California, suggests that the turn of
this century will most likely bring the founding of another wave of ethnic
Catholic colleges in these states, which today have few Catholic colleges.
It will also be interesting to see whether the phenomenal growth of fun-
damentalist Protestantism among Latinos will lead to the founding of new
institutions.

Recently some of the smaller and curricularly limited Catholic colleges
have undergone drastic changes. Many have secularized their boards of
trustees and numerous teaching faculty have given up their religious voca-
tions as well. Today the faculties of many Catholic colleges are predominantly
lay persons. Moreover, some colleges have imposed wholly innovative curricula and teaching practices, taking a leading role in expanding educational
outreach, especially to adult students (see Alverno College, Chapter 7).

COLLEGES FOR AFRICAN-AMERICANS

If Catholic colleges are the most florid response to multiculturalism, historically black colleges, although a critical and important sector of today's
educationally diverse mosaic, were at first tolerated by whites as an effort to
limit their attendance on otherwise white campuses. The impulse that created them was not pluralism, but separatism. Negro colleges first appeared
between the Civil War and World War I. Most often they were not founded
by empowered African-Americans but by whites, who, while they rejected
African-American enrollment in white institutions, saw higher education for
African-Americans as means of maintaining social control, providing useful
vocational and trade training, and, for the most altruistic, "improving the
race." Unlike the idealistic antislavery advocates who inspired such colleges
as Oberlin, Amherst, and Bowdoin to accept negroes in the 1820s and 1830s,

such organizations as the Freedmans' Bureau and the American Missionary Association, which founded over 200 private African-American colleges in the South after the Civil War, did not seek racially integrated institutions.

Legally prohibited in the South from learning to read before emancipation, most former slaves, not unlike the children of unskilled white immigrants, had far more pressing needs than higher education. As a consequence, the early successful institutions trained African-Americans in useful trades, providing the skills which might earn a living. Such institutions as Hampton and Tuskegee met such needs and were financed modestly by whites. Booker T. Washington spoke forcefully to whites about "industrial education" for African-Americans, and later W.E.B. DuBois urged the training of "the talented tenth" as teachers for African-Americans.

In 1896 the Supreme Court's *Plessey v. Ferguson* decision sanctioned separatism by requiring land grant universities either to admit African-Americans or to establish "separate but equal" colleges. This led to the founding of some thirty segregated state institutions, mostly agricultural and technical colleges, between 1890 and 1945. Historically black colleges, while serving a critical role for African-Americans during a dark period of officially sanctioned racism, represent a rejection of pluralism. With some notable exceptions, many continue to this day to experience the financial deprivation wrought by a separatist response by higher education.

Nonetheless, the early vision of leaders like Washington and DuBois established the foundation for those institutions which today continue to serve the largest numbers of African-American students and whose success in producing graduates and African-American leaders far exceeds the experience of other institutions. Based upon such experiences and evidence, the role of ethnic and culturally distinct colleges and universities in achieving access and success for underserved populations needs reexamining.

COLLEGES FOR HISPANICS

Although Spanish-speaking explorers and settlers are the earliest European citizens of the Americas, permanent Hispanic settlements in what is now the United States were confined to outposts in Florida, Texas, California and the Southwest. Mission schools brought schooling to these areas, but university-level education was restricted to metropolitan areas of the New World, not its outposts. The University of Mexico (1553), and the University of San Marcos (1572) provided the higher learning thought necessary, and those who required otherwise traveled to Spain. Unlike the New England Puritans, who planted the seeds for higher learning as soon as the cultural frost was off the ground, Spaniards created no colonial antecedents for higher learning in what is now the territorial United States.

Although increasingly large Spanish-speaking populations appeared in New York City, Miami, Los Angeles, and areas of south Texas, New Mexico, and Arizona, not until the 1960s did social demand for special services to Latinos become generally felt in higher education. Today significant statistical differences exist among the various Spanish-speaking populations—Americans of Mexican, Cuban, Puerto Rican, Haitian, Dominican, Central and South American origins. Mexican-Americans, for instance, grew by 93 percent between 1970 and 1980, while the overall increase for Hispanics was a still remarkable 61 percent. Income levels vary considerably among Hispanic national groups. Despite these differences, Hispanic-Americans as a group stand especially in need of access to higher education. Although Hispanics number 19 million and make up 8.2 percent of the age 18–24 population, they constitute only only 4.3 percent of the college-enrolled youth. Only 62.9 percent of Hispanics 18–24 graduate from high school (compared to 83.6 percent for Anglo-Whites and 75.6 percent for African-Americans), and only 48 percent of these enroll in higher education, well over half in community colleges. In 1985, Hispanics earned 2.7 percent of the bachelor's degrees awarded in the United States.[4]

Within the federal government, the Fund for the Improvement of Post Secondary Education was among the first agencies to perceive the need and to respond with institutional grants. Boricua College in New York and Washington, DC, was among the first, and its founder, Victor Alicea, broke innovative ground in gaining legal and financial support for its programs in 1974. Hostos Community College in CUNY also gained important recognition and support from FIPSE and other philanthropic organizations. Today Hostos offers a bilingual program which allows students to earn credit in academic subjects taught in the Spanish language, even while they learn English through English as a Second Language (ESL) programs. The result, according to Hostos president Isaura Santiago, is the highest proportion (87 percent) of Hispanic enrollment in any public college. The SUNY college at Old Westbury enrolls a significant proportion of Latinos.

TRIBAL COLLEGES

The same kind of support for ethnic, unicultural colleges now seems likely to develop for Native American institutions. A recent study by the Carnegie Foundation for the Advancement of Teaching shows that, by 1986, more than 90,000 Native Americans attended college, mostly at the two-year level. But the rate of growth in completion of bachelor's degrees is quite striking. From only 66 graduates in 1961 and less than 200 in 1968, almost 4,000 Native Americans received undergraduate degrees in 1987. Nonetheless, completion rates are not high, and the environment for native Americans at most colleges has been less than fully supportive. The Carnegie study focuses on an important exception: the "tribal college."

The first tribal college began in 1968; by 1988, twenty-four such colleges enrolled 4,400 students. These colleges are located within Indian communities, and most offer associate degrees in vocational and paraprofessional fields. These tribal colleges include, for example, Little Big Horn, Standing Rock, Turtle Mountain, Sinte Gleska, and Fond DuLac.[5] Federal financial support comes in very modest amounts through the Tribally-Controlled Community College Assistance Act of 1978. In 1989, the Carnegie Foundation for the Advancement of Teaching, building on the pioneering work of a handful of Native American colleges begun In the 1960s, announced a comprehensive and coordinated plan to strengthen these institutions through increased financial and philanthropic activity.

Only today is the positive role of these ethnic colleges coming to be better understood. It is no accident that essentially all of the African-American leadership during the 1960s and beyond were graduates of historically black colleges. Nor is it surprising that the rate of graduation and subsequent success is far higher for African-American graduates of these colleges than for African-americans who attend pluralistic, largely white, institutions. At a time when all of education is seeking to improve its ability to enroll heretofore underserved populations and avoid the revolving door, the expe- riences of these unicultural institutions could provide innovative lessons and new possibilities. Colleges which emphasize ethnicity, which are designed expressly for Latinos, Japanese, Native Americans, Roman Catholics, or Muslims, seem increasingly likely to emerge as innovative responses to pluralism and multiculturalism in America.

Higher education, however, does resist pluralism in other ways. One common example is the formation of a kind of cartel for the awarding of academic credit. In this arrangement, certifiable, accredited learning is a packaged commodity, available only from those member organizations that have met and that continue to meet the regulations of the presegmented market. Such accredited learning, in the form of degrees, diplomas, and certificates, is a regulated substance and, as such, is available only to students who come to the proper establishment, present the appropriate prescription, and proceed according to the instructions on the label. For adult students, in particular, such restrictions often precluded, until very recently, the achievement of a college degree.

Innovation and improvisation are adversely affected by such resistance to pluralism. Pluralism, which permits student choice and stimulates institutional competition, does not function well within a regulated environment, for regulation tends to limit educational options, to restrict the search for new programs and approaches. Of course, regulation can function positively—for the student consumer, by protecting the quality of academic standards and services—and for colleges, by limiting competition and allowing faculty to set standards of scholarship and practice. But regulation becomes less attractive for the student consumer when it segments the market, limits student admissions, restricts an institution's programs or outreach, and so minimizes the choices available to the consumer.

Consider, as an example, the prevailing means of evaluation or grading in higher education. Current grading systems are designed to recognize the most talented students and to reject or discourage those who do not compete in the upper quartile of talent. Faculty, especially in the exact sciences, are deeply committed to this evaluation strategy as it is believed central to maintaining excellence and quality. Yet one wonders if that system doesn't screen out from further participation large numbers of students who could perform many highly skilled functions accurately and consistently, given time and opportunity to master the subject in question. Given the growing national need for skilled workers, one wonders further if we can still afford the social waste of allowing so many to fail or lose interest.

It is just possible that a conceptual alternative more responsive to the American pluralistic value could actually produce a higher quality final result overall. For example, a change that could make a great difference would be to replace or supplement current evaluation processes which screen students out, which exclude those who do not rank "above the average," with evaluation strategies which measure student competency and subject mastery, while deemphasizing comparisons with class performance. While such a strategy may seem less strenuous and demanding, in reality it removes or reduces the importance of the factor of time in performance.

To a considerable extent the factor of time has driven our current selection and evaluation systems because fiscal cost and scarce resources have severely limited the support available to individual students. For many students, there has been insufficient time to determine a student's objective ability or inability to perform. When the cost of supporting a student's mastery of a subject is aided by technology—by computer-paced presentation, trial, and repetition—will the time and cost factor associated with the on-campus, classroom method be significantly lowered so as to permit greater access? Such a question is difficult to answer satisfactorily, but it presents a beguiling area for experimentation in the future.

Amy Gutmann notes that college admissions committees may "give weight to the wrong non-academic characteristics—conformity rather than creativity, ambition rather than motivation to help others, lust for power rather than leadership, good manners rather than good character."[6] Application of the values of pluralism to our systems of selection and evaluation seem necessary changes if higher education is to respond adequately to the multicultural needs of our time.

Pluralism thus presents a real conundrum. From a very early time, the American college has struggled with two opposing tendencies: the centripetal need to define and limit the curriculum, to squirrel in one nest the necessary teachers and books and to hold together a transient and sometimes fickle student body; and the centrifugal desire to respond to the highly diverse external population's values and requirements. Balancing these two tendencies may well be impossible within a single institution, but the American decentralized, laissez-faire approach to higher education has allowed each new group or an enterprising educator to initiate an institution or program. Pluralism is a powerful value for change. Multiculturalism, as the more active and positive aspect of pluralism, may prove even more potent as a force for innovation in the years immediately ahead.

To illustrate, one might think that the creation of new colleges would have stopped in recent times, especially with the increased attempts to regulate by statewide coordinating bodies and voluntary regional accrediting associations. But new colleges have continued to appear at a surprising rate. Between 1970 and 1981, 725 *new* institutions were founded. Many of these are very small colleges with close religious affiliations, not unlike those which appeared in many towns of the "Old West" between 1800 and 1820. Native American tribal colleges, noted earlier, account for twenty-four new institutions. In New York State, for example, twenty-three new postsecondary institutions appeared after 1970 and exemplify the pluralistic value. Eight are Jewish Rabbinical seminaries with very tiny enrollments; one is Roman Catholic with less than 150 students; eleven others are technical, proprietary, or branches of established community colleges, which enroll 21,500 students, largely in career programs. The remaining three institutions offer non-traditional programs and serve large numbers of students: Hispanic Boricua in New York City, Regents College of the New York State Education Department, and Empire State College of SUNY.

Together these last three non-traditional baccalaureate-level colleges serve nearly 25,000 students. Most of them are adult students, individuals who, for a variety of reasons, were unable to complete college degrees during the "traditional" years of ages 18 to 22. And these colleges are not alone in reflecting a pronounced trend to older registrants. The mean age of all students in American higher education has risen markedly in recent years, a dramatic change from the 14- and 15-year-olds who populated the nineteenth-century college. The number of programs now available to older students is a pluralistic phenomenon that represents one of the most important areas for innovation in American higher education today.

There is a pronounced tendency, then, for educational institutions to divide and multiply, to reach out, to expand their services, to embrace more groups of potential students. Accordingly, it is possible to understand the history and trajectory of American higher education as an ever-widening circle, gradually encompassing more people, in increasingly responsive programs and flexible curricula, and by more varied criteria leading to certification or to a degree.

Understanding this dynamic and plural response explains the evolution of a peculiarly American approach to higher education. It also puts into perspective some of the many perplexing changes of recent years. Finally, it may provide insight into the likely course of development for the remainder of this century, especially as the new interactive communications technologies become firmly established in supporting university extension and outreach. In the next chapter we shall see how pluralism serves the purposes of older students.

NOTES

1. Martin E. Marty, "Secular Humanism," *The University of Chicago Magazine*, vol. 79, no. 4 (Summer 1987): p. 12.
2. David Riesman, *On Education: The Academic Enterprise in an Era of Rising Student Consumerism* (San Francisco: Jossey-Bass, 1980).
3. Detailed information regarding Catholic colleges may be found in Christopher Jencks and David Riesman, *The Academic Revolution* (Garden City, NY: Doubleday, 1968), pp. 334–405; and Robert Hassenger (ed.), *The Shape of Catholic Higher Education* (Chicago: Chicago University Press, 1967).
4. Cheryl Fields, "The Hispanic Pipeline," *Change*, vol. 20, no. 3 (May/June 1988): pp. 20–27.
5. Carnegie Foundation for the Advancement of Teaching, "Native Americans and Higher Education: New Mood of Optimism," *Change*, vol. 22, no. 1, (Jan./Feb. 1990), pp. 27–30.
6. Amy Gutmann, *Democratic Education* (Princeton, NJ: Princeton University Press, 1987), p. 200.

Chapter 6

Continuing Higher Education and Adult Part-time Students

No contemporary social circumstance has required such substantial response and innovation from the university as the dramatic shift from first-time, full-time, usually residential students, to part-time, usually commuting, almost always older students. Although this shift has now become the most pervasive, widely accepted higher learning innovation of the twentieth century, higher education, with exceptions at some urban universities, has historically regarded part-time students as second class citizens, carefully segregating programs for part-time and older students from those offered to full-time, "regular" students. Educational apartheid has been the rule. But that pattern is now changing.

A few years ago the Commission on Higher Education and the Adult Learner said:

> There is a significant resistance within many four-year colleges and universities
> to making the accommodation necessary to serve adult learners with full and
> equal effectiveness. This is attested to by representatives of business, industry,
> and other organizations who have sought to negotiate with universities and
> colleges for undergraduate and graduate level educational programs. And state
> higher education officials note the lack of pressure from public universities
> for programs, services and funding to meet adult learner needs. In spite of the
> recent evidence of change on many campuses, higher education institutions
> themselves remain a major impediment to addressing the nation's needs for
> resources for adult learning. They appear unready to recognize the magnitude
> of the need and confront the requisite changes.[1]

Adult part-time study for academic credit or degrees beyond the boundaries of the daytime classroom developed slowly and faced difficult hurdles in its evolution. Yet, the notion that learning might occur at times and places other than "the eight-o-clock bell" or in the old school house had been around for a long time. Evening schools were offered in the eighteenth century for those who, like apprentices, were "confined in Business in the Day-time."[2] And such a colonial organization as Benjamin Franklin's Junto in Philadelphia and its many nineteenth-century imitations offered study opportunities for adults through "mutual improvement" societies.

It is odd that education for adults was not comprehended earlier within the formal schooling system. After all, in a rapidly growing economy, new immigrants, factory workers, incipient merchants, and newly hatched professionals represented a large potential demand for education. In the period between the War of 1812 and the Civil War, other social units did respond to this substantial adult demand for learning. But colleges were not among them, perhaps because, as noted earlier, they were still bound by a limited mission.

The developing factory system, however, was responsive. As the industrial revolution gained strength in America, newly developing factories and textile mills along eastern rivers required large numbers of new employees. Sons and daughters of mostly rural folk required immediate training so that they could undertake highly specialized tasks. In fact, in the dynamic society of the early 1800s, the factory system was widely understood to be the key to improving the overall quality of life. Believing that they could improve upon the "despised English industrial system," some industrialists designed whole factories from scratch that, presumably, offered a wholesome environment for workers and their families.[3] Some companies provided adult learning opportunities, even before public education became widely available. In this period, when entirely new technology, machinery, and processes appeared with regularity, in-house education and training was essential to forge a competitive workforce. As early as the 1870s, schooling within corporations offered education and training to employees. While at one end of the educational spectrum, literacy programs in the English language sought to acculturate immigrant employees, at the other, a few companies began to offer management training. Some of these programs apparently compared well with instruction offered in the public schools of that period, especially in such matters as student responsiveness and mental discipline.[4]

Another important organization for adult learners was the Sunday School. As these religious schools swept the nation, they used the Bible to provide significant instruction in reading and writing. Rhee's *Manual of Public Libraries* lists over 50,000 libraries in the country in 1859, with 30,000 of these found in Sunday Schools![5] The Lyceum movement, founded by Josiah Holbrook in 1826, also tapped into a considerable adult demand for education largely unmet by existing colleges. Through participation in the Lyceum, thousands of Americans in nearly every town across New England and, to a lesser extent, in the West and South, attended weekly lectures on the most up-to-date ideas of the age—topics largely excluded from the college curriculum. Similarly, the American Tract Society, anti-slavery organizations, and many others provided important educational opportunities for adults. By the latter part of the nineteenth century, the Chatauqua idea, based upon the summer lectures on Lake Chatauqua in western New York, spread throughout the country. Under hastily erected tents, lectures, and Round Tables were offered on such topics as Milton, Temperance, Geology, Relations of Science and Religion, and the American Constitution.[6] But the American college was not involved, resisting these popular innovations for adults in order to maintain a classical curriculum for a handful of youth. But by this time, the American college was becoming only one part—and increasingly, minor one—of higher education. The time of the university had come.

As one looks back across the history of the university in America, much change is closely associated with the coming of extension. Such efforts began slowly, perhaps only as an undefined potential in The Morrill Act of 1862. That Act authorized the creation of land grant colleges and stimulated the first courses in agricultural and technical subjects. Gradually the benefits for farmers were extended by the agricultural research and experimental stations established by the Hatch Act of 1878 and direct annual federal support authorized by the second Morrill Land Grant Act of 1890. The Cooperative Extension Service, established in 1914 under the Smith-Lever Act, enabled farmers far from a university campus to learn about the benefits of agricultural research. Meanwhile, general extension units began to appear in the 1880s and 90s.

As higher education grew and prospered into the twentieth century, the university scrambled to build a strong reputation for scholarship, whereas liberal arts colleges served almost exclusively full-time students of liberal culture (Chapter 2). Resistance to older, part-time students continued. When higher education did respond through the universities, it created new and separate structures which, for better or worse, maintained apartheid for older, part-time students. These structures became known as the "division," "school," or "college" of "evening," "continuing," "extension," or "adult" education and paralleled cooperative (agricultural) extension. Interestingly, and largely for political reasons state by state, cooperative extension was quite separate until the last two or three decades in most public institutions. "Continuing" education, as nomenclature, came later, after World War II.

Under these structures, universities otherwise occupied with quite traditional research and departmental instruction, could offer a wide variety of service courses to non-resident part-time students, both on and off-campus. Those engaged to teach were not necessarily traditionally trained faculty. And as some of these programs gained supporters, they became anchored within the traditional structure. Continuing education, then, acted as the lightning rod of the university, transmitting new social currents into the university, giving the university an outlet into the wider community. Populist notions in vogue around the turn of the century nurtured the idea that the university and society could infuse one another productively. In 1904, Charles Van Hise, president of the University of Wisconsin, proposed the "Wisconsin Idea," introducing general extension and making "the boundaries of the University campus coterminous with the boundaries of the state." For the first time popular and technical subjects were offered across the entire state through extension and correspondence courses.

Unlike the nineteenth-century colleges, which generally refused to incorporate into their pristine academic settings the thriving adult education found beyond its walls, the land grant universities responded rapidly. Some leaders of those institutions recognized that the adult world was changing rapidly, with need for further education. But within the liberal arts college, resistance continued, as it does to this day. Such spurious arguments as that "people would not sustain their interest through successive lectures," or that "time given by the professoriate for such lectures would inevitably weaken their classroom effort, where serious, real learning took place," were offered as reasons to resist.[7] Nonetheless, City College of New York did extend its courses into the evening hours in 1909 to allow students to pursue a degree at night. Other institutions, such as Chicago, Columbia, Wisconsin, and Minnesota, began to offer special courses for adults. Nicholas Murray Butler, president of Columbia, proposed "to extend the classroom and laboratory work in the evening in New York City and in the neighboring parts of New Jersey, New York, and Connecticut; and, in addition, evening classes will be organized which may be taken advantage of by wage workers." The University of California, Berkeley, first offered extension courses in 1891 and correspondence study in 1913. (Today, University Extension serves 50,000 students in 2,000 courses, covering every area of university study.) Later, these were joined by such universities as Wayne State (Michigan), Cincinnati (Ohio), and New York University, which built its early reputation through service to part-time and evening students in its professional schools.

Yet even with these new capabilities, no real adult degree—a program designed primarily for adults with special scheduling *and* curriculum—was available. Although the notion of offering a college degree to off-campus students was germinated in newly created extension divisions of universities, its realization was to take a long time. By the late 1950s, however, special off-campus degree programs for adult students appeared at several universities in the form of extension degrees. The best known were at Oklahoma, Syracuse, Roosevelt, and Brooklyn (CUNY). Although these degrees featured cross-disciplinary curricula, the Bachelor in Liberal Studies (B.L.S.) or some variant other than the classical B.A. was awarded, reflecting reservations held by the traditional faculty.

Probably the earliest program designed expressly for the adult working student was the Special Baccalaureate Degree Program for Adults (SBDPA) at Brooklyn College. Initiated with assistance from the Ford Foundation by President Harry Gideonse in 1954, the program was headed by Bernard H. Stern from the outset until his retirement in 1971. The program also awarded credit for knowledge gained through experience, by equating such knowledge with existing college courses. Seminars with broad academic content replaced certain prescribed courses, enabling adults to attend classes at times suitable to working people. Enrollment, originally limited to twenty-five students, had doubled by 1965.[8] When Stern retired from CUNY, he brought his experiences with him to Empire State College, where he became the first Dean of its New York City center in 1971.

Such new adult degree programs liberated the degree from the requirements of the traditional academic department, with its negotiated course sequences and major. These changes, while not earthshaking in their departure from the prevailing norms at the outset, prepared the way for a much more thoroughgoing reconceptualization of the entire educational process for adult students and so were important. They also confirmed that continuing education, in its many forms, would become the most responsive, most innovative sector of American higher education in the twentieth century.

Who are these older, part-time students invading the college campus? There are four categories of part-time students. One group are *students pursuing a regular degree program on a less than full-time basis.* These toilers often have similar purposes for study as students studying full-time, but they frequently exhibit higher motivation. They differ from full-timers in that they have chosen to study part-time because they have financial restraints, family, or work obligations that prohibit them from studying full-time.

Another important group are *students seeking additional professional training or upgrading* on a recurrent part-time basis. Already many professional associations require periodic retraining or upgrading to maintain certification or licensure, and this group seems to increase in number as new organizations and states dictate new expectations for professionals. Milton R. Stern, dean of University Extension at Berkeley, in noting the paradoxical need for those already well-educated to require yet more education, says that we "are in the process of extending compulsory education beyond childhood, beyond adolescence, to the end of professional careers."[9]

Students pursuing a particular interest, whether for credit or not, through university extension or continuing education constitute the largest group of part-time students. Either as a product of their own personal growth or because of their perceptions of changing social and technological situations, many adults feel the need to prepare for a new career. In recent years there has been a pronounced movement to establish some form of recognition for such study, and the Continuing Education Unit (CEU) has a validity which deserves wider recognition as a measurement of accomplishment.

Finally, *students attend credit or non-credit conferences, workshops, or institutes* held occasionally for a limited period of time. These intensive learning opportunities, temporarily full-time, seem likely to multiply as part-time students seek group experiences of greater depth and intensity and as colleges respond more creatively to the work and family responsibilities of individual students.[10]

In recent years few institutions have been untouched by the rapid shift away from full-time recent school graduates toward increasing numbers of these part-time, older students. In fall 1988, of the 12.8 million degree credit students who enrolled in colleges, 5.5 million, or 43 percent, attended part-time.[11] Moreover, part-time status correlates well with age; the enrollment of part-time students is roughly equal to the number of students aged 25 or over. If one included formal non-credit studies, then adult students would easily constitute the overwhelming majority of students in and about the college campus. Those data don't mesh well with the still widely held myth about the character of the American college. The reality is that, except at the more selective of liberal arts colleges, the mythical model is largely extinct.

A widely circulated 1984 report of the National Institute of Education described these changing patterns of college-going: "One in three of our freshmen have delayed entry to college after high school, more than two in five undergraduates attend college part-time, and over half of the bachelor's degree recipients take more than the traditional four years to complete the degree."[12] In a 1986 report prepared for the American Association of State Colleges and Universities, a call went out to public universities to recognize the needs of older part-time students. The report went further, calling for significant structural reform in order to respond adequately.

> In order to respond to these needs, state colleges and universities should restructure their modes of delivery of instruction and services to give adult and part-time students full access to undergraduate and graduate programs. Specifically, institutions committed to serving adult learners should build on tested cooperative models: work-study programs, instructional television, instruction at the work place, and faculty-designed computer-aided instruction.[13]

One development certain to bring increased numbers of adults into higher education is the large number of older persons who complete their school diplomas through the tests of General Educational Development, the GED. Since 1967, the number of people taking GED tests each year has increased from 218,000 to nearly 800,000. Today almost one in seven persons earns a diploma by this alternative route. The average age of the candidates is in the mid-twenties, and about half indicate that they plan to pursue further education.[14]

For many institutions, it is now certain that future growth and financial stability will depend in large measure on their ability to attract and organize services for older part-time students. Such a capability is more easily asserted than executed and presents new problems for old institutions.

For the residential college, service to adults sets new challenges. For one thing, most adults study part-time. Although a part-time student's course tuition provides only a fractional part of college revenue, each person represents *one whole student* in demand upon college services. Part-time students can require as much college effort as full-time students, especially in such operations as library, admissions, records, placement, student accounting, advising and counseling, food services, and, not incidentally, parking. Moreover, older part-time students can be demanding, insistent on gaining access to costly services, and vocal about the need for flexible practices.[15] Most obvious is the need to extend the hours of college services beyond the usual academic workday into evening and weekend hours. Unfortunately, most budgeting formulas fail to recognize this increased institutional workload, a distinct disincentive for academic departments to serve part-time students.

To make matters still more challenging, the needs and demands of part-timers are as variable as the students themselves. Far from the relatively common background and experience brought to the campus by callow secondary school graduates, older students come with widely diverse interests and preparation. College faculty cannot assume a common level of preparation, nor can they necessarily conduct their classrooms in the same ways as they have done and expect to remain aloof from student challenge. Once they have their feet planted firmly on the unfamiliar classroom terrain, adults tend to speak their minds, engage faculty as peers, and thereby create a very different, though stimulating, intellectual climate.

Another characteristic of institutional resistance is elitism; this can also create problems for part-time students. One of the compelling factors within the dynamics of higher education which moves universities away from service to adult part-time students is the almost universal faculty desire to be as selective as possible in admitting students. Prestigious New York University, for example, grew in the earlier years of the twentieth century, largely by serving regional clienteles drawn from the lower socio-economic groups of New York City. Today NYU competes internationally for students and finds service to general regional needs costly and not well aligned with its research mission. Its professional schools, which once catered to part-time evening students struggling to gain necessary credentials, now admit primarily full-time candidates or offer continuing advanced professional education to practitioners. Although the School of Continuing Education offers credit toward a B.A. in Liberal Arts and an M.S. in Real Estate Investment and Development, the great bulk of its students are non-credit, non-degree candidates. Nonetheless, this School has grown rapidly in recent years and represents an important educational service for adults in the New York metropolitan region. NYU's Albert Gallatin Division is a more non-traditional program, offering individually planned degrees, with students able to pursue undergraduate and masters degrees in the regular university academic departments. But the professional schools at NYU, as at many other research universities, focus heavily upon graduate level, tuition supported, continuing education for professionals. At the undergraduate level, CUNY has assumed much of the regional mission in serving part-time adults. Unfortunately, even the public colleges and universities, operating under funded enrollment caps, tend to eliminate part-time and off-campus clienteles to make room for full-time students. Given a choice, university faculties will opt for full-time, on-campus students.

Many adult programs, especially for off-campus offerings, fail to provide adequate resources for learning—the books, study guides, communication networks, and timely, incisive faculty feedback to students—that are central to serious study. Vague promises that students have "access" to the libraries of other colleges may not have much value unless specific arrangements have been made between the institutions. Adult education programs need to gauge that degree of resource support and accessibility which is essential, without necessarily providing the equivalent of the Bodleian Library (as some external evaluators sometimes seem to suggest) to each student. Clearly, off-campus programs should not be expected to provide a level of resources which is seldom duplicated at even the strongest of residential campuses.

In this connection, the importance of the library as the intellectual center of the university, the spark plug of the campus, can be often exaggerated. Strong colleges may spend as much as 10 percent of their annual operating budget in purchasing and cataloging volumes and in providing specialists to assist scholars and students in reference, periodicals, and bibliography. But most do not. The irony is that the library is so little used. A 1984 survey of undergraduates conducted by the Carnegie Foundation for the Advancement of Teaching, showed that about a quarter of undergraduate students do not typically use the library at all, and another quarter use it less than two hours per week. The variation in this pattern was relatively small, whether the student attended a public or private institution, a research university or liberal arts college.[16]

Nonetheless, part-time adult students do need books, and they need them in time for the beginning of a course. This goal has proven difficult for many programs to meet, especially for off-campus students. Empire State College, for example, ships books directly to students by parcel post with a 24-hour order turnaround. Central Michigan University has developed library services which can quickly respond to students studying at its many centers throughout the nation. Although some programs designed explicitly for adult students, such as the British Open University, the International University Consortium, and the Public Broadcasting Service, have made large investments in expensive course packages, including printed texts, the area most amenable for innovation in the future is likely to be in the provision of print resources through electronic data bases (Chapter 9). Already, some colleges offer their entire library catalogue by satellite or dial-up telephone transmission, and, assuming that copyright policies keep pace with the technology, transmission of full texts directly into student homes will be feasible when the incredible capacity of fiber optic cable becomes more generally available. Such technological innovations should do much to help overcome the problem of scarce and costly resources for adult off-campus and part-time students.

Another problem of adult continuing education is the tendency for colleges in need of funds to turn to special off-campus courses for adults as a way to turn a quick profit. Educational gimmickry is sometimes the result. Although the place of study ought to be irrelevant to learning, courses offered in shopping centers, on commuter trains, by newspaper column, and on cruise ships do present serious issues of quality assurance. Worse yet, a few "universities" advertise promises of quick whole degrees, tailored to the academic level and field of the student's desire, and almost by return mail. The potential student cannot always evaluate the difference between legitimacy and fraudulence. Without some form of regulation, the unwary adult student becomes easy prey for unscrupulous operators.[17] Recently, regional accreditation has given more attention to off-campus operations and imposed a level of requirements for them. Even so, out-and-out diploma mills remain untouched, oblivious to the need for accreditation or sometimes inventing their own spurious accreditation!

Of course, some well-established academic programs for off-campus students employ outreach techniques that bring education close to the student and are responsive to the student's learning style. These techniques may be the basis for a very strong program and so should not be hastily dismissed. Instead evaluation of a particular program should rest on certain definable measures. In general, a program should be suspect if it suggests that it can offer an exceptionally wide range of kinds and levels of degrees, proposes a very short time in which the degree can be earned, tells students that they will gain nearly all of the required credit for the degree from "experience," employs part-time adjunct teachers exclusively, or asks the student to send money before receiving any information or services.

Problems of cost and financing exist for adult students. Even employed students may find current levels of college tuition difficult to meet on a regular basis. Costs are not an issue for those who have employee tuition reimbursement plans, but many employers do not sponsor these plans. The Internal Revenue Service once permitted the deduction of education expenses for certain purposes, but its regulations have been tightened considerably in recent years. Finally, those adults most in need of education, including the poor, bypassed minorities, part-time workers, and some self-employed, usually receive no aid at all. Recent changes in the eligibility rules for financial aid now allow some assistance to part-time students, and this provision, if expanded, could greatly improve the financial picture for older students.

There are educational issues, as well, that colleges need to understand if they are to meet adult student needs effectively. Despite some views to the contrary, most scholars of the adult learning process agree that continuing higher education students require a more learner-centered than teacher-centered approach. Many adult students seem to benefit from greater participation in, even control of, the educational process. They are motivated by helping to establish educational goals and define the ways in which they will be fulfilled.[18] The adult's prior experience can also be an important motivator in learning, and is likely to lead to a more problem (i.e., solution)-centered rather than discipline-centered approach to curriculum. Although some disagree about the capacity of many adults to be self-directed learners, certainly the relationship between professor and adult student tends to become less hierarchical, less controlled by the traditional authority of the academic subject or of the professor. Leonard Freedman says it nicely: "the expert is on tap, not on top!"[19] Such parity is also encouraged when continuing higher education schools engage faculty not bound to or by the traditional academic department. Some of them are more willing to experiment with alternative methods in the classroom and beyond.

Continuing higher education, then, is much more student centered than "regular" instruction. Some might say that it is consumer-centered, since the necessity of offering what the marketplace will buy is a primary factor in putting the student at the center of continuing education. If we set aside the continuing education courses required for professionals who must take refresher courses to maintain certification or licensure, much of CHE is undertaken voluntarily. Although strong motivations certainly exist for adult students to study, the most common being to qualify for job promotion, nonetheless the decision to pursue continuing education is the consumer's choice. And as I have argued earlier in these pages, university response to student choice and initiative is the single most powerful force for innovation and change. That factor alone, then, would make continuing education the most likely place to find significant novelty within higher education. But application of theories about adult learning can unleash quite powerful forces for educational innovation as well.

Three such important forces are attrition, acquisition of necessary learning resources, and the diversity of student background. The majority of university-level continuing education students hold some previously earned college credits, with many already holding an associate or bachelor's degree. This is especially the case for continuing education students at major university centers. Because CHE is so largely discretionary for potential students, other temporarily more important or pressing life matters can easily cause a student to terminate or abruptly suspend study, thus confirming an unusually high attrition rate for continuing education students. Efforts to reduce such attrition, especially those which make education more convenient for the busy student, can stimulate innovation and change. In such cases, innovative approaches as to when courses are scheduled or where instruction is located are obvious changes. Solutions to the problem of getting learning resources to students are also catalytic in bringing change. Finally, the wide range of student preparation within a single CE class leads to the need for experimentation in instruction and evaluation, and these areas are at the very center of educational innovation.

Adult students test the possibilities and the limits of pluralism in the American university. They encourage the university, more than any other single group, to reach out, to extend, to indulge its centrifugal desire. As George Herbert Palmer said in 1892, this creates dangers for the university. But the tendency for adult higher education to continue to grow and extend American higher education seems likely to continue. As in the nineteenth century, beyond the programs of accredited academic institutions, there is an abundance of non-collegiate postsecondary study available for motivated adults. Labor unions offer technical training to thousands of journeyman apprentices. Corporations have extensive internal training programs for executives, managers, sales personnel, and other professional and clerical staff. Government, at its many levels, sponsors countless seminars of every conceivable variety. Organizations, such as the American Institute of Banking, American Board of Realtors, the health, insurance, and travel industries, make available thousands of workshops, courses, home-study packages for agents, physicians, underwriters, brokers, and bankers. The list is almost endless. Estimates of the numbers of people engaged in some form of tertiary or post-tertiary education range into the tens of millions. In America, adult further education appears to be as much a family sport as Sunday football.

In both numbers of persons served and total level of expenditures, corporate education and university education may be virtually comparable. Few recognize the extent of formal learning already offered by corporations to their employees. Although difficult to assemble comparable and precise data from such a diverse group of providers, the American Society for Training and Development and a number of commentators estimate that corporate expenditures for formal employee training in the United States will approach $50 billion by 1990. When compared to nearly $200 billion in expenditures projected for all of higher education, the proportion is significant and growing rapidly.[20] Whatever the actual expenditure, it is clear that corporate education is now a major factor in tertiary and post-tertiary education and likely to continue to grow rapidly. IBM, for example, supports 7,000 instructors and course developers, teaching 390,000 employees.[21] Xerox, AT&T, Ford, General Motors, GTE and many others have extensive programs. The course catalogue at Sperry (Unisys) Long Island is comparable in size and number of courses offered to that of a small university.

Although many of these courses of instruction are highly job and employer specific, increasingly the range of courses offered look like many of the courses offered at colleges and universities. As Nell Eurich emphasizes, the sharp difference that academics like to draw between *education* and *training* is becoming fuzzy. From courses in basic literacy to advanced technical subjects, to fully accredited degree programs at the doctoral level, "America's business has become its own educational provider."[22] Although the most extensive, structured, and formal educational programs are usually found at the national and international corporations, smaller companies are increasingly discovering the importance of in-house educational programs in building and maintaining a competitive workforce. Joining with company-based labor unions through negotiated contract benefits for education, corporate support for education is spreading through all employee levels.

The irony here is that although the university is vaguely aware of such programs, academics continue to devalue their quality and significance. Yet these corporate programs, as much as the university's programs, are a direct response to social and economic need. Consequently, despite some ebb and flow with changing economic conditions, they possess a validity and staying power that must be reckoned with by higher education.

Helping higher education to make that reckoning is Project LEARN, a comprehensive project sponsored by the Council for the Advancement of Adult and Experiential Learning (CAEL), designed to increase national awareness of the need for lifelong learning. The project, partially funded by the Kellogg Foundation during the 1980s, ultimately has affected over 1 million adult learners in over 1,500 institutions, especially in increasing recognition of the need for adult support systems. Among its accomplishments are improved adult advisement and counseling systems, assessment of extracollegiate learning, changes in federal and state laws, accommodation of college academic patterns to adult needs and schedules, and establishment of new connections between adult educators and between colleges and universities.[23]

The results of such innovation are encouraging. Extended degree programs which collaborate with external non-collegiate organizations are now offered by many regional state colleges and universities. One of the most notable examples is at the School of Extended Learning of Central Michigan University. A traditional public institution with 17,000 on-campus students, its Institute for Personal and Career Development began in 1971 (the magic year for new programs) by offering classes at Wurtsmith Air Force Base in Michigan. By the late 1970s, IPCD offered courses for many off-campus sponsors, about one third at military bases and the remainder in corporate, health, government, and labor settings. Today the program operates forty-seven centers across the nation. As with other successful programs, the long-term leadership of its dean, John Yantis, has provided the clarity of vision and continuity essential to success. Central Michigan University claims over 25,000 extended degree alumni.[24]

In conclusion, those who seek opportunities for innovation in the education of adults and part-time students will find much to do. Adults are fascinating students. Adults are highly diverse, and face problems of time, cost, and lack of confidence. Although they usually come to college with strong motivation toward career or vocational studies, they are as literate, if not more so, than younger students. Moreover, they often prove to be highly interested in exploring liberal studies as these emerge from their career interests. They are highly selective in seeking out institutions which meet their needs, and outspoken if conditions and policies are not satisfactory. They see themselves as "persistent, having leadership ability, and an ability to handle stress."[25]

The experience of almost all adult programs shows a need for extensive student academic advisement and planning to set goals and provide the psychological transition from home, job, and community back to college study. Concern for confidence building may also be necessary at early points of student reentry, so that students can gain assurance and direction.[26]

But if these special needs are met, adults who attend school part-time prove to be superb and stimulating students. When institutions respond vigorously to these students, they demonstrate most fully the innovative force of continuing higher education on the American university. And perhaps the most important effect of adult learning upon the university is that all of higher education is forced to redefine our notions of who the "learners" are—persons of all ages, with highly specific but diverse interests and a range of learning styles. The net effect could be a much more responsive, much better undergraduate education for *all* students. Tolerated by American commitments to the values of pluralism, such innovations might ultimately transform the university we know into the educational multiplex that society now requires.

NOTES

1. The Commission on Higher Education and the Adult Learner, *Adult Learners: Key to the Nation's Future*, Morris T. Keeton, Chair (Columbia, MD, 1984), p. 7.

2. Bernard Bailyn, *Education in the Forming of American Society* (New York: Random House, 1960), pp. 32–37.

3. Nell P. Eurich, *Corporate Classrooms: The Learning Business* (Princeton, NJ: The Carnegie Foundation for the Advancement of Teaching, 1985), p. 26.

4. Eurich, p. 38, as quoted from Harold F. Clark and Harold S. Sloan, *Classrooms in the Factories* (NY: Fairleigh Dickenson Press, 1958), p. 6.

5. Alice Felt Tyler, *Freedom's Ferment: Phases of American Social History from the Colonial Period to the Outbreak of the Civil War* (New York: Harper & Row, 1944), p. 261.

6. See Joseph E. Gould, *The Chatauqua Movement* (Albany, NY: SUNY Press, 1961); and Bruce Swanson, "An Early American Experiment in Distance Education," *ICDE Bulletin*, vol. 16 (January 1989): 39–42.

7. George Herbert Palmer, "Doubts About University Extension," *Atlantic*, vol. 69 (March 1892): 367–374.

8. Murray M. Horowitz, *Brooklyn College: The First Half-Century* (New York: Brooklyn College Press, 1981), p. 59. See also Bernard H. Stern, *Never Too Late For College* (Chicago: Center for the Study of Liberal Education for Adults, 1963).

9. Milton R. Stern (ed.), *Power and Conflict in Continuing Professional Education* (Belmont, CA: Wadsworth, 1983), p. ix; see also Milton R. Stern, "Universities in Continuing Education," in H. J. Alford (ed.), *Power and Conflict in Continuing Education* (Belmont, CA: Wadsworth, 1980).

10. James W. Hall et al., *State University of New York and the Part-Time Student*. Report of the Task Force on Part-Time Students (Saratoga Springs, NY: 1976).

11. U.S. Department of Education, Center for Educational Statistics, "Early Estimates," CS 89-315 (December 1988).

12. National Institute of Education, *Involvement in Learning* (Washington, DC: Department of Education, 1984), p. 7.

13. Terrel H. Bell, Chair, *To Secure the Blessings of Liberty* (Washington, DC: The American Association of State Colleges and Universities, 1986), p. 24.

14. "The GED: A Growing Alternative Route to Higher Education," *Change*, vol. 21, no. 4 (July/August 1989), pp. 35–39.

15. James W. Hall et al., *State University of New York and the Part-Time Student* (Saratoga Springs, NY: Empire State College, 1976).

16. Ernest L. Boyer, *College: The Undergraduate Experience in America* (New York: Harper & Row, 1987), pp. 160–161.

17. For a thorough discussion of fraudulent practices, see David W. Stewart and Henry A. Spille, *Diploma Mills: Degrees of Fraud* (New York: American Council on Education and Macmillan, 1988).

18. See Stephen B. Brookfield, *Understanding and Facilitating Adult Learning* (San Francisco: Jossey-Bass, 1986); David A. Peterson, *Facilitating Education for Older Learners* (San Francisco: Jossey-Bass, 1983); and Malcolm Knowles, *The Adult Learner: A Neglected Species*, 2nd edition (Houston,TX: Gulf Publishing, 1978).

19. Leonard Freedman, *Quality in Continuing Education: Principles, Practices, and Standards for Colleges and Universities* (San Francisco: Jossey-Bass, 1987), p. 64.

20. See Jack E. Bowsher, *Educating America: Lessons Learned in the Nation's Corporations* (New York: Wiley & Sons, 1989), for a corporate viewpoint of the level of need and some new strategies to meet it. Also David R. Powers, et al., *Higher Education in Partnership with Industry* (San Francisco: Jossey-Bass, 1988).

21. Bowsher, p. 41.

22. Eurich, p. 1.

23. Morris T. Keeton, "The Outcomes of Project LEARN," unpublished report, February 24, 1986.

24. Robert Trullinger (ed.), *Annual Report of IPCD, 1987-88* (Mt. Pleasant, MI: CMU Press, 1989).

25. See Elizabeth Steltenpohl and Jane Shipton, *Life/Career/Educational Planning for Adults* (Saratoga Springs, NY: Empire State College 1976); Timothy Lehmann and Virginia Lester, *Adult Learning in the Context of Adult Development* (Empire State College Research Series, 1978); Ernest G. Palola and A. Paul Bradley, *Ten Out of Thirty* (Empire State College, 1973); *Student Learning and Quality Education* (ESC, 1984); *The Adult Learner in Non-Traditional Programs* (ESC, 1986).

26. The most complete examination of adult learning needs is found in K. Patricia Cross, *Adults as Learners: Increasing Participation and Facilitating Learning* (San Francisco: Jossey-Bass, 1981).

Chapter 7

Extending the College Campus: External and Competency Degrees

The need for access, student problems of time and place of study, and the proclivity of Americans to move frequently over a vast country, prompted the American university, or more often its surrogate, extension arm, to move beyond the walls of the campus and to offer instruction and evaluation to students who seldom, if ever, appeared on the campus. One of the most far-reaching worldwide innovations in higher education, the growth of external instruction and degrees has greatly increased access for students throughout the world and more recently in the United States. Today there are several dozen institutions, from Pakistan and India to Costa Rica and Thailand, which specialize in distance learning. They are serving over 10 million college-level students, and there appears to be no upper limit to their growth.

External degrees, per se, came late to the United States, although they build upon earlier established patterns of extension of university services to a larger and more widely dispersed public. At first the outward spread of higher education occurred through the proliferation of small residential college campuses into the hinterlands (Chapter 2); later the technical extension offerings of the land-grant universities (Chapter 2), and the spread of community colleges (Chapter 4) brought higher education closer to students' homes. Correspondence education for university credit began in the late nineteenth century, but only in the late 1950s were extension and adult programs able to offer credit and degree programs to students who accomplished much of their study off-campus (Chapter 6).

Although Cyril O. Houle points out that the concept of a degree awarded by an authority external to the university dates to 1534, when the Archbishop of Canterbury was given the right to grant degrees, it is the founding of the University of London in 1836, and especially its revised charter in 1858, that marks the more familiar antecedent. Until 1900 this university's sole function was to examine students who prepared at other institutions or completely on their own. Most of London's students were citizens of the British Empire, later the Commonwealth, eager to earn a degree from a British university, but unable to travel to Britain to do so. Many thousands of distant students gained degrees in this way. But the University of London itself, while it offered course reading lists and sample examinations, provided no instruction to these students. Admissions was not open. Students were required to pass a matriculation qualification. Given the great value of distance education for remote geographic areas where residential university resources were far-removed from students, it is not surprising that external distance learning programs came early to British dominions in South Africa, Australia, and Canada. By much the same rationale, the land-grant and regional universities of the United States offered correspondence courses in a variety of subjects to students who could not come to the campus. Usually, however, these correspondence programs did not, short of a period of minimum student residence on the campus, lead to a university degree.

Although the University of London pioneered the external degree, it fell into disfavor during the 1970s[1], especially with the growth of the British Open University. More recently, Malcolm Tight tells us, the external examination degree has been rejuvenated on a self-funding basis and enrolls nearly 25,000 students.[2] As such it remains one of the truly original and successful innovations in higher education.

Houle provides a taxonomy of external degrees, which is useful.[3] He defines *extension* degrees, *adult* degrees, and *assessment* degrees. Houle says that "at the heart of [the external degree's] advocacy lies the deep and perennial egalitarianism of the American ethos, rooted in the belief that the individual should have as much education as he needs or wishes to develop his potentialities."[4]

As with so many innovations in American higher education, the impulse for external study came from outside the university. In the United States, the impulse came from the Department of Defense, which needed a system that would allow members of the military, moved periodically from base to base at home or abroad, to earn college degrees. Moreover, many technical training programs (based upon Military Occupational Specialties) offered by the military itself were comparable to courses offered in community colleges. With the guidance of Cornelius Turner, in 1945 the American Council on Education published its first *Guide to the Evaluation of Educational Experiences in the Armed Services*. Institutions of higher education everywhere were encouraged to accept for academic credit non-collegiate programs evaluated by the newly created Commission on the Accreditation of Service Experiences (now the Center for Adult Learning and Educational Credentials).

The Department of Defense, through its United States Armed Forces Institute (USAFI), offered standardized tests in academic subjects. In 1974 USAFI was recast as the Defense Activity for Non-Traditional Education Support (DANTES), whose tests were evaluated for academic credit by ACE. The same year the American Council, working with the New York State Education Department, initiated the Program on Non-Collegiate Sponsored Instruction (PONSI) to conduct evaluations whose purpose was to assign academic equivalency to educational programs offered by businesses, voluntary associations, government agencies, and labor unions. These were ground-breaking innovations at the time, establishing precedents that were soon applied more broadly. In a 1948 ACE publication, Alonzo Grace said, "Out of the experience of the armed services in the training of twelve million men it is clear that new concepts have emerged...the importance of the objective, the need for curricular revision in the light of social change and scientific advancement, the desirability of adjusting the curriculum to the individual, the relatively greater effectiveness of learning experiences that involve doing rather than only listening or reading...and the power of motivation and a learner purpose in attaining objectives."[5] Here was a call for the application of learning principles which would appear only much later in the concept of a "Serviceman's Opportunity College."

In the meantime at Columbia Teachers College in the 1950s, Jack Arbolino and Ewald Nyquist permitted some of their students to test out of required courses through examination. With the burgeoning of student applications for admission in the 1960s, some colleges permitted students to complete a portion of their course requirements through challenge examinations. These students gained advanced placement, thereby shortening the length of time and lessening the expense of obtaining a college degree. By the mid-1960s the College Entrance Examination Board, with Arbolino now directing its Advanced Placement and College Level Examination Program (CLEP), developed, with major financial support from the Carnegie Corporation, standardized college-level (CLEP, 1966) examinations which, over time, came to be used by more and more colleges. During the same period, with Nyquist now Deputy Commissioner of the State Education Department (Regents), New York developed college proficiency tests (CPEP, 1961) in many subjects and found a growing market for them. CLEP and CPEP now made it possible for colleges, through a selective use of these exams, to evaluate with considerable efficiency a student's broad liberal knowledge and specific disciplinary competence—two important dimensions of a college education forming the basis of a degree.

Although the idea of an off-campus degree has distant antecedents, it was not until 1970 that Alan Pifer, President of the Carnegie Corporation of New York, sounded a trumpet call for large-scale examination of external models in his article "Is it Time for an External Degree?"[6] As a logical evolution of the repeated American pattern for extension of learning beyond the campus and to less than full-time students, the external degree was a necessary invention.

The American system of credit and credentialing[7] parallels the nation's approach to status. In the Old World, land holding, property rights, and titles gave automatic status to those who inherited them. Perhaps education was desirable for some, but it was not a requirement for advancement in status. Lacking a landed aristocracy, a form of quasi-meritocracy became a necessary route to achieve status in America. In the nineteenth century a grammar school education was recognized as one way to improve one's personal status. By the twentieth century, those with more education became increasingly "meritorious" and able to advance economically and socially. The college degree, and especially a professional diploma, offered a commoner's route to advanced income and social status, and it was "gained through individual effort.

The Carnegie system of 1906, which formalized the counting of college credit hours, when combined with the elective course system, permitted a student to accumulate interchangeable "credit" segments toward a degree, an ideal expression of democratic choice. Students of differing talents, backgrounds, and interests could now weave together a curriculum of parts. No longer was the curriculum a unitary, prescribed sequence of study but a series of interchangeable parts which could be assembled and reassembled to meet the student's predilections. Although the implications of this kind of flexibility were probably not encompassed in the conceptual design of Eliot's curriculum at Harvard, the logical outworking of his concept, within the pluralistic American educational environment, traces a clear lineage to such contemporary "innovations" as transfer, articulation agreements between two- and four-year colleges, international educational exchanges, credit-banks, advanced placement examinations, and assessment of prior experiential learning.

Although the key conceptual innovation was the acceptance of advanced placement by institutions (i.e., the granting of their own academic credit to students who had never sat in their classrooms), the announcement in September 1970 by Commissioner Ewald Nyquist of the New York Regents of the possibility of a student earning an entire degree by examination was a major organizational innovation. At first Nyquist wanted the Educational Testing Service (ETS) to offer a degree for completion of New York State competency tests. When this could not be done, he proposed that the Regents themselves grant the degree. In this way, the Regents External Degree Program (now Regents College) was born. Some others imitated the approach. Thomas A. Edison College of New Jersey was founded in 1972, initially using many of the New York Regents examinations. Connecticut's Charter Oak College appeared in 1973. For the first time, new and separate organizations, not individual colleges or universities as one might have recognized them, appeared as university surrogates. Generally speaking, they are statewide or regional in application, with no physical campus. They are capable of responding to students at great distances so long as materials can be received and proctored examinations can be administered.

Their full-time staff are not teaching faculty, but administrators. These administrators convene professors from other universities as consultants, asking them to define the content of the degrees offered and to write the examinations used to certify the student's meeting of those requirements. Academic policy is reviewed by such faculty committees.

The examining university or external degree approach offers several significant new ideas in furthering university outreach. First, unlike most campus-based programs, they define the degree in very broad terms. The kind of departmental compromises required for campus agreement are avoided, freeing the curriculum from the tyranny of the departmental major.

Second, not having the student in the classroom, the faculty are required to focus on the specific outcomes and performance expected from the educated student rather than the more subtle and usually unarticulated nuances of the campus experience. Third, the approach offers to all comers a chance to try. The usual inhibitors to access, such as physical space, limited faculty to teach course sections, and scarce library volumes, do not limit the ability to serve the student. Consequently students no longer need to be preselected and ranked for admission. A *standard of graduation* supplants a *standard for admission*. The approach becomes essentially an open one.

Of course there are weaknesses and problems which the external approach exacerbates. There is little or no instruction available for students. Students may enroll at other traditional colleges or they may use independent study guides and the like, but otherwise they are on their own. That gives a distinct advantage to the well-motivated and literate student. Others need help. A new potential exists for an incoherent university degree. Although this is a problem that is easily avoided, in some student programs a mishmash of credits may add up to something, or perhaps nothing.

A potentially more serious problem is that the faculty can be disenfranchised. Although the various existing external degree programs handle the implications of this situation differently, in all programs administrators retain the initiative to establish the curricular agenda, to call meetings, and to select those academics who are employed as consultants. For example, although many highly qualified professors participated intensely in the first creation of the Regents Degree, none would define that work as being central to his or her career or reputation. They accepted assignments, often for very modest remuneration, because they were committed to the new concept. But administrators were able to manage the discussion of both policy and substance.

Another innovative approach, somewhat related to the external examination degree, is the *degree by demonstration of competency*. The idea that individual performance should be the measure of a college degree gave rise to a number of innovative models which proposed to award the degree on the basis of student demonstration of competency across a number of areas. The idea had already been found useful in some corporate training programs (e.g., AT & T after World War II). David Riesman sees the demand for a competence-based approach to learning as a "dialectic common throughout American life and American education of oscillation between an emphasis on liberty for individual achievement seen in highly competitive and individualistic terms, and an insistence on equality of outcome."[8] As developed at Alverno (Wisconsin), Minnesota Metropolitan, Mars Hill (North Carolina), Loretto Heights (Colorado), and Northeast Missouri State, the model replaced all traditional time, course, and credit requirements with highly detailed, required competencies.

The best known is probably Alverno College, where Sr. Joel Read led her faculty, beginning in 1968, through a thorough reexamination of the curriculum. By 1971 the idea of an outcome-based approach surfaced and by 1973 was applied to all first-year students. By 1976 all four years of the curriculum were competency-based.[9] For example, not only are students expected to demonstrate strong writing, communication, and analytic skills, but to demonstrate these skills at ever higher specified levels, over time. Most liberal arts colleges do indicate in the introduction to the catalogue that students will develop these skills, but they seldom explicitly try to find out in any systematic way if students in fact achieve them. At Alverno, students might prepare to demonstrate competency in a variety of traditional or informal ways, including enrollment in courses offered by the college. Often the evidence of competency is demonstrated by the performance of tasks or activities rather than by completion of a written examination.

The degree by competency, unlike the external examination degree, continues to involve faculty directly with students. But the faculty role is shifted significantly toward explicit definition of student learning goals and effective methods of teaching. Competence-based education has proved to be a difficult and exacting form of learning for students and faculty alike, and it has its detractors as well as strong advocates.[10] Nonetheless, the degree by competency is a development which has had a substantial impact upon higher education and which may become more important with greater future use of independent study and technology. Moreover, the recent widespread efforts to develop better measures to assess institutional outcomes and performance could benefit greatly from competency approaches.

In sum, these new approaches are potent innovations in response to American values. They broaden the concept of the degree, offer flexibility in meeting requirements, and open opportunity for students to try, even while bringing the professionalism of academic advise and consent into the process. Because all students can attempt the tests without an admission requirement, *equal access* is promoted. It shows the continuing importance of *pluralism* by creating a wholly new path, an alternative route, to achievement of a degree. It responds to the American individual obsession with *mobility* by freeing the student from the traditional requirements of space and time. And finally it provides a new way to recognize individual *merit*. Large numbers of people have responded enthusiastically to a mechanism which allows them to demonstrate, in a degree-conscious employment environment, what they already know.

Distance and open universities are as much political movements as educational ones. Spawned as nationwide approaches to the burgeoning demands of lower school graduates, these institutions are powerful tools of massification and, in some cases, democratization. Called into existence by the social and economic imperatives for modernization and competition, distance universities confront, as do few other institutions, the often conflicting claims of educational access and intellectual achievement. Such institutions are already a major force for change in higher education in much of the rest of the world. Whether or not education external to the university campus becomes of comparable importance in the United States remains to be seen.

NOTES

1. The University of London had developed a substantial traditional campus over the years, and the external programs were, for a time, considered a less desirable legacy of the past.

2. Malcolm Tight, "London University External Developments," *Open Learning* (June 1987): 49–51.

3. Cyril O. Houle, *The External Degree*, a publication of the Commission on Non-Traditional Study (San Francisco: Jossey-Bass, 1973).

4. Houle, p. 64.

5. A. P. Grace, *Educational Lessons from Wartime Training: The General Report of the Commission on Implications of Armed Services Educational Programs* (Washington, DC: ACE, 1948), p. 99, as quoted in Gerald Grant et al., *On Competence: A Critical Analysis of Competence-Based Reforms in Higher Education* (San Francisco: Jossey-Bass, 1979), p. 84.

6. *The College Board Review*, no. 78 (Winter 1970–71): 5–10.

7. See Jerry W. Miller and Olive Mills (eds.), *Credentialing Educational Accomplishment* (Washington, DC: ACE, 1978).

8. David Riesman, "Society's Demands for Competence," in Grant et al., p. 39.

9. See Thomas Ewens, "Transforming a Liberal Arts Curriculum: Alverno College," in Grant et al., pp. 259–298; also Sr. Joel Read, "A Degree by Any Other Name ...The Alverno Plan," in John F. Hughes and Olive Mills (eds.), *Formulating Policy in Postsecondary Education* (Washington, DC: ACE, 1975).

10. See Zelda Gamson, "Understanding the Difficulties of Implementing a Competence-Based Curriculum," in Grant, et al., pp. 224–258.

Chapter 8

Educating Individuals: Beyond the Ivy-Covered Walls

In fall 1970, when Alan Pifer, president of the Carnegie Corporation, answered positively his own question "Is it Time for an External Degree,"[1] he defined two models: an examining university which offered no instruction, and a teaching university which employed new instructional methods to reach distant or off-campus students. Although several versions of Pifer's second model were already on the drawing boards, his call signaled the launching of several lasting and more or less healthy innovations designed for off-campus students. Among these new institutions were the University-Without-Walls (UWW) with its nationally distributed collaborating institutions; Empire State College in New York State; and Minnesota Metropolitan State College in the Twin Cities. Experiential learning, as developed at Antioch College and in international education, also moved the university beyond the ivy-covered walls of academe, into the wider, even world, community.

In extending the outreach of the campus, each of these institutions or approaches was responding to American egalitarian demands for access, mainly by serving new students—mostly adults who were unable to come routinely to the campus. They responded, as well, to pluralism, by introducing diverse new options into higher education's inventory. But most of all, they responded to American individualism with innovative programs, offering uniquely crafted curricula and tailored programs for each student. These approaches built on the goals of the individual, integrating a student's knowledge gained prior to study with a unique plan of study, sometimes through the pedagogic device of individualized contracts or study plans. They are also approaches with which I have had considerable experience at Empire State College: I am acutely aware both of their considerable strengths and persistent problems.

THE UNIVERSITY-WITHOUT-WALLS

The idea for a "university-without-walls" originated with the Union for Experimenting Colleges and Universities, a consortium of 18 colleges and univer-

90

sities headed by Samuel Baskin. That experimenting consortium began in the early 1960s, a collaboration instigated by Royce ("Tim") Pitkin, founder of Goddard College in Vermont, and James Dixon, president of Antioch.[2] The Union, headquartered at Antioch College in Yellow Springs, Ohio, had been the first publisher of *Change Magazine*, a journal dedicated to encouraging innovation and reform. Evolving from proposals developed in the late 1960s, the formal organization of the University-Without-Walls included among its early members Antioch, Bard, Chicago State, Friends World, Goddard, Howard, Loretto Heights, Morgan State, New College (South Florida), New York University, Northeastern Illinois, Roger Williams, Shaw, Skidmore, Staten Island Community, Stephens, Massachusetts (Amherst), Minnesota, South Carolina, and Westminster. Although for the most part these highly diverse public and private institutions created new and separate educational structures, in most cases, the degree itself was awarded by the UWW consortium.

> Baskin described the program as a "university-without-walls" because "it abandons the tradition of a sharply circumscribed campus and provides education for students wherever they may be—at work, in their homes, through internships, independent study and field experience, within areas of special social problems, at one or more colleges, and in travel and service abroad. It abandons the tradition of a fixed age group (18–22) and recognizes that persons as young as 16 and as old as 60 may benefit from its program. It abandons the traditional classroom as the principal instrument of instruction, as well as the prescribed curriculum, the grades and credit points which, however they are added or averaged, do not yield a satisfactory measure of education. It enlarges the faculty to include knowledgeable people from outside the academic world …it places strong emphasis on student self-direction in learning, while still maintaining close teaching-learning relationships…. [3]

Baskin's dream captured, as well as any statement before or since, the dual objectives toward which many pressed in that fertile time of educational experimentation: flexibility in the time and place of study, *and* flexibility which tailored the curriculum to meet individual student requirements.

Supported by a $415,000 grant from the federal government (HEW) and an additional $400,000 from the Ford Foundation, UWW was a comprehensive response to the student pressures which had already shattered many practices and programs on the traditional college campus. Fred Hechinger, writing in *The New York Times* of December 17, 1970, understood that if such approaches were not to "slide into dilettantism" there would need to be a careful selection of students who could "demonstrate commitment, maturity and independence…and intellectual integrity." But again, reflecting the urgency of the times, Hechinger believed that the greatest potential would be to "release the 'freewheeling' minority from the confining structure devised for the majority" and "in the process even soften the mold of tradition for that majority."

Although suggesting some of Hechinger's worst fears, George Keller contributed to the hype of it all in the September 1971 *Seventeen*, in "Get Ready for Off-Campus Colleges." Keller's advice to teenagers was distinctly practical and romantic but caught the flavor of Madison Avenue: "Think in terms of designing your own life, as you would design your dream bedroom." Keller suggested "a short period of intensive study of the cello in Puerto Rico with a protégé of Pablo Casals", or perhaps "a Spring term holed up in a small house on North Carolina's Outer Banks," reading Thoreau, Burroughs, and Muir. Although such a response to individualism might easily become narcissistic or precious, it did capture, for a time, the ethos of a generation of Americans.

The idea was dramatic and soon a topic of wide discussion among lower schools and colleges and in international arenas. The first students were admitted to UWW programs in fall 1971. Although the UWW concept is a form of "external" degree, one major and intentional difference between degrees by examination (Chapter 7) and the university-without-walls concept is delineated in Baskin's original proposal. "It is not the intent of the University-Without-Walls to award a degree in recognition solely on what students have learned and achieved *prior* to entering UWW." The key was to craft, sometimes to negotiate with the faculty, a uniquely individual program of study.

Baskin's UWW was solidly rooted in American social values. He emphasized the crisis in university governance, the rapid expansion of knowledge, the influx of huge numbers of students into the academy, and so focused his interest on small numbers of students in highly discrete programs. While Baskin understood that the usefulness of and demand for the UWW educational approach might have implications for the problems associated with the recent massive expansion of college-going, his model lacked the capability to respond to large numbers. Each member of the consortium had certain latitude in determining its particular academic policies and could either choose to offer its own degree or have the degree conferred by the consortium. But the Union itself could prescribe little more than a set of principles and ideals.

At Skidmore College in New York, for example, the idea to join the UWW consortium originated in the college's Education Department. But Virginia Lester,[4] a member of the president's office, took responsibility for making the effort college-wide. When the Skidmore faculty adopted the UWW program and agreed to award the Skidmore degree, Skidmore's affiliation with the Union gradually ended, an outcome undoubtedly contemplated and applauded by Baskin. Yet today only a few of the original UWW affiliates, such as New College at the University of Alabama and Skidmore, continue to function. Raised as orphans at the periphery of the traditional colleges, many of the UWW programs have disappeared. More recently, the Union (today, The Union Institute in Cincinnati) has developed a national off-campus doctoral program. As a series of nationally distributed pilots, UWW demonstrated that individual students could be served effectively without sitting in the traditional classroom. But the subsequent demise of many of its units also shows the difficulty of sustaining an innovation based upon a consortium structure.

EMPIRE STATE COLLEGE

Begun at about the same point in time as UWW, Empire State College (ESC) of the State University of New York required a different structure in order to serve the large and diverse citizenry of New York. Like a number of other institutions, ESC attempted to address a field of educational and logistical problems which faced higher education in the late 1960s. Although ESC developed a number of experimental practices employed elsewhere, such as contract learning, faculty mentorship, experiential learning, credit for prior learning, the use of instructional resources, and distance education, the principal and unique innovation of the college is structural.

The key structural concepts are a mentor-based approach to student academic planning and evaluation and an administrative capability to bring precisely the necessary academic resources from the multicampus State University of New York, or from the community, to the service of a single student's educational needs. In this way the off-campus student can pursue a wide range of academic studies and do so in a variety of different educational modes, while remaining at home or continuing to work. Such a comprehensive effort in educational outreach had never before been attempted on a statewide basis. And despite its highly individualized approach, it is also efficient, for it uses the existing resources of SUNY selectively, including SUNY faculty as tutors and SUNY libraries. Such a complex system of student matriculation, educational delivery, and evaluation requires a structure that is at once conceptually clear, administratively strong, educationally sure, and individually flexible.

ESC was very much the child of its time, providing an alternative way to solve some of SUNY's problems of space, duplication, and unserved citizens. Enrollment in the late 1960s was surging beyond the extant or expected future capacity of campus space and facilities and was firmly anticipated to continue to do so. An off-campus plan which might serve as many as 10 percent of SUNY's students seemed helpful. In an earlier attempt to address both the unparalleled enrollment growth and some of the turmoil of the 1960s, SUNY had invested a substantial but largely unproductive effort in media and off-campus instruction, such as television, radio, and correspondence (Chapter 9). Now SUNY sought to move education beyond the campus, but while also linking the student to a more effective academic planning, delivery, and evaluation mechanism. Shifting the place of study to the home, the workplace, or even to an international site would help to alleviate the space crunch.

The creation of an entire institution that could meet students outside the classroom and provide flexibility in time and place of study was a new approach to the problem of more efficient campus use. Empire State College actually increased the capacity of SUNY to meet its obligation to many older, working, disabled, or distant students for whom the campus, for reasons of schedule or distance, proved inconvenient or inaccessible.

ESC also helped SUNY to address the systemwide problem of statewide demands for duplicative and highly specialized curricula. Empire State College drew upon SUNY-wide faculty expertise to offer such a program to a few or even to a single student at virtually any location, avoiding the cost of duplicating entire departments across the state. The college also provided unique programs of study for individual students who did not fit easily within existing curricula. Just as university-without-walls units allowed traditional colleges to serve highly diverse students, ESC offered individual academic programs to students while reducing friction within the system.

SUNY also sought to reach out to government, business, and labor. By incorporating experiential field study, internships, and on-the-job learning into student programs, ESC brought higher education closer to the working population who required further education for job promotion or self-improvement. This individual, experiential approach helped both student and employer.

The University also wanted to find a way to recognize the astounding number of talented individuals who had earned large numbers of college credits, but could not translate these credits and the knowledge which they represented—into a college degree. Still other persons demonstrated substantial college-level learning in the performance of their jobs and lives but were blocked from career advancement by the lack of a degree. By recognizing such learning by assessing prior learning for credit, Empire State College enabled many otherwise talented people to move forward personal educational goals.

In these ways, ESC was shaped by the social needs of the times as interpreted by the University. But the particular response to those conditions was crafted by the particular individuals who joined ESC at its founding, including this writer. We were attracted to the opportunities which ESC promised, allowing us to test new educational theories while solving real problems. Many experienced and creative academics left successful careers elsewhere, bringing their personal agendas to this risky venture. Our agendas included such issues as individualizing education, the testing of a human development model for learning, new interdisciplinary approaches to curriculum, and the exploration of human values within the undergraduate experience. In many respects these issues were not radically different from those which had motivated the curriculum reformers at the liberal arts colleges (Chapter 3) or the continuing education specialists (Chapter 6). But the structure of ESC became a nexus for a number of educational innovators whose varied educational threads could be woven by the institution into a rich fabric for individual students. The result was multiple and engaging goals which, when implemented, provided diverse options and flexibility to individual students.

For example, the question of values in the curriculum, a longtime goal of the liberal education innovators, was approached at ESC by explicitly imbedding implicit, but often unarticulated, values in the educational process. American egalitarian, individual, and plural values found their expression in the individual degree program. As students pursued individual personal and educational struggles as deeply as possible, they grappled with and applied important social, economic, and intellectual principles within an emerging framework of personal and intellectual maturity.

The structure also attracted those, such as William R. Dodge and John H. Jacobson, interested in developing student independent study through the use of instructional resources. Provided with a purposeful and flexible system of academic planning and advisement, students could be motivated to use a wide range of resources for independent study, including televised and programmed courses. Nor were students locked to a mono-modal form of instruction, as with some earlier mediated learning forms. Students could select among technologies, using those which best served their needs for a given project. The best resources available for a given curriculum could be selected to support an individual student's purposes. In particular, the off-campus student now began to have available, as a practical matter, the educational advisement, faculty feedback, and rich resources comparable to those available to residential students.

Faculty, such as historian Loren Baritz, philosopher Bernard Parker, physicists Victor Montana and Fernand Brunschwig, and Wordsworth specialist Kenneth Abrams, with strong interests in interdisciplinary teaching and freed from the highly differentiated courses of the traditional curriculum, were able to create course guides for independent study. They could respond to students who sought holistic, idea-, or problem-centered curricula. Several hundred interdisciplinary study guides were written by many of the nation's best-known scholars, and literally thousands of individual permutations were pursued by students. In this way Empire State College was an important innovation in curriculum design.

But most significantly, ESC provided a way to focus attention on student learning. Traditional departmental emphasis on the discipline was now balanced by the student's goals and learning needs. Those with interests in learning and human development, such as psychologists Arthur Chickering and F. Thomas Clark, found at ESC a challenging opportunity to engage with each student in educational goal setting and planning. None could avoid the implications of the student's central position in the academic process. Knowledge about how students learn, differences in individual learning styles, and the relationships between learning and human development were essential. The student could use the process as a means to examine personal objectives, his or her preparedness to grow, and then participate in setting educational goals. Both faculty and students had to address these issues in order to succeed.

In responding individually rather than collectively, ESC needs to bring expertise and resources directly to the student. That response begins with a single student and faculty mentor at one of forty-two college offices across the state. Together they "contract" an individual study plan. This plan specifies the studies to be pursued, the tutors, courses, or experiences to be used, the books or other resources needed, and the means and criteria for student evaluation. Reviewed by a faculty committee, this program, when completed, earns credit toward an individual degree program. Previous learning, including knowledge gained through non-formal experiential learning, may be applied toward completion of the degree requirement. A student's program may include learning approaches as diverse as an independent reading program, international travel, or registration in a formal classroom course. The structure allows an appropriate mix of modes to meet a particular student's needs and conditions.

Recognizing that such an experiment would be watched closely by those who doubted the capability of these approaches to ensure excellence, ESC invested considerable effort in research about its students and graduates. If the individual student curriculum was sometimes idiosyncratic, the college was able to demonstrate that the level of student performance and accomplishment could meet the expectations of accreditors and graduate schools. Nearly half of the graduates have entered graduate study and performed well. Gradually, ESC transcripts were recognized as representing graduates of high quality and promise.

The danger, of course, is that the centrality of the student in the process will elicit the worst aspects of student consumerism. The student is indeed a consumer who is central to the learning process, defining needs, means, and ends. But, although the academic structure of the college requires that these be initiated by the student, they are negotiated with the faculty mentor in interaction with established faculty policies and degree expectations. In practice, this structure seems to deflect, or in some cases co-opt, the consumerist tendency, moving students instead, through their own motivation, toward sound realizations of a college degree. That structure has also proved to be adaptable to changing conditions as the needs of education have evolved through the 1970s and the 1980s.

EXPERIENTIAL LEARNING

Experiential learning is a closely related form of individualized off-campus education. Originating in the small liberal arts colleges, experiential innovations, strongly influenced by the philosophy of John Dewey, offer curricula which feature a high reliance upon experiential, practical applications of theoretical learning. Such colleges as Bennington (1925) and Sarah Lawrence (1926), with their emphasis on the fine arts, and a reborn Antioch (originally founded 1852), with its tradition of social activism, are older examples of this approach. Under President Arthur E. Morgan in the 1920s, Antioch developed a work-study curriculum which encouraged students to alternate periods of study on-campus with work in various job sites. Liberal education was integrated with work experience and social training through a plan of study for each student. Much of the normal coursework was pursued independently (although all individual plans had to meet both general education and major field requirements). Although planned as a five-year program, by taking examinations which permitted waiver of entry-level courses, about half of the students could complete the program within four years.

This notion of bringing undergraduate students into contact with the complexities and tensions of the workplace and community was a novel addition to the concept of the well-educated man or woman and an approach which was far ahead of its time.[5] Certainly few institutions copied the scheme at the time. In fact, a later Antioch President, Samuel B. Gould, tells the story that he had won a major foundation grant in order to support Antioch faculty in campus/work exchanges, similar to those established for students. When not a single faculty member volunteered to participate, Gould reluctantly returned the grant unused. Although Antioch did not consciously seek to spread its innovative program, it joined with Ralph Tyler and others in the late 1950s to form the National Council for Cooperative Education and helped get legislation enacted in support of cooperative education. Cooperative education has since become a most important activity at community colleges, its linkage of students with work an important variety of experiential learning.

With few imitators, Antioch replicated itself, beginning with the Antioch Putney Graduate School of Education in 1964 and other centers at Los Angeles, Philadelphia, San Francisco, Seattle, Boston, Santa Barbara, a law school in Washington and an international division. Antioch operated a "college in dispersion," difficult to manage given its geographical "campus," but well placed for dissemination of its experiential learning model. Antioch was also able to increase its ethnic diversity and broaden its academic palette toward internationalism and urbanization. More recently the experience of each Antioch center has varied considerably, especially in financial success, and some centers have been closed or cut back.

But experience-based learning as a part of the liberal culture of a student's education has gained other adherents. Over 300 undergraduate institutions are reported to assess prior learning for credit, and a number of these also recognize informally gained learning, utilizing portfolio assessment as a means for awarding advanced standing. Some otherwise traditional universities now award at least the equivalent of one academic term (15–16 credits) for experience-based learning, and some offer considerably more. Such credit is especially common to academic programs which include as part of the degree requirement an interneship, community service project, or apprenticeship. And although it now seems to be passing out of fashion, the January term, or 4-1-4 calendar, often incorporates experiential learning, including certain forms of international study, into the curriculum.[6]

At the College of Human Services (New York City), the curriculum is based almost entirely upon experiential learning. In the late 1960s President Audrey Cohen forged a unique model, which started out as a training grant for women in the human services professions and in which the traditional patterns of book learning and extensive writing were substantially replaced by student demonstrations of competency in a core of professional abilities. About 200 students, with the assistance of a faculty of 20, undertake "constructive actions," the term used for demonstrations of particular competencies. Although completion rates have been rather low, the College of Human Services has attracted high-risk students, many of whom, unprepared to engage in a traditional academic setting, have succeeded. [7]

The Empire State Youth Theatre Institute (ESYTI) is another fascinating example of experiential learning. Although ESYTI itself does not award academic credit, it is a teaching and performing company within the State University of New York. Theatre students from university campuses undertake yearlong internships for credit with the company, gaining firsthand experience in professional acting and production. Fully supported by state appropriation, its professional actors are also teachers who perform and teach at schools throughout the state. Its founder, Patricia Snyder, has created a highly innovative model for experiential training in the fine arts.

Metropolitan State University of the Minnesota State System, founded by Chancellor Theodore Mitau and President David Sweet, admitted its first students in fall 1972. It combines a mentor-student relationship with a competency-based degree. Its 3,700 upper-division and graduate students are served by a core of full-time faculty and by several hundred part-time "community" faculty. These community-based specialists are drawn from many areas of activity, including the professions, business and industry, labor, and social and political agencies. Each shares his or her particular expertise with an individual student as together they plan a program of study, evaluate competency, and pursue learning.

The degree at Metro is defined as competence in communication, community, vocation, culture, science and tradition, and avocation—an unusual and distinctive group of collegiate abilities. Although these competencies are often achieved through traditional means of study in the arts, sciences, and applied disciplines, the college also encourages students to develop these skills through actual experience and application to real problems. The community faculty provides the necessary link for such experiential learning.[8]

Experiential and open learning is by no means limited to bachelor's-level institutions. Numerous community colleges have successfully offered the first half of an undergraduate education through assessment of informal and experiential learning, sometimes through demonstration of student competency in defined skills and knowledge, sometimes through individual learning contracts with students. Community colleges that participate in the League for Innovation in the Community College are among the leaders of this group, examples including Bunker Hill (Massachusetts), Delaware County (Pennsylvania), Kingsborough (New York), and Rockland (New York).

One of the most interesting is the Community College of Vermont, for it has no campus and operates through more than a dozen community sites throughout Vermont. Like many other experimental programs, it began in 1970–71 under President Peter Smith, later the Lt. Governor of Vermont. In 1972 it became a part of the Vermont State College system and since 1975 has handled assessment of educational portfolios for the system. The majority of its students are not degree students, the reasons perhaps best expressed in one student's comment: "It sure is easy to get started but awfully tough to finish at CCV." Over 1,500 part-time instructors offer courses and evaluation to slightly over 3,000 enrolled students. In the early 1980s, CCV, under the leadership of Dean Myrna Miller, adapted its program to some of the emerging career-oriented needs of Vermont and grew significantly in size. Miller, who came to CCV from Empire State College, has since served as president of two other community colleges.[9]

Most of the students in this and other experiential off-campus programs are adults. For these students, the willingness of a college to recognize the rich and extensive learning gained through experience is a critical flexibility. The growing importance of assessing such informal prior learning led many of the university-without-walls programs in 1974 to join in the formation of the Cooperative Assessment of Experiential Learning (CAEL; today the Council for Adult and Experiential Learning). This organization, initially funded by the Carnegie Corporation and quartered at the Educational Testing Service (ETS) in Princeton, has played an important role, both in helping to codify good practice and by encouraging the spread and acceptance of experiential credit to hundreds of colleges and universities.[10] Under the presidency of Morris T. Keeton, CAEL became what could best be termed "a movement." Writing about its history and importance, Zelda Gamson shows how CAEL captured the "imagination of leaders" at the W. K. Kellogg Foundation, at the Educational Testing Service, the American Council on Education, the American College Testing Program, the Council for Postsecondary Accreditation, the Fund for the Improvement of Postsecondary Education, the Carnegie Foundation, and numerous others, to become "the responsible innovator."[11]

CAEL has become the most visible expression of the wide diversity of reforms and alternatives from the 1970s and 1980s. A network of very diverse individuals and interests, it has served as a generator and disseminator of ideas, especially in the areas of assessment of prior learning and service to adult students. Moreover, it has been an activist organization, promoting change in corporate, governmental, and university educational and training settings. Gamson concedes that CAEL has been successful in improving acceptance of educational alternatives within higher education and in improving access and service for older students. But she notes, significantly, that for all its size, energy, and committed network of people, it never "penetrated the academic establishment." Instead, she argues, CAEL has really stimulated a "periphery that was fast growing into a structure parallel to traditional higher education."[12] In short, CAEL's experience lends verity to Warren Bryan Martin's thesis that in the United States a "two-track" educational system has emerged. One track is the traditional, "narrowly academic" institutions; the other is the "broadly educational" institutions.[13] CAEL has given a unified voice to the second track.

INTERNATIONAL EDUCATION

International education is perhaps the most optimistic expression of American university outreach, the ultimate university-without-walls. In its earliest variations as an extended grand tour for maturing aristocrats before World War II, student study in an international location was an exotic education promoted by a few progressive institutions. For example, in the 1930s New College, an undergraduate experiment of Teacher's College, Columbia University, had a curriculum that featured a year abroad either as student or assistant teacher, and also six months in industry, and at least a summer on a farm. Thus, some students spent their junior year teaching the English language in a French lycée.

International programs for a wider clientele became more widely available in the 1960s. As with other innovations, the stimulus for international study programs came from external political and economic pressures. After World War II, knowledge of the world, especially of Europe, became an important part of the liberal learning of future politicians, businessmen, diplomats, and others. Many universities developed area studies programs, and new academic majors, such as African, Latin American, or Southeast Asian Studies resulted. The American national interest required such knowledge, as the scope of American activities spread from Europe and Japan to an increasingly worldwide field. The continued stationing of the military in foreign ports, the idealistic efforts of many young people through the programs of President Kennedy's Peace Corps, and the scholarly exchanges supported by the Fulbright Scholars Program, all encouraged the university to reach out to international settings.

Initially American students were treated with kid gloves, reflecting the paternalistic customs of the home campus. Although the international program provided a legitimate *in situ* experience, the American undergraduate student was guided and protected by a transplanted American college structure. While foreign language instruction was often a part of the program, English was usually the language of instruction, and classes were commonly restricted to Americans. Field trips, housing, and other supports were also usually handled by an American coordinator. In short, most of these early programs replicated the traditional instructional pattern of the home campus, including the use of English language. This allowed the sponsoring American college to maintain integrity and control.

More recently, international education has begun to explore the individualized and experiential aspects of foreign study, employing some of the innovative approaches of a university-without-walls. This could be especially fortuitous for adult students, most of whom cannot spend more than a few weeks abroad at one time. An adult student, under careful college direction, might make a short intensive visit to a region or single city and accomplish a precisely defined learning goal. Such an approach would be especially helpful for corporate employees, undertaken as an experiential learning activity. For corporations engaged more and more in international trade, this approach offers an individually tailored way to enhance an employee's cultural knowledge, sophistication, and understanding. Experientially based international education is a growing arena for innovation in university extension and outreach and a prime example of how the American university, especially through continuing *professional* education, can respond to a growing external need. But even in undergraduate education, the focus of this volume, there are splendid opportunities for invention in international study.

NOTES

1. Alan Pifer, *College Board Review*, (Winter 1970–71): 78, 5.
2. See Ann Giles Benson and Frank Adams (eds.), *To Know for Real: Royce S. Pitkin and Goddard College* (Adamant, VT: Adamant Press, 1987, p. 157).
3. Samuel Baskin, "University Without Walls: A Proposal for an Experimental Degree Program in Undergraduate Education," unpublished (Yellow Springs, Ohio, September 28, 1970).
4. Virginia Lester moved to Empire State College, then to the presidency of Mary Baldwin College where she continued to implement innovative programs.
5. Park College, by the 1870s, and Berea College, by the 1890s, are reported to have included work on campus as part of the educational program. The University of Cincinnati required alternating work and study in its schools of business and engineering as early as 1906 but was not considered an effort in general or liberal education.
6. See Carnegie Commission on Higher Education, *Toward a Learning Society: Alternative Channels to Life, Work, and Service* (New York: McGraw-Hill, 1973).
7. See Gerald Grant, "Creating a Nontraditional College for New Careers: The College for Human Services," in Grant et al., *On Competence*, pp. 299–334.
8. Cf. *Self-Study Report* (St. Paul: Metropolitan State University, March 1980).
9. Community College of Vermont, *15th Anniversary Celebration* (Waterbury, VT, 1985).
10. Morris T. Keeton & Associates, *Experiential Learning: Rationale, Characteristics, and Assessment* (San Francisco: Jossey-Bass, 1976).
11. Zelda F. Gamson, *Higher Education and the Real World: The Story of CAEL* (Wolfeboro, NH: Longwood Academic, 1989), p. x.
12. Gamson, p. xvi.
13. Warren Bryan Martin, "The New Two-Track System of Higher Education," in James W. Hall (ed.), with Barbara L. Kevles, *In Opposition to Core Curriculum: Alternative Models for Undergraduate Education*, Westport, CT: Greenwood Press, 1982), pp. 173–180.

PART THREE

THE FUTURE: BRINGING ABOUT SUCCESSFUL INNOVATION

Academic leaders who wish to bring about constructive change will need to be attentive to those social forces and American values which have stimulated innovation in the past. Each generation of educational leaders must reinterpret the cultural context and, hence, relative importance of egalitarian, individualistic, and pluralistic American values; each generation will inevitably respond through institution-specific opportunities.

A sea change is occurring in the conditions of American life. The change is hastened upon us by two new circumstances: by the reality of world economic competition, which has, in a short time, confronted the hegemony of American manufacturing and commerce in international trade; and by rapid transformation in the way knowledge and information is transmitted, manipulated, and processed. The need for American institutions to respond is great, and the university is not exempt from this need.

Part Three focuses on where and how to ensure as much as possible that the innovative responses to these changes meet with success. Chapter 9, on the "*electronic university*," examines transforming opportunities in the uses of technology. Chapter 10 explores the changing college faculty role. Chapter 11 offers a case study in how innovations can become stable and effect lasting change. The question of financing innovation is the subject of Chapter 12. Chapter 13 offers some observations about management, with some practical suggestions about how to undertake innovative leadership and management in the future. The Conclusion makes some predictions about the future course of innovation in higher learning in America.

Chapter 9

The "Electronic University" and Distance Education

Suppose that the college and university of the future is not a *campus* at all, that technology could reduce the traditional separation of on-campus study and off-campus study to one of mere convenience. Is it possible that the "halls of ivy" could become the "electronic university"? Jacob Schwartz, in a synthesizing paper, "Dreamworld," asks us to

> Imagine a computerized environment with a large wrap-around screen on which one can display many high-resolution images, both computer-generated and retrieved from videodisk, simultaneously or separately, in various sizes and tempos. Imagine that it is possible to access all of the world's books within this environment, and that elaborate indexes, cross-references, and illustrations are instantly available. Suppose that the images of all the world's great works of art are also available, along with images of all notable buildings, landscapes, and other scenes, the whole providing a "universal museum" of art, architecture, culture, and landscape. Within the virtual concert and performance halls of this museum, all the world's concerts, operas and dramas are continually in performance. Imagine that the museum visitor, seated at a console that gives unlimited access to this universal library and museum, can soar freely through any part of it simply by moving a joystick; can summon up any work of literature, any existing audio or video dramatization of a literary work, any photograph or film relevant to a scientific or historical text, simply by touching the screen. Imagine that moderately personalized cost-free tutoring is available to any student wishing to master some part of this immense edifice of knowledge and information. Finally, imagine that artists and scientists continually contribute to the content of this universal library and museum, and that scholars, critics, and educators constantly add to the fabric of cross-reference, comparison, and explanation that ties it all together.[1]

This imaginative description of the electronic university, shorthand for higher education using the whole range of video, computing, and communications technologies for learning purposes, portrays a capability that remains underutilized. Although many experiments have been attempted in past decades and intense trials are now underway in many quarters, successful modeling of university instruction with the electronic technology as its principal medium for instruction does not yet exist. But the technology which makes this "dream" feasible is already available experimentally and is likely to become more generally available at reasonable cost within a very few years. Indeed, the electronic university promises to provide one of the most fertile areas for innovation in higher education. Why has it not done so up to now?

The promise of an instructional media revolution, heralded so loudly for two decades, remains largely unfulfilled—despite the fact that new and powerful aids to learning abound. Almost daily, often through the academy's own research, new and more powerful technologies become available. Few imagined the desktop computer when the first computation by ENIAC, a monster of 30 tons and 18,000 vacuum tubes, initiated the computer era in 1946. ENIAC (Electronic Numerical Integrator and Computer) was one thousand times faster than its electromechanical contemporaries. In 1950 there were no operating systems; users, had to write their own. Even as late as 1972, operating systems were comprehensible only to a trained programmer. But today these old cabalistic systems are irrelevant to the user, who can communicate with the machine in normal language. Word scanners can translate printed documents into computer language automatically, and human voice recognition removes even the need to type on a keyboard. Ease of use for the most untrained operator is nearly a reality.

Rapid increases in computer speed and memory, and corresponding decreases in cost, permit expanded uses of the computer in daily human activities and bring the cost, like electricity, within reach of almost everyone. And miniaturization has brought desktop convenience and portability.[2] Frank Rhodes, president of Cornell University, catches the dimensions in his 1985 quote of a Washington journalist:

> Had the automobile developed at a pace equivalent to that of the computer during the past 20 years, today a Rolls Royce would cost less than $3, get 3 million miles to the gallon, deliver enough power to drive the QE II, and six of them would fit on the head of a pin.

Daniel Bell defines three kinds of technological impacts: "*Niche* technologies," which do specialized tasks; "*domain* technologies," which extend the uses of existing technologies; and "*transforming* technologies," which, like the electric motor or transistor, actually replace previous technologies and cause major structural changes in society.[3] The new interactive capacity of telecommunications technology possesses a transforming character which has the potential to alter dramatically the structure of the university, providing flexibility, convenience, and individual feedback and evaluation of both residential and off-campus students. At the very least, its early impact on the capabilities of university extension and outreach will be fundamental, making possible the next major advance of American higher education in offering access to its services.

Many of the innovations described earlier in this volume represent significant steps toward extending the capability and quality of service of the

college and university beyond the walls of the campus. They represent important milestones along the American university's historic continuum toward
outreach and extension. The various units of the University-Without-Walls,
Empire State College, the Fielding Institute, the Regents College Degree,
and Metropolitan State University, are important programs which allow students to pursue education beyond the campus. But they are also, in a way,
halfway houses. They represent the best capabilities of the present, but they
are circumscribed in their efforts to make possible the realization of a lifelong pattern of learning for the off-campus student. They aim at increased
flexibility of time and place of study, but they have been constrained in
reaching the learner by the absence of an adequate contextual resource;
their technical capability until recently has not been sufficient to bring about
the changes. Dreams have so far been…dreams! These programs have been
limited in providing the necessary rich and varied learning resources and
texts for student study directly from data and bibliographic bases. Some have
created their own materials but at extremely high cost. Until now, then, the
most advanced programs have operated, figuratively, halfway between the
campus and the home.

And so a conceptual design for an electronic university proves easier to
talk about than to implement. Facile descriptions of the electronic landscape
of a decade hence do not help us to understand how incremental change
might occur in the intervening years. Moreover, a good deal of misunderstanding continues to exist between the practitioners of technology and the
theorists of learning. Key questions about the uses of technology need more
widely considered and understood responses:

1. How extensively will residential and off-campus students be served by
   telecommunications?
2. What changes, if any, may be required in faculty and curricular academic structures?
3. Does the use of technology require new ways of thinking about the
   prerogatives of the teacher?
4. How will academic quality be assured?
5. Are the considerable costs fundable?

Finding comprehensive answers to these fundamental questions, and others
yet to be determined, is essential if higher education is to move beyond the
current piecemeal, small-scale, highly expensive, and marginal efforts.[4]

Planning the electronic university should not begin, as has too often been
the case, with iconoclasm directed toward the existing university. Rather, it
should begin with an assumption that the university's strengths and enduring
values can be adjusted structurally so that the qualitative essentials—faculty,
scholarly capacities, and pedagogies—can be extended to reach students
not now well served. In this way the electronic university could fulfill more

adequately the promises of university extension while it actually transforms the quality of its service. Quality in extension could conceivably approach that of the best traditional campus instruction, possible because the faculty, pedagogies, and resources of the residential campus would be practically available to the off-campus student. As these changes occur, the long-standing distinctions between residential and off-campus study, whether in the home, workplace, library, or community center, will diminish in importance. This is an important area toward which innovative leadership should be directed.

Of course serious problems must be overcome. Perhaps the central difficulty will be the illusion of easy access. The medium, it happens, is not the message. All that has changed is that a system of communications, between students and faculty and students and learning resources, has been put in place. Well-conceived learning strategies and engaging courses will still be required, and this is precisely the area in which failure has been greatest in the past. Non-traditional modes of instruction, including correspondence, television, and computer-mediated, do a reasonable job in helping the student acquire factual knowledge and communication skills. These are essential building blocks for a solid advanced education. But, in themselves, they do not adequately enable the student to attain those higher skills which ought to characterize a high-quality education. These higher intellectual and personal dimensions of a baccalaureate education are seldom treated systematically in off-campus delivery and, indeed, they are achieved only occasionally by the most effective traditional classroom delivery. Nonetheless, if the new technology-assisted education is to achieve recognized quality, something like the broad range of intellectual and personal competencies described by most colleges as the goals of an undergraduate education need to be elicited by the system.[5]

The problem remains the issue of human contact. In 1984, CitiBank required that all of its customers transacting business of less than $5,000 use the Automated Teller Machine (ATM). The result was that customers rebelled and soon moved their business to other banks. The ATM was able to meet the technical requirements of the transaction, and the cost analysis clearly showed that small-value transactions at a teller's window were very expensive to the bank. But somehow the human dimension of the transaction was missed by the bank. Entrepreneurs of educational technology have made the same miscalculation, and made it repeatedly.

Today *interactive* technologies and expert software systems hold forth the promise to allow for teaching and learning which nurtures and elicits advanced skills from the student. But those who work with these innovations will need to be guided by well-defined concepts of what higher learning is really about and how to stimulate real student involvement. This is the real challenge. Remember Henry David Thoreau's timely comment regarding the technology of the 1840s: "We are in great haste to construct a magnetic telegraph from Maine to Texas; but Maine and Texas, it may be, have nothing important to communicate."[6] That might be paraphrased for us today: With the most extraordinary technology, will we have a worthwhile education to deliver?

FAILURES IN INNOVATION

Not all innovation is successful, and the area of technology provides an unhealthy share of failures. But it can be instructive to consider innovation that either has not worked or has not established itself successfully. One of the more interesting chronicles of this kind is the University of the Air experiment undertaken by State University of New York (SUNY) in the mid-1960s. An early effort to create the "campusless college," it represents a highly innovative effort which failed because it appeared too far in front of student demand, because the underlying technical capacity was not sufficiently advanced, and because no degree concept guided the student.

In the *SUNY Master Plan for 1964*, the new chancellor, Samuel B. Gould, makes brief reference to "new teaching devices" by which was meant films, tapes, and closed circuit television. But it is a passing notation and merely indicates the intention to "encourage the faculty in the development of educational techniques to make optimum use of new instructional devices." This was all delicate enough. But the real kicker appeared two pages later. Under the heading "Television for Education and Communication," Gould trumpeted the first call for an educational television network which, "used in conjunction with advanced placement and competency examinations,...will enable many persons to study at home."

Here was an emerging educational agenda of the 1960s. Gould had been the president of Antioch, and after a stint at U.C. Santa Barbara, president of New York's station WNET. Gould had both the vision and experience to bring technological innovation to New York. But bureaucratic obstacles lay ahead.

SUNY was enlarging existing campuses and building new ones as rapidly as concrete could be poured. In 1964 SUNY employed 15,300 faculty and staff. In fall 1965 that increased by 3,666 positions, in fall 1966 by 3,663 more positions, and, incredibly, again in fall 1967 by another 2,508 to a total of 25,137. Gould's plan was to use the projected scarcity of campus places for students as a basis for developing off-campus delivery systems. He was encouraged as well by McGeorge Bundy, president of the Ford Foundation, who was also interested in the British University of the Air (later the British Open University; see Chapter 10).

In 1965 the state legislature made its first appropriation of $625,000 to support a statewide educational television network. SUNY was responsible for development and operation of the network and for production and broadcast of all higher and continuing education programs. For several years this appropriation was increased annually, with endorsement from Governor Nelson Rockefeller, who supported "an expansion in the University-wide use of television, computers and other devices of modern educational technology."[7]

There followed a comprehensive effort to implement and to gain acceptance of educational technology. The first two sample courses for the University of the Air were broadcast in spring 1966 and 1967 with 2,400 student registrants; Stony Brook conducted an experimental study of the use of computers for programmed learning using computer linkages to neighboring institutions; and a statewide microwave network was shortly expected to tie the entire state together. Educational radio was also in use.

But the *Master Plan of 1968* of SUNY revealed the first sign of problems. Television broadcast, it said, was confined to weekends "because of the scarcity of air time." The broadcast signal could not as yet be received by those who might make the greatest use of the network, those who lived in the most remote regions of the state. Perhaps most significantly, the Plan urged that "more definite goals" be set for students, allowing "regularly matriculated students on all campuses...to complete appropriate portions of their academic programs through the University of the Air." [8] Here one notes the continued separation of the technology from the mainstream of campus instruction and the resistance of campus faculties to accept such courses as part of a degree program.

By 1969, New York State, with fiscal problems beginning, established workload measures for the University of the Air and noted that non-credit course enrollments exceeded credit enrollments by a ratio of four to one (2,800 non-credit, 650 credit). The 1970 *Executive Budget* significantly reduced the appropriation (albeit at the high level of $2.3 million), shifted the emphasis to direct campus funds for improved course usage, and again noted the sharp increase in non-credit users relative to credit students. Emphasized again was the rationale that "large numbers of students will take ETV courses in order to relieve enrollment pressures on the community colleges."[9]

Finally in the fiscal crisis of 1971 the curtain was drawn. The University of the Air was disbanded, most of its personnel were dismissed, and the nation's most vigorous and well-funded innovation in educational technology ended. The ETV stations breathed a sigh of relief, for they could now concentrate on competing with regular commercial television while continuing to receive their state subvention.

Such failure was not limited to SUNY. Well-funded programs at the University of Nebraska (SUN), later the University of Mid-America, and finally the American Open University (AOU), sponsored by the ten large midwestern universities, with an additional $2 million annually from the National Institute of Education (NIE), closed their offices by the mid-1980s. Substantial innovation done there by some of America's most talented educational media specialists makes this latter failure especially discouraging. More recently, the International University Consortium (IUC), with initial support from the Carnegie Corporation, struggles to develop a body of course users sufficient to offset development and operational costs. Linkage to some of the emerging technologies may, in time, revivify this promising program, now joined with Maryland's University College.

What lessons were learned? Most importantly, the flimsy original justification that ETV in New York State would relieve campus enrollment pressures simply dissolved when new enrollment projections indicated that SUNY would soon be overbuilt in the face of declining numbers of high school graduates. Future justification of educational technology would need to be based upon qualitative improvements in learning and improved access, especially for off-campus students, rather than relief of campus facilities.

Second lesson: Using technology as an adjunct to campus teaching was challenged as a productive line of development. In 1971 it seemed questionable that traditional faculty would be willing to include such courses as part of a degree program. A separate faculty committed to this purpose would be needed.

Third lesson: It was fiscally impossible to develop and maintain sufficient numbers of programmed courses to allow a student a reasonable range of university curricula. A more flexible system, which could assemble comprehensive and flexible curricula for each student, was required.

These problems and the lessons learned actually led directly to the creation of Empire State College, which was charged with developing new strategies to serve students whose responsibilities and circumstances prevented them from coming to campus regularly. The 1972 *Executive Budget* shifted a substantial portion of the terminated University of the Air budget to the new college. Empire State College would attempt to offer study more responsive to individual students, would use an integrated mixture of instructional modes and strategies rather than rely on a mono-modal technology, and would offer varied tracks leading to a degree (Chapter 8).

INNOVATIONS WITH PROMISE FOR THE FUTURE

But there are already other new programs which are using the newer technologies to their advantage. The National Technological University (NTU) [10] is one of the most promising, substantively organized, and well-sponsored new examples of instructional television. Actually a consortium of twenty-nine engineering schools [11] and seventy sponsoring organizations, this "university" transmits, by satellite, graduate-level engineering courses from a participating university directly into nearly 250 corporate worksites. The collaboration began in 1984 as an effort to permit some of the nation's most distinguished schools of engineering to extend their highly specialized courses directly into the workplace. Supported initially by subscriptions by a number of the nation's largest corporations (e.g., Hewlett-Packard, Eastman Kodak, IBM, DEC), NTU is also beamed into some of the major scientific laboratories.

Participating schools transmit by electronic uplink live classes currently offered on the university campus. Students in distant corporate settings receive the transmission by satellite downlink, and may use the telephone or electronic mail to communicate questions back to the course instructor. NTU, drawing upon the course offerings of many engineering schools, can offer a much richer and deeper palette of course specialties than would be possible at a single university. Moreover, the question of adequate class size, an economic issue for all university courses offered in one location, is no longer an issue. Students may select courses from the most knowledgeable and up-to-date instructors, a very important factor in the rapidly changing technological fields. Students also gain flexibility of schedule by videotaping courses and watching them at a later time. Degrees are conferred by NTU and, since 1986, accredited by the North Central Association.

Although this television approach encounters many of the same deficiencies which have characterized other such experiments in the past, these problems are overcome by the highly specialized character of the courses offered, the high motivation and need of the students, and the availability of direct corporate financial support to program and student. NTU fills four color ITV channels each workday. Lionel Baldwin, founding president, reports that over 325 courses are now available through this system. During 1988–89, NTU offered over 10,000 hours of graduate instruction and 1,000 hours of interactive continuing education and research conferencing. Most recently, NTU has initiated a master's program in technology management. NTU projects to expand its offerings to over 150 major corporations at over 1,000 sites.

Other institutions are also extending their efforts. The systemwide efforts by the California State University are of the greatest immediate application for satellite transmission of courses to remote classroom sites. Chico State, for example, offers an M.S. degree to subscribing companies across the continent. Its library catalogue of nearly 2 million items can be accessed by computer terminal anywhere. Stanislaus State broadcasts nearly 100 courses over three channels to five counties. New multi-campus organizations, such as the National University Teleconferencing Network (NUTN), founded in 1982 with 125 institutional members, makes possible program sharing, pooling of telecommunications costs, and wide geographic coverage for off-campus students. Innovations like these are in important experimental phases, and their success or failure will be indicators for the immediate future.

Although the British Open University is a successful innovation, real ferment exists today in the United Kingdom for subdegree training and continuing education by open learning. In the late 1970s a planning group developed the concept of "Open Tech," which developed many projects. Now the concept has become "Open College." In fall 1987 this new concept was intiated with the cooperation of Channel 4, a new network with strong commitments to continuing education. Open College explicitly is a coordinating and planning organization, which expects to offer students somewhat individualized options for study. Most of the early courses are vocational, technical or business-related topics, although basic and general education areas are planned.[12]

Today in the United States, television and video courses are used by over 800 institutions, preponderantly community colleges. Course producers include Coast Telecourses (Coastline Community), Maryland Public Television, Miami-Dade Community, Dallas County, and Great Plains National. Although some generate internal funding for capital investment in new courses, most rely on foundation grants, in particular grants from the Annenberg/CPB Project. That project, funded by a $150 million, fifteen year pledge from *TV Guide* owner Walter H. Annenberg, has supported the creation of eighteen credit courses, with fourteen additional courses in progress.[13]

But the more important aspect of the Annenberg project's work is likely to be its gingerly and modest encouragement of technology experiments which link computing and telecommunications systems to the use of these courses. Access through telecommunications can be costly. On the other hand, these costs are likely to be a good deal less than the costs of regular transportation to a campus.

A number of highly promising developments in computer instruction are underway. The innovative approaches of such early pioneers as Arnold Arons and John Anderson have moved computer usage well beyond the earlier dull routine of "page turning" of texts and have developed engaging tutor systems which provide individualized drill and highly interactive laboratory simulations. Arons says, "The last thing we want to do is cultivate dependence on the reinforcement supplied by computer instruction. Rather, we want to cultivate the skills underlying genuinely independent study.... The computer can help many students to the threshold of these higher intellectual skills."[14]

And fortunately, more and more students are being asked to purchase computers upon entering college, and this has not thus far appeared as a bar to student enrollment. With large numbers of students now word-processing, and linked through hardwiring to a college's central computing system (usually a VAX), more and more of the faculty are communicating with residential students through the computer. Given the greater purchasing power of adults, it seems reasonable to expect off-campus students to possess computers and to use the telephone as a large, perhaps dominant, form of communication with on-campus faculty. The British Open University, with a grant from the Department of Trade and Industry, now leases computers directly to students. By 1988 over 11,000 "home computing" students were enrolled.[15]

There are those who believe that interactive computer technology is threatening to the university as it currently exists and that the technology will ultimately cause the university to be a much smaller, though essential, institution. Francis Fisher, a lawyer with wide experience in technology administration in the federal government and at Harvard University, sees the impact of the computer learning station, with its capacity to eliminate the geographic imperatives of time and place, as helping students from grade school onward to learn much more, and faster. He sees movement toward near universal learning, but in *other* places than the college campus.[16] Certainly technology, through drill and mastery learning techniques, gives us the capacity to afford students the time to persevere to success, and that is an entirely startling possibility.

There have been a number of research projects aimed at determining the relative value of learning through technology, both computer- and video-based systems. These studies tend to show that faculty evaluations of student performance are higher when work is individualized through technology. Unfortunately the methodologies used tend to focus on command and retention of specific information, an easily measured factor which is enhanced simply by additional time on the task. Moreover, most studies are unable to make a real determination about the enhanced intellectual capability of the student. Yet this aspect of learning, admittedly difficult to measure, is the most significant component in the teacher-student relationship.

The recent rapid growth of the use of computers by faculty, mostly for word processing but increasingly for electronic messaging and student communication, shows an irresistable quality of technology. Even the most traditional of professors, some of whom until recently flatly refused to use a computer for word processing, have succumbed. As Bruce Pulling of NYNEX said at a 1985 conference in Saratoga Springs, "Technology is pervasive, it cannot be regulated, and will go anywhere." Given the evidence thus far, the use of electronic communications would seem to be the most important area for breakthroughs in educational innovation for the remainder of this century. Certainly it supports the view that the college of the future may not be a campus.

NOTES

1. Jacob T. Schwartz, "Dreamworld," *Daedalus*, vol. 116, no. 3 (Summer 1987): 165–166.
2. Frederic G. Worthington, "Limits of Key Technologies," *Educom Bulletin*, vol. 19, no.4 (Winter 1984): 2–4.
3. Daniel Bell, "The World and The United States in 2013," *Daedalus*, vol. 116, no. 3 (Summer 1987): 1–31.
4. Empire State College, *A Report on the Electronic University of the Future*, proceedings of a conference supported by The Sloan Foundation, Saratoga Springs, New York, 1985.
5. As one example, see James W. Hall with Barbara L. Kevles, "A Model College Education," James W. Hall (ed.), with Barbara L. Kevles, *In Opposition to Core Curriculum: Alternative Models for Undergraduate Education* (Westport, CT: Greenwood, 1982), p. 205.
6. Henry David Thoreau, "Economy," in *Walden*, Norman Holmes Pierson (ed.), (New York: Holt, Rinehart & Winston, 1948), p. 42.
7. State of New York, *The Executive Budget (1967–1968)*, p. M27.

8. *Master Plan of 1968*, Albany, New York, 1968, p. 22.

9. New York State, *The Executive Budget, 1970,* Albany, New York, 1970, p. 366.

10. National Technological University, *1988–1989 Annual Report*, Fort Collins, CO, 1989.

11. Including such universities as Arizona State, Boston, Florida, Maryland, Minnesota, Purdue, SMU, and Wisconsin.

12. Robin Moss and David Grugeon, "Open College of the Air," *Open Learning*, (November 1986): 40–43.

13. As of January, 1990, as reported by Annenberg/CPB staff, Mara Mayor, Director, Washington, DC. Unfortunately this program will soon terminate.

14. A. B. Arons, "Computer-Based Intructional Dialogs in Science Courses," *Science*, vol. 224, no. 4653 (June 8, 1984): 1056.

15. Adrian Kirkwood, "Evaluating a Major Innovation in Distance Education: The Home Computing Policy of the U.K. Open University," *Research in Distance Education*, vol. I, no. 2 (July 1989): 5–6.

16. Francis Dummer Fisher, "Higher Education circa 2005," *Change*, (January/February 1987): 40–45.

Chapter 10

Changing Undergraduate Faculty Roles

Because the faculty stands at the very center of college instruction, any innovation directly affects the faculty role and organization. New curricula, extension and outreach, adult continuing education, open universities, universities-without-walls, experiential and competency learning—all of these require faculty to assume different and, frequently, unaccustomed roles. These innovative teaching roles significantly differ from the traditional professor/investigator/lecturer model imported from the nineteenth-century European university. Indeed, any contemplation of the new dispensations compels one to explore the changing role of the undergraduate faculty.

A common assumption is that faculty and innovation are in opposition. Many faculty do sometimes wonder whether new programs are part of a strategy aimed at replacing them with computers, programmed textbooks, and evaluative instruments. This may not be an entirely unjustified fear, for in fact some educators and government officials tend to think of innovations in educational delivery, at least those which they may be willing to fund, as ways to reduce faculty costs and increase "efficiency." For my part, I believe that the faculty concern is genuine only as it affects them in their need to learn more about adapting their teaching in an age of technology. Many disciplines have benefited from the use of technology in research. Now it's time to expand this use to teaching as well.

But I want to emphasize with equal force my belief that no innovation which omits or diminishes the critical faculty role is likely to be recognizable as higher learning. Without a faculty, there is no committed body which maintains the currency and rigor of the academic offering, provides important evaluative feedback to students, or sets expectations for a university degree. Clearly innovation without a faculty is fraudulent. But innovation does often require new or sharply redefined faculty roles.

In fact the role of the American college professor has undergone significant change in the past. The stock image of the tweedy university scholar, emitting an air of modest preoccupation with unworldly things, hardly reflects the reality of today's professor. Nor does the campus/Washington jetset specialist featured by the mass media typify those who carry the teaching load of undergraduates. More ancient models of the teacher might be useful—

116

Socrates on the steps of the Agora, unkempt and bawdy scholars wandering about Europe, or perhaps more elegantly attired court servants tutoring the children of the eighteenth century gentry.

But today, two distinctly contrasting roles can be found in American colleges and universities: the university research scholar and lecturer, and the increasingly specialized undergraduate teacher, once champion of liberal learning. Unfortunately these roles divide two functions which should be co-equal aspects of the undergraduate teaching role: the pursuit of *scholarly knowledge*, with competence in research skills, analysis, reasoning, and explication; and stimulation of *student learning*, with competence in adapting pedagogy to the student and applying critical skills in Socratic and evaluative processes. Rooted in "traditional" collegiate patterns, the most successful of undergraduate faculty combine both functions, though not easily. And innovation can occur in both functions.

The discovery and use of new knowledge is an academically central, visible, and sharable form of "original work" for most scholar-teachers. Because such visible scholarship is widely recognized and rewarded, the possibilities for innovation in the teaching/learning function are often ignored, or even studiously avoided, by faculty, as they are overshadowed by the requirements of scholarly innovation. This leads course content to be stressed above concern for student learning. Derek Bok says "the fascination with curriculum, so typical of American undergraduate education, protects traditional faculty prerogatives at the cost of diverting attention away from the kinds of inquiry and discussion that are most likely to improve the process of learning."[1] For this reason, it is typically college-wide efforts, as opposed to individual faculty efforts, which seek to strengthen the voice of the student in the teaching/learning duet or to focus on innovations in the teaching/learning function of the faculty. Such innovations shift the student's learning to center stage, with the academic subject matter played differently for the individual student.

Until relatively recently the scholar has not had an easy time of it in the American university. Especially the research role, imported from Germany in the later nineteenth century, was not at first honored by Americans. No American scholar was addressed as "Herr Doktor Professor," with the attendant ritual of academic regalia, and respectful students stamping the floor at his entry into the lecture hall. Only in the too frequently monotoned recital of the scholar's current research might one find a pale example of the continental model. Moreover, the American university failed to invest the university professor with "all the rights and privileges which pertained to the Ph.D." in the European university. From colonial times, the board of trustees and president have exercised a higher measure of authority in matters of university policy than was accorded to administrators by the traditional European university faculty.[2]

Teachers in early American colleges, dealing with somewhat younger students than today's undergraduates, were necessarily school master, disciplinarian, and dormitory resident. Perhaps the egalitarian social value introduced suspicion about elitism or abstract knowledge; it may be that individualism and concern for the "self" was best served by a style of teaching which promoted a high level of interaction between teacher and student. Certainly American undergraduate students, except for the most intellectually committed, respond to the human side of the teacher, who, in addition to a rapt classroom style, is encouraged to display himself in athletic contests, engage in frequent private office appointments, or perform in the faculty play. So early in the twentieth century, when President Woodrow Wilson introduced what he considered his most important innovation at Princeton, the "preceptorship" role, he was responding to a prevailing value which resisted the fashionable Germanic faculty model. The preceptorial teaching method linked four or five students to a young academic whose interest and concern for the student's development had both academic and personal dimensions. Individualism, expressed in concern for a student's personal growth, was very much alive in the American university. Wilson once described Princeton not as "a place where a lad finds his profession, but a place where he finds himself." In defining this purpose for the college, Wilson also described a faculty role which, countering the professorial model of the graduate school, became normative in the private liberal arts college.

But with the growth and modernization of colleges and universities after World War II, the pattern of the research university was increasingly imprinted upon the faculty role at those regional colleges that had previously had a tradition of student-oriented teaching. Young scholars and administrators, prepared in standards of modern scholarship at the most prestigious graduate schools, came to the regional or provincial college with more "professional" expectations and aspirations for their role as members of faculty. Rapid expansion of graduate study drew faculty away from undergraduates, and informal advisement systems withered. Needs of students and interests of faculty were increasingly mismatched. In many cases the impact was disjunctive for older collegiate faculty, a frustrating career-end for otherwise useful teachers who found themselves pushed aside by sometimes arrogant new colleagues. In this period of rapid growth, new administrators aspired to replicate the same ethos, curriculum, and practices of their own ivy institution. In the process, little support was offered to old-fashioned, homegrown innovations, some of which might have been more responsive to the needs of local students. For a time, individual students were muted behind the intellectual scrim of the university, pluralism of choice was replaced by standardized requirements, and a general effort to admit always more qualified students limited diversity and access.

New college faculty were prodded by professional pressures to fulfill the scholarly research role. But with the explosion of new knowledge and increasing faculty size came increased division and differentiation. The European historian, for example, was no longer a generalist but a specialist in the early Baroque culture of Lombardy. Although his or her own writing was even more specialized than this, the scholar was expected to offer the department's courses on such "general" topics as the Counter-Reformation, the Holy Roman Empire, Seventeenth-Century Europe, and, alas, Western Civilization. Evaluated for tenure on the basis of the number and quality of publications, such a scholar had little time to consider college-wide issues of student learning and innovation, other than those directly connected with his or her own scholarship or teaching. Collaboration with colleagues, even within the department, was difficult. Participation in general education outside of the department was thereby discouraged and unlikely to be rewarded by the department.

Presidents and deans have since worried about how to interest the faculty not only in what is taught but how it is taught and whether students learn anything. One suspects that President Wilson influenced the Princeton faculty in this regard no more effectively than the recent voice of Harvard President Bok, who urges faculty members of research universities to take a greater interest in how well students learn. Bok concedes that the inherent demands of disciplinary scholarship command most of a professor's time and interest.[3] Bok's dean, Henry Rosovsky, in a widely circulated but judicious and politically cautious document,[4] urges substantial change in Harvard's undergraduate non-concentration area. But Rosovsky's real concern goes beyond curriculum to the style of teaching and learning, which he defines in a phrase from Eton Master William Cory in 1861, who said, "You are not engaged so much in acquiring knowledge as in making mental efforts under criticism."

But these occasional voices can seldom prevail in the face of a dominant faculty pattern in which students are often left to fend for themselves. The result is too frequently sterile teaching and student apathy toward learning. "At Berkeley," says Martin Trow, "the tensions that arise from this disparity [between undergraduate education and graduate training and research] are felt by every student, teacher, and administrator . . . and these tensions reflect themselves in various kinds of troubles and discontents on that campus."[5]

Studies consistently show that student learning occurs best when the teacher engages the individual student in projects and seminars, builds on a student's interest and motivation, and provides frequent feedback and positive evaluation.[6] The tension between the scholar as teacher, and the teacher as student's mentor can be found in any reading of student evaluations of faculty. Even in the great research universities student action as a force for change doesn't work either, Bok says, because when students select a college on the basis of institutional prestige, no pressure for change is generated. Thus most real reform in teaching occurs in small, largely non-selective colleges that must compete for students. "The schools that have the greatest chance of influencing other institutions through successful innovation are the ones least likely to be venturesome."[7]

There are countercurrents, of course. Many of the innovations in curriculum described in Chapter 3 are attempts to recreate the climate of the small liberal arts college. In these colleges, faculty often emphasized individual work with students. As liberally educated scholars, they participated in the *general* as well as *specific* education of students. Students could turn to their faculty teachers for advisement in the design of their total undergraduate program or could explore with them their own struggles with important moral and ethical questions. But these faculty commitments were almost never established within separate lasting structures which might support new faculty roles. In the 1960s, partly in response to student demands, universities vigorously shucked off the responsibilities of parenting, including rigorous separation of the sexes by invigilated dormitory hours and regulations and strict attention to classroom attendance and proctored examinations. To replace these former regulations, a few reformers advocated programs which allowed young students to address values of human character and other issues once considered fundamental to a liberally educated person.

One such effort was advanced by the Danforth Foundation of St. Louis, which for two decades supported graduate students who as college teachers might assume a special role in relation to the moral and ethical development of students. Spearheaded by Kenneth I. Brown, the Foundation's president, the Danforth program represented the American idea that the university college should deal with the whole development of the student. It addressed the problem by trying to coopt the faculty role within the existing disciplinary structure, planting well-trained scholars across the American academic landscape.

One major university system, the State University of New York, stimulated a program of instruction across its many campuses which enabled students to work with faculty in "Values Seminars," wrestling with key social, moral, and ethical questions. The approach was short lived but did draw the enthusiastic interest of a number of faculty who responded to this effort. But few of these efforts were rooted in a new *structure* which could support a modified faculty role.

Installing new faculty roles within an existing faculty structure is virtually impossible. Change of this magnitude cannot be imposed by administrative fiat; existing academic departments, buttressed by collegewide faculty governance or, in some cases, by contractual agreements of unions, will reject any effort to establish a new role. Even when such a new role does somehow emerge, its life may be brief. It will either not be accepted by the traditional faculty as a proper activity for them and so becomes part of the administration or "staff," or, if created initially as a faculty role, it will sooner or later be transformed toward the traditional model. Arthur Levine argues, on the basis of his research at SUNY Buffalo, that, although innovation should ideally be conducted within existing universities, the risk of backsliding and even program discontinuation is much higher than would be the case in a separate new structure.[8]

It was this issue of faculty role and appropriate structure which motivated most of the efforts of the 1970s to create new departments (e.g., Black Studies,

Womens' Studies), special enclaves for different learning (e.g., Tussman or Johnston Colleges; see Chapter 3), or, wholly new institutional structures (e.g, the British Open University and Empire State College; see Chapter 11). In theory the necessary tasks could have been accomplished within an existing university, but experience had demonstrated its practical impossibility. Even within a successful new faculty structure, new faculty are employed who do not share the founding vision. "One fine morning," say Jencks and Riesman, "the true believers discover they have become a minority...and the more traditional norms of the academic profession begin to reassert themselves."[9]

Yet even with this scenario, there are a number of current academic structures which have, thus far, implemented new faculty roles with success. Two examples of innovation, one representing the student teaching role, the second the scholarly research role, are described below. Several others are mentioned briefly.

THE FACULTY MENTOR

One of the earliest appearances of the professor as faculty mentor developed at Goddard College under President Royce S. (Tim) Pitkin. Samuel Baskin introduced a similar role in the University-Without-Walls. About the same time Arthur W. Chickering, a faculty member at Goddard College and associate of Pitkin, produced his important study *Education and Identity*.[10] This study examined a number of institutions with an eye to the effect of conscious teaching strategies on student development, arguing that "colleges and universities will be educationally effective only if they reach students 'where they live,' only if they connect with those concerns of central importance to their students."

Chickering brought this conviction to the newly created Empire State College (SUNY) as its vice president for Academic Affairs. He and this writer, who had planned the SUNY-wide Values project mentioned earlier, found a common ground. In working with the SUNY Planning Committee for Empire State College, I had devised a new academic teaching role in which a faculty member would facilitate an individual student's link with appropriate learning opportunities in the resource-rich SUNY network. Chickering added the critical conceptual dimension of individual academic planning and feedback, suggesting a faculty/student relationship which was responsive to a student's interests, initiatives, and educational goals. During the early years of development, this mentorship role was fully developed through experience, debate, and modification.

F. Thomas Clark (formerly an Empire State College dean) describes the new faculty role in this way: "Traditional higher education prescribes a series of courses in academic subjects' generally to transmit the knowledge, skills and values of one highly educated generation to the next....The professor determines what students should study, when and how. The professor is also the sole judge of how well the student learns. Nontraditional college education, in contrast, often puts the student rather than the professor in the center ring, then adjusts the objectives, the content, the teaching style, the learning experiences and even the method of evaluation to fit the unique differences of that individual."[11] At its best, this teaching role provides the "cogent, compelling, and realistic advising" which makes education, Grant and Riesman advise, "responsive to [the students'] needs rather than to their wants."[12]

THE FACULTY COURSE DEVELOPER

A second new faculty role is a nontraditional variation of the scholar-teacher function. If the *mentor* role reunites a variety of closely related educational functions which had been broken apart within the rapid expansion of the modern university, the faculty course-developer role does just the opposite. This role differentiates the faculty role yet further. For example, at the British Open University the variety of traditional instructional activities normally performed by the classroom teacher were unbundled, with each function assigned to a specialist.

At the center of the BOU model are the scholars who create the courses. Except for possible involvement in a summer residency, these academics never actually see or speak to a student. Their role is to bring their academic expertise to the course material. Working with a course team of ten to fifteen persons, specialists handle even pedagogic issues such as the manner of presentation of ideas and the formatting of examinations. When a course is completed, they are responsible for maintaining its currency, monitoring its effective use by students, preparing examinations, and thinking about the next complete course revision.

Student learning begins when the student receives the course materials by post. Conceptually, the student who requires no further assistance can study these materials and books, complete assignments, pass the examinations, and so succeed. In practice, most students seek some interaction regarding their performance on papers or require assistance in understanding the reading or assignment. To meet this need, BOU also created the roles of part-time Study Tutor and Counsellor, persons engaged on an overload basis from other institutions in a geographic region.

Organizing such a vast network as is required for the 125,000 students throughout the UK requires a regional link to the university faculties. Thus BOU created the position of Staff Tutor (full-time), placing (ideally) two such tutors for each academic faculty (i.e., Arts, Social Sciences, Science, Education, Business) in each regional office. Although these tutors are technically members of one of the BOU faculties, their role is quite different. Although they do participate occasionally in course teams, lecture in the summer session, and participate in university governance committees, most of their time is devoted to facilitating the hiring, orientation to courses, and coordination of the part-time study tutors. Their typical week includes two days in the regional office, two days on the road visiting the myriad local study centers and arranging local links, and one day on reading and university governance.

A full-time Staff Counsellor is also a member of the regional office, and is responsible for hiring and coordinating both part-time tutors and counsellors. Part-time counsellors provide advice to students about course election and, in the process, bear a lot of student anxiety and personal difficulties.

BOU has found it difficult to separate the tutor and counsellor roles cleanly, and in practice the two often merge serendipitously in the same person. Typically in the first year of employment, an individual tutors a course; the second year he or she again tutors the course but continues with the first-year group as an academic advisor and counsellor. In this way academic advisement and the tutor role are linked. In payment for these services, the part-timer receives a flat stipend for each course tutored, an additional stipend for each student enrolled, and yet another stipend for each student paper marked.

But when tutors or facilitators manage courses created by other scholars, the separation can undermine the freshness, intention, commitment, and therefore the quality of the academic experience for both tutor and student. BOU has noted such criticism of its part-time tutors from time to time.[13]

In another example of faculty innovation, the New York Regents Degree may appear to have dispensed with faculty altogether: students send transcripts of previous college study by mail, take proficiency examinations, and are awarded a degree by mail. But in actuality, if invisibly, panels of senior faculty from other universities exercise responsibility in setting degree requirements, defining the competencies to be examined, and determining adequate levels of student performance. These faculty, although they do not instruct, are the scholars who create curricula and course requirements.

COMMUNITY FACULTY

Metropolitan University (St. Paul) has created a part-time "community faculty" role. Using specialists who work and live in the students' milieu, the linkage of professional skills and liberal education are achieved. Both Metropolitan and some units of the University-Without-Walls use an *academic advisor* who helps students plan programs of study and links them with specialist faculty tutors.

Models such as these, though not widely used today beyond the examples cited, are effective with many students and hold significant promise for the future. Part-time faculty roles present certain structural inequities but are likely to continue to increase as many colleges attempt to provide expertise to cover the needs of highly diverse students and expanded curricula. These arrangements require more careful planning than has been the case in the past, ensuring that part-time faculty meet rigorous academic standards, are brought into the life of the college, and have some teaching security.

NEW FACULTY ROLES FOR THE FUTURE

The coming changes in student body composition and new approaches to teaching and learning bring three pressing issues involving future faculty roles to the fore. They are: (1) teaching adult and part-time students; (2) developing the capacity to handle remedial learning; and (3) using educational technology in instruction, and for mastery learning in particular.

Clearly all faculties, graduate as well as undergraduate, given the rapid change in the age and enrollment status of large numbers of students, need to adapt their skills to relate to adults in new and meaningful ways. While such faculty adaptation is occurring gradually as student profiles change, certain conscious efforts to improve and facilitate performance would be helpful. Given the pedagogic and stylistic needs of older students (see Chapter 6), faculty development and sensitizing seems an important agenda. For some years, programs in adult continuing education have recognized such needs and have offered, even required, special training, especially for part-time, adjunct faculty.

The second issue grows out of the increasing urgency to enroll and teach less prepared students. This teaching role is already of great importance as underprepared students try to gain necessary, college-level, specialized skills, such as writing and mathematics. One of the key problems faced by CUNY in the open admissions innovation of 1969–1976 (see Chapter 4) was the dearth of faculty prepared to undertake this role. Brooklyn College's President John Kneller, in his assessment of open admissions, acknowledged that "nobody was equipped to deal with the problems of the underprepared.... Our faculty was divided among those who were very eager and willing to deal with the underprepared student and those who were not....Moreover, the whole question of the underprepared became a matter of political difference... between faculty and faculty.[14] Here is a whole emerging area for which a new faculty role and support structure is required. In fact, a new teaching specialization (or subspecialization by discipline) is growing at the collegiate level and bears examination.

In recent years some undergraduate colleges have developed special attention and expertise among faculty in improving student writing skills. The concept of "writing across the curriculum" engages faculty in disciplines other than English in this task. But these programs still assume a basic level of literacy upon entrance and probably would be inadequate to deal with students severely lacking in basic reading and writing skills. Bilingual programs, designed to allow entering students time to make a transition to English instruction, have been helpful in a few colleges. But such programs are very rare, and have also become a politically controversial subject in some states. Specialists in rapid skill development for underprepared students is an important new faculty role which the university will need to recognize and reward.

Finally, the use of the new technologies in instruction, especially for distance students, will also require new faculty roles. Many scholars will be needed to create the instructional software that will support courses, student interaction, and evaluation. As at the BOU, specialists in facilitating student learning will also be essential to provide help when needed. The facilitative faculty role may be increasingly recognized. As corporations, medical facilities, government agencies, and community centers engage in on-site forms of continuing professional education, skilled teachers will teach students located far from the campus classroom, providing the crucial motivation and expertise to students who use a variety of learning resources. Currently the IBM Corporation alone employs several hundred specialists in instructional design. Offered as a graduate specialization by only a handful of institutions, a large and growing market exists for this faculty role.

In recent years it has been possible to attract adequate numbers of well-qualified academics to these new roles. In part, the academic market place has had a surplus of talent, and some have been willing to accept positions distinctly different than those they had anticipated. This, of course, leads in some instances to some career dissatisfaction. Still others are drawn to new ventures by choice, out of a conviction that the new role is more satisfying in meeting their professional goals. Grant and Riesman point out perceptively that faculty drawn to innovative colleges are "united in their opposition [to the multiversity]," but seldom united as to their "aspirations."[15]

Clark offers a catalogue of these new roles, contrasting traditional faculty roles, which include disciplinary or subject expertise, "knowledge-dispenser" and "judge," with a number of non-traditional faculty roles. He includes the following roles:

Facilitator-counsel

Broker-negotiator

Instructor-tutor

Evaluator

Administrator

Developer and coordinator of learning resources

Creator and user of instructional materials

Planner of individualized programs[16]

All of these new or modified faculty roles, although often quite different from the traditional model, offer solutions to the problems of engaging more fully with students in the learning process. By exploring such innovations intelligently, these roles need not undermine the academic profession but actually bring new life and possibility to meeting important concerns of our institutions of higher learning.

NOTES

1. Derek Bok, *Higher Learning* (Cambridge, MA: Harvard University Press, 1986), p. 71.

2. Extended treatment of different facets of the traditional academic role and its struggle for recognition in America is found in Richard Hofstadter and Walter P. Metzger, *The Development of Academic Freedom in America* (New York: Columbia University Press, 1955); Richard Hofstadter, *Anti-Intellectualism in American Life* (New York: Vintage Press, 1962); and Christopher Jencks and David Riesman, *The Academic Revolution* (Chicago: University of Chicago Press, 1968).

3. Derek Bok, *Higher Learning*.

4. *Undergraduate Education: Defining the Issues,* Report of the Dean, 1975–1976.

5. Martin Trow, "Bell, Book and Berkeley," in Carlos Kruytbosch & Sheldon Messinger (eds.), *The State of the University* (Beverly Hills, CA: Sage Publications, 1968), pp. 295–308.

6. Cf. *Involvement in Learning* (Washington, DC: National Institute of Education, 1984).

7. Bok, p. 186.

8. Arthur Levine, *Why Innovation Fails* (Albany, New York: SUNY Press, 1980), p. 5.

9. Jencks and Riesman, p. 502.

10. Arthur W. Chickering, *Education and Identity* (San Francisco: Jossey-Bass, 1969).

11. F. Thomas Clark, "The Non-traditional Setting," in *Designing Teaching Improvement Programs* (Berkley, CA: Pacific Soundings Press, 1978), pp. 163–206.

12. Gerald Grant and David Riesman, *The Perpetual Dream* (Chicago: University of Chicago Press, 1978), p. 358.

13. Judith Fage and Roger Mills, "Student-Tutor Feedback in the Open University," *Open Learning* (November 1986): 44–46.

14. Murray M. Horowitz, *Brooklyn College: The First Half-Century* (New York: Brooklyn College Press, 1981), pp.169–170.

15. Grant and Riesman, p. 360.

16. Clark, "The Non-traditional setting."

Chapter 11

Institutionalizing Innovation

Innovation and institutionalization seem to be antithetical processes. The one makes new, the other makes the new old. Yet in the introduction I stressed the two minds of the university, at once protective of its traditions and practices and at the same time seeking new knowledge, new audiences, and structures. Initially, of course, even the slightest proposal for educational change encounters the sturdy rampart-like rigidity of skepticism and tradition. Even after acceptance, a promising new program will be only an ornamental appendage to an existing college or university. Such a tenuous position within an organizational structure limits its claim to permanent budgetary allocations for staff, facilities, library books, and equipment. Most often a new program is expected to pay its own way rather than share the subsidy available to core university programs. Under such conditions, an innovation which has flourished in response to an emerging market demand declines rapidly when that demand lags. In other cases an innovation is so identified with a particular founder that it cannot survive the loss of that individual's influence. As a result of changing conditions, an innovative program in the university may either slowly wither or be subject to abrupt termination.

But some innovations do succeed and prevail. These innovations, not necessarily superior in concept or quality to those that fail, succeed because they find a vital place in an institutional structure. Why some innovations find a stable place while others do not is difficult to assess.

One way to analyze why and how some innovations "take" might be to reflect on institutional choices. From the first days of a new experiment, important, determining, and often irreversible choices are made. These early choices give shape to a new program, and they also set in motion other patterns which govern subsequent choices. To a considerable extent these choices also help to put in place what David Riesman calls an institution's "saga" and what Thomas Peters calls "culture and shared values."[1]

Two excellent examples for the purpose of case study are the Open University of the United Kingdom (BOU) and Empire State College of the State University of New York (ESC). I select these two cases for several reasons. Both experiments have operated successfully for twenty years and have gained wide recognition. They have achieved relatively stable places within their respective environments and have earned public and institutional support. Although BOU is not American, its early influence upon American reform in the late 1960s and early 1970s was considerable. Both BOU and ESC serve students over large geographical areas and employ the resources of other academic institutions, so their impact goes considerably beyond their own immediate structure.

Most significantly, both institutions have been efforts quite consistently and boldly determined to grapple with much larger cultural and socio-economic issues which have confronted their societies. Both, for example, focused on the student in new ways, recognizing that in much of higher learning the student had become invisible. Both were innovations in the process of learning as well, and this is the most difficult form of innovation to institutionalize. Innovation in *content*, so long as it fits within accepted constructs and paradigms, is expected, accepted, and integrated. But innovation in *process* brings resistance and tension, forces confrontation between the traditional and the new.

Finally, as the founding president of Empire State College, I took part in these choices, seldom with the analytic aftersight described here. With no models to follow, our educational instincts and intuitive sense were frequently the only guide. We did watch the Open University, however, noting its experiences and successes as it evolved from the earliest days. I find this a useful way, then, to think about how innovation can become organizationally stable. Thus a consideration of key choices made in the development of these two educational programs can provide solid clues as to how these new degree-granting entities became institutionalized, forward-looking models for a changing higher education structure.

Most basic, of course, was the choice of *a clear educational purpose, or mission*. For both the British Open University and Empire State College that purpose, simply put, was to provide alternative paths to a higher education for students unable or unwilling to pursue formal study through a campus classroom. During the late 1960s there was wide social and political recognition that a great many perfectly capable individuals were not able to connect with the existing educational system. For both BOU and ESC, inventing a wholly alternative academic program and delivery system of creditable quality for these off-campus students presented a distinctive challenge. It required a series of unique choices regarding the nature of the curriculum, the character of the faculty, the structure of the administration, and the methods by which the institutions would relate to the student.

State University of New York's chancellor, Ernest L. Boyer, said at the time of Empire State College's creation, "the university of tomorrow will be more like a public library than a private club, not a place of confinement but a point of departure, a place of renewal, a staging ground for learning."[2] As president, I emphasized in my investiture address that ESC "incorporated student views at the point where it matters most—in the design of each individual's education." Such an approach, I said, "impels us to seek alternatives that will demonstrate that individual learning and mass education need not be contradictory."[3] From the very beginning, then, Boyer and I expressed a dual mission for the college: not only to increase accessibility to students of all ages but also to extend and improve American higher education through focus on the individual student.

Professor Walter Perry, now Lord Perry of Walton, became the first vice chancellor of the British Open University in 1968.[4] He was not an educational theorist by training, but a pharmacologist, then vice principal of the University of Edinburgh, who "had never been interested in adult education... knew nothing of educational technology... [and] was wholly ignorant of the new developments in educational theory and philosophy that were challenging established patterns and practices."[5] Clearly this founder did not match, at least at the time of his appointment, the familiar model of an innovator or educational reformer. Yet Perry quickly grasped the prevailing climate in Britain. For some years public support had been mounting for expanded opportunities for school leavers and for adults who wished to continue their studies. Several proposals for addressing the problem yielded, in 1963, the concept for a National Extension College and, in the same year, an election campaign pledge by the new Labor government to create a "University of the Air" by linking higher education with the BBC. Within a short time Harold Wilson's call for a "University of the Air" was paralleled by Governor Nelson Rockefeller's support for SUNY's proposed "University of the Air" in New York (Chapter 9).

Neither of these early plans resembled closely the subsequent form of the Open University or Empire State College. But they were important conceptual and political antecedents which expressed the larger social need for alternative and more egalitarian approaches to education. And for both institutions, they provided an inheritance of a clearly defined mission that would set the direction for the future. Both institutions shared another important characteristic from the beginning: they sought to improve not only access through new instructional delivery systems, but the quality of teaching and learning for those students as well. Consider, therefore, ten choices for change.

1. Institutional independence
2. Collaboration with others
3. Geographic outreach
4. Planning versus operation
5. Role of faculty
6. Status of faculty
7. Nature of academic program
8. Initial capital priorities
9. Administrative structure
10. Academic standards and quality

1. *The British Open University and Empire State College were established as independent institutions.* Jennie Lee, a member of Parliament and undersecretary of state for education and science, established a parliamentary committee whose white paper of February 1966 essentially outlined Britain's "University of the Air." She apparently decided from the first that the new organization "would be a an independent university, offering its own degrees, ...and offering an opportunity to all, without any entrance qualification."[6] Later, she and the planning committee, which included as its chair the future BOU pro-chancellor, Sir Peter Venables, "rejected any idea of a consortium of universities acting as an examining and organising body." The Open University was conceived as having its own faculties and was granted a Royal Charter, with all of the rights and responsibilities which that autonomy implied for all British universities.

In New York, Empire State College was also planned as a completely separate unit within the multicampus SUNY system. It was a recommendation made courageously by Chancellor Boyer, a decision endorsed by the SUNY Board of Trustees on January 27, 1971 and shortly thereafter confirmed by the Board of Regents and Governor Rockefeller through the statewide master planning procedure. This action established "...a non-residential degree-granting college...within the State University of New York...[which would] under its own administrative organization, draw upon the resources of the entire university to devise new patterns of independent study and flexible approaches to learning thereby providing accessibility for young people and adults for whom an off-campus individualized pattern will be more effective...."[7] That decision was of the most fundamental importance. From the beginning, Empire State College was established not as an evening division or extension program, not a school, not even as an office within the SUNY central administration, but as a college. As a college, Empire State had the authority to define its own academic program and to recommend degree candidates directly to the SUNY board.

It would be difficult to overemphasize this not entirely obvious choice for independence. In fact, for the majority of new programs founded in that highly experimental period, a different choice was made. In 1971, for example, the California State University system created the "Consortium," or "Thousand Mile Campus," which, as the name implies, was a coordinating office located within a central administration, subject to the university-wide senate and the academic policies of each of nineteen campuses. The educational mandate for the Consortium grew out of the same concerns which led to the founding of BOU and ESC. But the Consortium was linked to a statewide and multicampus governance structure. Although the California Consortium offered much needed and unique programs to students, it never fully realized its enormous potential. In 1989, the Consortium was terminated, its few successful programs assigned to participating campuses.

Similarly, the University-Without-Walls, Sam Baskin's innovative creation at the Union for Experimenting Universities and Colleges (Chapter 8) was a consortium of some twenty prominent universities and colleges, each with its independent UWW educational unit and academic policies. But today only a few of those very creative and promising UWW units remain in operation. While it may be politically and economically easier to initiate, it seems that the consortium concept presents some problems which undermine organizational stability and success.

Early in 1971, one of the candidates for the presidency of Empire State College proposed that the new institution become, in fact, a federation of units, each located on an existing SUNY campus and operated by local administration and faculty. Such a plan was attractive indeed, for it promised to provide both immediate faculty and campus-based resources for students, as well as more easy acceptance and endorsement of the new concept. Fortunately, in retrospect, neither the planning committee nor the chancellor recommended that pattern in New York State. Empire State College gained its autonomy.

Of course establishing such autonomy required the creation of governing and advisory boards of recognized stature. The BOU planning committee included such luminaries as Sir Eric Ashby, Professor Asa Briggs, Lord Fulton, and Sir Peter Venables. For ESC, Governor Rockefeller named an outstanding council of public citizens headed by a New York attorney, Elliot H. Goodwin, and Chancellor Boyer appointed a panel of distinguished SUNY professors to guide and advise ESC's early planning.

Significant external endorsement was also an important aid to acceptance of a separate institution. McGeorge Bundy, president of the Ford Foundation, was very keen on exploring the use of television as a medium of instruction, and his interest ultimately led both Ford and the Carnegie Corporation to provide substantial grants to initiate ESC's development. Such powerful endorsements gave the new college much more than dollars. They accorded significant external credibility to the new venture.

Choice of location also fostered the perception of independence. BOU was located neither in London nor on the premises of the British Broadcasting Company, but rather accepted the invitation to locate in a new town on the periphery of Greater London called, appropriately, Milton Keynes. The coordinating location for ESC was intentionally located in the small town of Saratoga Springs, forty miles away from the center of political power and activity in Albany. Independence, as well as the motivation for these new institutions to stand on their own legs, was aided by removing them promptly from the proximity of the British education ministry or the SUNY headquarters.

2. A second key choice was that *these institutions would be collaborators, not competitors* within their existing contexts. Both sought to emphasize an interdependence of forces and resources. Empire State College was charged by the SUNY trustees to "build upon the strengths and resources" of the largest single university system in the world. State University of New York had recently developed new systemwide policies which improved service to the student, irrespective of specific campus matriculation. Among these new policies were (1) the expectation that students could cross-register for courses among campuses, (2) that students could transfer predictably and routinely from lower-division community colleges to upper-division senior colleges, and (3) that the libraries and other educational services of all campuses were open for the use of all citizens of the state. So this policy of university-wide cooperation was naturally imbedded in the ESC concept. It left ESC to focus on the individual student's needs and to find ways to bring to that student supporting resources, wherever they might be identified. It also meant that ESC could work easily with other SUNY colleges in developing these new approaches, new educational alternatives, helping everyone to serve non-resident students more effectively. Collaboration, not competition, was a fundamental choice.

The Open University, in much the same sense, would need to rely not only on the considerable capabilities of the British Broadcasting Company but on the faculties and facilities of the other educational institutions. Clearly BOU's intention was to transcend the limits of a single university faculty and to draw upon the richness of international cultural and scientific knowledge. And pressures in the United Kingdom augured for a distribution of labor for the new concept. Lord Briggs, for example, thought that, in setting up the University of the Air, additional financial support should be directed to organizations already serving adult students. In any event, "the new organisation should not be centralised in any sense, but should depend . . . on full consultation with local bodies."[8] BOU's plan envisioned that students would attend summer residential schools. This required complex arrangements for facilities at many universities and colleges throughout the UK. Cooperation also involved arrangements for the numerous part-time tutors and counsellors who were needed to assist students in moving through BOU courses. These part-timers were to be located in each region of the UK, easily accessible to students, and were to be drafted from the full-time permanent staffs of other institutions. So, like ESC, the new delivery model really presupposed academic collaboration rather than competition. BOU even went one step further to ensure that it was not viewed as a competitor—it restricted admission to adults over 21 years of age.

3. A third key choice was that Empire State College and the British Open University must be, as their names implied, respectively, *a statewide college and a national university with no other arbitrary geographic boundaries*. ESC was to serve a population base of nearly 18 million persons, while BOU reached 55 million British citizens. In New York, less than 10 percent of the adult population held a four-year college degree in 1971, while in Britain the comparable group was still smaller. Boyer said, "The new system must ... permit each student to study what he wants, when he wants it, and at a place convenient to him." If students could not come to a campus, then the college must be prepared and empowered to go to the student, wherever in New York State or the United Kingdom that student might be. The founders of BOU often spoke picturesquely of serving those who lived at the most remote of British outposts—"in a lighthouse on the Orkney Islands." From the first, BOU established twelve (now thirteen) regional centers, with over 200 smaller study centers encompassing all of the United Kingdom. OU was not to be English, Irish, Welsh, or Scottish, but British!

The territorial principle was challenged in two early instances at ESC. The first occurred when the planning committee invited an external panel of distinguished experts to critique the initial plan. One member of the visiting group, a regent from Syracuse protective of local institutions, endorsed the plan with enthusiasm, but added, "of course, ESC will not locate in Syracuse!" The second challenge to statewide operation was raised, quite understandably, by the New York State Division of the Budget. While DOB expressed strong support for the new concept, it wanted to fund only a single "pilot center," probably in Albany, so that the concept could be tested and proven before a larger commitment was made. ESC argued strongly that such a geographically limited pilot would undermine the efficacy of the extended university concept itself. Although the immediate result was an agreement to fund only two regional centers, ESC also gained the concession that, unlike other SUNY residential colleges, it would not be required to seek separate approval for each new service site as the college expanded to meet its statewide goal. Even as centers opened at Albany and New York City in September 1971, plans were under way for additional centers in Rochester and Long Island. By 1975, at some risk of spreading its limited resources too thinly, Empire State was established in twenty locations, a reasonably effective statewide presence. And by 1980 the college operated through over forty locations.

4. A fourth choice was *to begin operations almost immediately*. The principle was to develop flexible institutions that could adapt and change based upon practice, experience, and ongoing practitioner research. Planning avoided an abstract, theoretical model. If students were to be the fulcrum of these institutions, then the new structure would need to be shaped *with* students. In hindsight, this created many short-term logistical and administrative problems for both ESC and BOU. But subsequent events proved that the choice to move ahead was right on the money. During the 1960s other new colleges, such as SUNY's campus at Old Westbury or California's at Santa Cruz, opened their doors but only after planning periods of up to four years. Delay was distinctly counterproductive and many of these well-considered new programs dissolved in disagreement and disorganization during the academic upheavals of the late 1960s. By 1970, the prevailing mindset was against a lengthy, costly, and sometimes querulous planning period.

ESC took a rapid plunge into actual operation, enrolling the first students barely five months after its first public announcement. As it turned out, a major statewide budget crisis hit New York State in fall 1971, just as ESC began. Had ESC not already been operational, the subsequent freeze in hiring would have postponed its opening. And had that delay lasted until 1973, odds are that the new college would never have started.

BOU had barely more than eighteen months to set up its elaborate network and create an entire curriculum. Dean John Ferguson noted that "the first group [of faculty] appointed were in post in the second half of 1969. The decision was taken to admit the first students in January, 1971. We knew that we could do with a more leisured run-in. But expectations had been aroused, and undue delay would be frustrating for students and stultifying for us." But the political choice was even more telling: "the Conservative victory of 1970 was already a clear prophecy. Unless the University was securely established, there was a distinct possibility that it might be disestablished."[9] For BOU, a dramatic change of government and a national postal strike occurred just as all was in readiness to begin. A choice to delay at that time might well have terminated the whole enterprise.

5. A fifth key choice had to do with *the structure and role of the faculty* (Chapter 10). Here BOU and ESC faced similar tasks of reaching off-campus students with an instructional network which could also assure high-quality education. But each pursued a quite different path, responsive to the needs of its particular constituency.

BOU created six entirely new faculties,[10] whose members were quartered at the Milton Keynes campus. These faculties had a singular responsibility, and, except for some summer residency lectures, they were not teaching in the traditional sense. Rather, organized into development teams, these scholars created, from whole cloth, multidisciplinary instructional course packages in print and video. These packages included not only the texts and guides for direct instruction but year-end student examinations as well. The teaching role included no direct contact with students. Vice Chancellor Perry said, "if the whole concept of teaching at a distance, of home-based study, of working in isolation, was valid, then we must dispense with face-to-face teaching. We must put faith in the idea that it was possible for students to achieve the same level of education without a significant face-to-face element."[11]

At ESC several optional approaches were considered. The notion of a full-time administrative staff to coordinate the occasional use of full-time faculty from other SUNY institutions was speedily rejected. And the notion that a small number of full-time faculty could coordinate and monitor legions of part-time adjuncts seemed only likely to perpetuate the tradition of third-rate off-campus learning for third-class students. Equally unsatisfactory at ESC was the British Open University option of a full-time resident faculty devoted to course development, with part-time study tutors in the field. ESC did actually experiment briefly with a BOU-model development faculty but soon discovered that, given the educational culture of New York State and the students' expectations, a fixed curriculum, developed centrally but offered wholly from afar by correspondence, was not likely to work very well. Empire State College opted for its own full-time resident faculty, who would be assigned to regional learning centers across the state to act as mentors to individual students. This created a balanced distribution of authority and responsibility across the entire state. It avoided the creation of a class structure within the college. Faculty were to have responsibility both to a regional center and to a college-wide academic area of study group, to both a regional as well as a collegewide committee and governance structure.

But while both ESC and BOU ultimately chose quite different faculty structures, neither could easily devolve into the departmental structure common to the traditional university. In both cases, the choice of innovative models for the organization of faculty was one of the most significant factors in their successful institutionalization.

6. Yet while both chose to create a distinctly non-traditional faculty structure, BOU and ESC also chose to *create true university faculties, with all of the criteria, expectations, and practices which that commanded* in the traditional university. Although additional criteria would be called for, faculty needed to hold the credentials and scholarly excellence expected for all university faculty. This choice was as vital for success as the non-traditional model. At ESC the actual day-to-day function of the faculty mentor, as he or she is called, was worked out over several years. Much discussion occurred around the "role of the mentor." Early debates centered on whether the mentor should be drawn from the ranks of trained counsellors or scholars from the academic disciplines of traditional departments and graduate schools. Was it possible to find mentors who were committed to wearing the two hats of both academic advisor and scholar? Finally, should this new role carry faculty status within SUNY, or should it be an administrative position? Although the *mentor* role was distinctly new and different, not really comparable either to traditional definitions of the professoriate or to administration, ESC, after considerable debate, was persuaded that the faculty's professional success would depend heavily on its identification within SUNY, and beyond, in the teaching faculty role.

At BOU many expected those faculty who opted to join the new venture to be "the rag, tag and bobtail of the academic profession. Nothing did more to establish the credibility of the Open University . . . than the quantity and quality of the applicants for these first posts."[12] Although these faculty did bring to BOU a somewhat wider range of experience and academic breadth than was typical of a new university lecturer and although they had idealized expectations for teaching, learning, and university governance, nonetheless they did bring as well the expectation that they would bear the full responsibilities and privileges of a university faculty.

A closely related sixth choice, then, was to opt for faculty rank, tenure, and centrality in the academic governance process. It was a choice made by very few of the new non-traditional programs. In making this choice, these two highly innovative institutions ensured that the focus of external interest would be on the substance of the academic program rather than deflected by a perceived devaluation of the professoriate. It was not an easy choice at ESC, for traditional tenure was viewed by some as the single most deadening aspect of the traditional college. As an issue which generated a lot of early tension at ESC, it reveals the kind of give-and-take which those who attempt change should anticipate between established conventions and innovative practices.

7. *Distinctiveness of academic program* was a seventh key decision. Although process was the overriding innovation, the substance of learning was also deeply affected. At ESC no one doubted that the curriculum would be an individual one, initiated by a single student with mentor guidance—Socratic dialogue—with approval by a faculty committee. By this educational strategy, the student gained tremendous leverage on the nature of his or her academic program, while the faculty retained its traditional corporate responsibility to set and approve curricula and to recommend students for degrees upon successful completion.

But the issue of what institutional limits would be placed upon the student's choice of study was at first left unresolved. Originally ESC expected that it could draw upon any academic resource from within SUNY in designing a program for a single student. But this open-ended individual curriculum posed a dilemma for SUNY and for the State Education Department (SED), both of which were required by law to review specific and highly detailed college curricula and to authorize or *register* each curriculum *before* it could be publicly offered. It was logistically impossible, not to say illegal, for SED to approve individually designed curricula after the fact. Some colleges were approved to offer individualized majors, but these were within tightly defined study areas. But at ESC the requirement for external prior approval of an individual curriculum seemed an unworkable plan.

Empire State College proposed a compromise solution: *broadly defined areas of study*, within or across which individual degree programs could be designed. The faculty for each Area of Study group was asked to create guidelines to provide a consistent basis for review and approval of individual degree programs across the college. Most of the broad areas of the Arts and Sciences could be accomodated in this way; a limited number of professional areas, such as Educational Studies, Business and Management, Labor Studies, and Allied Health, were also included. This organization of the academic offerings of the college provided a structure which enabled ESC to meet the State Education Department's accreditation requirements. It also helped clarify the college's program for outsiders. Most important, because it guided faculty mentors in understanding the possibilities for an individual student's curriculum, the college maintained its unique capability to design responsive degree programs for individual students. While the decision to create these area of study guidelines was highly controversial at the time, its durability in institutionalizing a central characteristic of the ESC program has been proved.

For BOU the curriculum problem was quite different. British university students traditionally *read* in a specific faculty or discipline, and, after three years of such preparation, they take comprehensive examinations for the baccalaureate. But this traditional process actually intersected poorly with the interests and needs of those students over the age of 21 whom the BOU wished to serve. Moreover, since most of the students were expected to study part-time, shorter segments for study and evaluation seemed likely to increase motivation through more frequent feedback. What BOU created, then, was the choice of study within a faculty, but only after completing two full courses in foundation, or multidisciplinary and interdisciplinary general education courses.[13] BOU chose, in this way, to respond both to the wide cultural interests of adults and to the possible lack of grounding in general or secondary education among its clientele.

In Britain, the BOU approach was most unusual and very innovative. It offered a solution for adult students to the tight traditional pattern of British education. In New York, ESC responded creatively to what was then a widely perceived condition of curricular confusion at traditional universities. ESC's choice was to offer a new and individualized path to organizing the curriculum.

8. As the result of their differing approaches to curriculum, BOU and ESC also diverged significantly in early choices about where to allocate capital investment funds. But each made a choice which proved responsive and appropriate for its particular cultural milieu. For ESC the eighth key choice was to *invest resources neither in hardware nor in curriculum development, but in people.* For BOU, the choice was to *invest resources in academically sophisticated, pedagogically engaging, and aesthetically attractive course materials* (written, of course, by people), supplemented by broadcast quality television segments for the BBC.

As obvious as these choices may seem today, the circumstances of 1970 offered other possible approaches. For one thing, the SUNY University of the Air and a closely related independent study program had received major dollar investments during the late 1960s. Research studies, which found these programs limited in effectiveness, reported that what those programs required for future success was a clearly defined set of courses leading to a degree goal and an improved student support system. SUNY had made an enormous investment at every residential campus in technological facilities and staff for instruction. So it is not surprising that many observers and supporters of the concept believed that ESC would play a major role in advancing educational television and programmed media instruction in New York State.

But ESC made a different choice. Its early planners believed that investments in courseware and facilities designed without evidence of student need and without consideration for student motivation would be but a refinement of notions already shown wanting in the United States. Therefore ESC sought to create an educational structure which directly interacted with the students first and which could then make available to them *any instructional resource* needed to facilitate their study. ESC did not reject useful resources but decided, at least until the need was demonstrated, that it would invest its limited dollars in faculty and a strong support network rather than costly and inflexible media courses.

On the other hand, BOU's capital investment in such courses is by now legendary. Never before had a university conceived and designed such superior and elegant print-based courses for home study. Over seventy full courses were created within the first five years, designed by course teams of ten to fifteen or more scholars and instructional specialists from BOU and other universities and with costly television and radio segments for each unit. It was a wise choice that proved especially appropriate for acceptance within the British university tradition. The courses demonstrated a rich fare of academic substance, and student achievement was verified through national course examinations, a widely understood process for evaluation.

9. Most other new programs of the 1960s and 1970s skimped in the provision of an adequate support and management structure. Consistent with the ethos of that time, structure, hierarchy, and clear organization were not favorite topics among innovative academics. But because BOU and ESC needed to provide their academic programs at considerable distances, through *de*centralized service locations, the ninth choice for both was a *centralized administrative organization, with highly accountable regional structures given clearly delegated tasks.*

ESC planned *a traditional central administration, accompanied by innovative regional structures close to the faculty and students.* Each regional center was to be a microcosm of the college as a whole. Eschewing departmental organization by separate academic disciplines, ESC devised a wellbalanced interdisciplinary model. Each center was small enough to maintain close academic and personal relationships among faculty and students but large enough to offer students a range of ideas, resources, and approaches. As regional centers became larger, they spawned new units to afford access to students in new areas of the state. In time, some of those units were spun off and became new regional centers. How could highly individual teaching and learning occur in what was expected to become a very large public college? The answer, ESC thought, was the replicability of small regional learning centers, with strong centralized coordination.

The centralized administrative and academic structures of BOU were extended and elaborated *by an intricate, carefully thought-out system for student interaction, support, advice, and monitoring.* For example, admissions involves a prescreening of applications in an otherwise open admissions process. There are followup orientation sessions, "getting started" packets, all of which precede the student's actual start of study by many months. During this waiting period, the student can elect to pursue many special study-skill courses offered by non-BOU collaborators.

But the core of the BOU delivery system is the Regional Center and its network of dozens of small Study Centers close to students. Usually each of the faculties maintains a full-time Staff Tutor at the Regional Center. In turn, the Staff Tutors employ large numbers of part-time study tutors, who meet with the students as needed, offer seminars to help them pursue particular courses, and mark students' written assignments. In addition, the regional center employs full-time Senior Counsellors, who in turn manage a number of part-time counsellors at the study centers. Not infrequently in practice, the part-time study tutors and counsellors are the same person, especially for foundation-level courses, thereby uniting the academic and advisory functions. These key persons provide the essential human face in the educational process.

Another way BOU adjusts its program is in response to the special needs of handicapped students. For example, examinations are individualized for place-bound or otherwise handicapped persons, tutorials are arranged for such students, and as the result, there seems to be a high level of such demand in the system. The system is also adjusted to work with prisoners as well. For both institutions, the capability to manage very complex and widely dispersed organizational activities is made possible by innovative initial choices about structure and management.

10. As a tenth choice, BOU and ESC insisted from the outset that *academic quality be a central concern*. Although each had academic opponents who resisted the new institutions for largely political and territorial reasons, some thoughtful people believed quite honestly that these off-campus approaches simply could not produce high-quality learning. Yet the conscious choice to emphasize academic quality set both institutions on a path which ultimately led appraisals of their work away from the stereotypes typically associated with off-campus programs in the academic mindset.

Unlike the wide variation that exists in the definition of the liberal arts degree in the United States, the definition of the B.A. is rather set in Britain. The BOU planning committee and vice chancellor had very good reasons, therefore, for setting as a goal the creation of an academic program as demanding as that of the traditional university. But, as Vice Chancellor Perry expressed it, "could equivalence in the status of the degree be achieved without falling into the old trap of designing a degree primarily to suit the scholars?"[14] The problem was even more difficult to solve since there was also the expectation that students would be admitted to study without an entrance qualification. Many students had learning and skill deficiencies and found the academic expectations presented by the very demanding foundation courses difficult to meet. But, at the least, BOU wanted students to have the opportunity to demonstrate what they could achieve. The foundation courses, then, were designed to engage students at whatever their initial levels of preparation might be and move them forward step by step, *gradus ad parnassum*, to be able to handle the more advanced expectations of the second-and third-level courses. By the completion of the program, however, all graduates were expected to have demonstrated a level of attainment comparable to that of university graduates elsewhere.

ESC, with no single prepared set of course materials for all students, held that individual student initiative and one-of-a-kind degree programs, including a hard look at a student's previous achievements, would not diminish the quality of learning but would strengthen it. ESC's individual curriculum defined clear expectations of students and provided detailed evaluation and feedback. The faculty mentor, supported by a faculty review committee, had to define clearly a program for each student, embodying the meaning of college-level study and credit. Consequently Empire State College was never a "do-your-own-thing" program. It was never unstructured but rather *uniquely* structured for the individual. Some referred to the college program as "an honors program for adults," an unintended result but one descriptive of the difficulty of the college's program. The college early gained a reputation for academic excellence and high student achievement.

It is noteworthy that these two institutions began, in theory, from opposite poles with respect to their orientation to the student. BOU posited an ideal curriculum for all students then planned how to deliver it. ESC began with the individual student's curriculum, then considered how to create the common resources and courses which might serve these diverse needs. For BOU, the study center with its intricately responsive capabilities provided the necessary human element in the delivery network. Conversely, ESC created a new faculty, The Center for Distance Learning, which provided a significant body of academically first-rate course materials for individual student use. Two solutions to a common problem.

These ten choices were critical in enabling these two pioneering institutions to become well established in the higher education structures of their respective nations. BOU currently enrolls nearly 125,000 students, is approaching its 100,000th graduate, and annually awards about 7,000 degrees. ESC enrolls about 6,500 students and has over 16,000 graduates.

BOU has become the most admired model for the development of distance learning institutions across the world. With distance learning the most dynamic and rapidly growing approach to higher education in much of the Third World[15], as well as in such populous nations as China and the Soviet Union, the BOU represents to the English-speaking world a contemporary, if benign, educational analogue to the political and economic importance of the nineteenth-century British Empire.

The international impact of ESC has been less dramatic, for its basic teaching/learning strategy requires a rich regional educational network and infrastructure, a condition not widely found in much of the world. Nonetheless, the ESC model is increasingly recognized as institutions find the need to introduce student/teacher/counsellor interactions to improve student progress. Even so, the highly individualized approach, which places a very heavy intellectual and emotional demand on the faculty mentors, is more in keeping with a characteristic American value which emphasizes the individual and his or her development.

ESC's demonstrated success in working with off-campus and adult learners is respected in the United States. But respect so far has not lead to its becoming a statewide model for an alternative which could provide academic planning and advisement, assessment of prior learning and student competency, and direct study through a variety of instructional modes including television and computer technology. Yet given the need for the university to reach out to new populations—to business, industry and labor—it is again time to consider the advantages of modes such as those offered by BOU and ESC. Especially in states with growing populations, such as California where new universities are on the drawing boards, shouldn't the possibility of one statewide institution offering these options be an important consideration? Wouldn't such an institution focus especially on the new possibilities for use of media and technology in educational instruction and outreach? Whatever the future holds, Empire State College continues to extend the historic pattern of educational outreach, a pattern for which American higher education is most noted in the world.

NOTES

1. Thomas J. Peters and Robert H. Waterman, Jr., *In Search of Excellence* (New York: Harper & Row, 1982), p. 26.
2. Ernest L. Boyer, from a memorandum to the SUNY Board of Trustees, January 27, 1971, providing background for the resolution creating Empire State College.
3. September 5, 1972, Saratoga Springs, NY.
4. Officially January 1, 1969.
5. Walter Perry, *The Open University* (San Francisco: Jossey-Bass, 1977), p. xv.
6. Perry, p.13.
7. The minutes of the SUNY Board of Trustees, January 27, 1971.
8. Perry, p.23.
9. John Ferguson, *The Open University From Within* (New York: NYU Press, 1976), p. 25.
10. Arts, Social Science, Educational Studies, Science, Mathematics, and Technology.
11. Perry, p. 65.
12. Ferguson, p. 35.
13. A full BOU course is roughly the equivalent of an American semester program, or 15–18 Carnegie credits. Six full courses are required for graduation (approximately three years equivalent), eight courses for an honors degree.
14. Perry, p. 54.
15. Hundreds of thousands of students are now enrolled in open and distance learning universities in such nations as India, Pakistan, Costa Rica, Spain, Venezuela, South Africa, Thailand, Sri Lanka, Italy, Norway, Australia, Canada, Nigeria, and Kenya.

Chapter 12

Financing Innovation

No issue impedes innovation more consistently than the matter of finances. Any initiative must have newly available financial resources to support the time of people who are assigned to the new tasks. Inevitably the money requirement, probably more tellingly than ideological issues, elicits resistance or outright opposition to change in an established organization or system. This chapter examines financial problems which affect innovation in higher education and offers recommendations which may alleviate them. It assumes that a novel program is to be developed within an existing structure.

Peter Drucker, in his volume *Innovation and Entrepreneurship*, stresses that "the entrepreneurial, the new, has to be organized separately from the old and existing."[1] If Drucker's structural condition for innovation is to be met, funds must be reallocated from ongoing programs to new ones. This condition forces managers of ongoing programs into immediate conflict over resources. In such competition, these managers find reasons to undermine the new program. Typical arguments are that the innovation is unneeded, is in conflict with institutional goals, or is unlikely to achieve the expectations set for it. Such competition often provides an occasion for latent conflicts to surface among individuals within an organization. As a consequence, whether or not the new program is established within an existing structure or, as Drucker proposes, separately, if an underlying problem is budget, it will surface quickly.

Frank Newman, president of the Education Commission of the States and principal author of the "Newman" report, described the situation in broad strokes in this way: "Higher education almost always at first resists change and inclusiveness. It resisted," he says, "the Land-Grant College Act; many argued vehemently against the G.I. Bill; others opposed the creation of community colleges; and the core university labored for years to keep adult students out of the mainstream." He goes on, "At first [higher education] said, 'this is an unwarranted intrusion on our autonomy.' Then we opined, 'it won't work.' Then we cried, 'but it costs too much.' But in the end, when the new change was irresistable, we turned around and claimed credit for the change."[2]

In fact, most of the sweeping innovations of the post-World War II period were supported by the addition of new funds rather than the reallocation of existing funds. Because the financial pie for all of higher education expanded rapidly, many new ideas, worthwhile or not, were able to be tried during that expansive era. Huge increases in tuition revenues, received from the rapidly growing student bodies, brought additional disposable income to old and new institutions, both public and private. Expanding federal financial aid programs ensured that a widening group of students could apply to college and be able to pay and that institutions could also gradually increase student fees without negatively affecting applications. Direct state appropriations for higher education provided new funds, often indiscriminately, for program expansion, new facilities in new locations, and new academic programs. As a consequence, the separation and dedication of funds for the new was a relatively easy matter for aggressive administrators. Older programs could be well supported even while new marginal funds were allocated to innovation.[3] Many of the innovations described in Part Two of this volume were made possible by a constantly expanding fiscal base.

Eleemosynary institutions also provided a major impetus to innovation. In the period after 1950, several very large foundations emerged as major forces for change. In earlier times wealthy individuals established entire institutions as expressions of personal philanthropy and perhaps vanity. Often the cost of naming a college was surprisingly modest by today's standards. Leland Stanford gave his name to one of the great institutions of America for a relatively small sum. But today, the grand personal gesture of institutional founding is rarely possible. Even the largest personal gifts in these times only build a building or endow a professorial chair. There are significant exceptions, such as Walter Annenberg's School of Communications at the University of Pennsylvania and his more recent grant of $150 million in support of the "electronic university" concept.

But recently philanthropy has been more likely to come from foundation boards of directors than from single benefactors. The shift of personal philanthropy to foundation boards of directors also shifted grant making away from endowing institutions and chairs and toward the support of innovation. As a matter of policy, foundations defined social goals worthy of encouragement, then funded proposals for programs which might advance those goals. Foundations perceived institutions of higher education as places where certain social changes might be stimulated in a responsible way. The principle was almost always the same: foundation dollars provided a separate budget for a new educational project, sometimes with matching university funds. Typically such grants were spread over several years, during which time the efficacy of the new program might be demonstrated. By the conclusion of the grant, the expectation was that a successful program would have been integrated into the regular college budget. Since in those post-war years of rapid growth new marginal funds could almost always be found, the process often worked well. When federal government grants became a significant force for new initiatives in the mid-1960s, the principle was usually the same. The private foundation model was substantially adopted by the U.S. Department of Education in 1973 with the formation of its own quasi-foundation, The Fund For The Improvement of Postsecondary Education (FIPSE), complete with its own board of directors for grant making.

Corporate giving to higher education has also been substantial, although its innovative grants have tended to go to well-established schools of business or engineering rather than more experimental colleges. Corporate matching gifts, correlated with the personal giving of employees, are more widely distributed across institutions, but such matching funds are usually dedicated to a college's general purpose annual budget, not to new and innovative projects.

A major foundation grant initiated Sam Baskin's University-Without-Walls. SUNY's Empire State College, the New York Regent's Degree Program, and Steven Bailey's Syracuse-based Five County Consortium, all began with Alan Pifer's single commitment of funds from the Carnegie Corporation, with parallel grants from the Ford Foundation. Carnegie has also supported CAEL, CLEP, and IUC with an extended series of grants. The Mellon and Kellogg Foundations made significant grants, supporting innovations in curriculum and adult education. Kellogg has almost wholly funded the development of New York and California external degrees in nursing. Exxon and Sloan have made important contributions. And FIPSE has supported literally hundreds of small, new colleges and programs which have offered new opportunities for access to higher education. Minnesota Metropolitan, Boricua in New York, Beacon in Washington and Boston, the College for Human Services (New York), and the University of Mid-America, all exemplify highly innovative outcomes of external grants.

Foundations, government agencies, and, to a lesser extent, corporations have functioned as powerful levers for change and innovation in higher education. With the writing of a check they have made possible an entire new venture or experiment. The benign fallout from those grants in terms of permanent change is more difficult to assess. Probably it is true that most grant-supported ventures ultimately wither or are terminated. Nonetheless, much change in the American university, from service to new clienteles, to improvements in curriculum and the enrichment of scholarly research, can be attributed to external grants.

Today's innovator faces significantly greater financial problems than did his or her predecessor of even a decade ago. Once upon a time, knight-errant program developers and directors could test the lists or pursue quests to capture prizes from foundations, corporations, and agencies. But the contemporary scene for external grants has turned more cautious. Although several foundations continue to approve grants to improve access for bypassed students, significant funds once available to higher education have been shifted to support the urgent problems of the lower schools and other priority areas of national need. Moreover, federal grants, except for traditional research and student financial aids, have all but dried up.

Second, incremental internal funding available to an earlier generation is no longer available. The prevailing ethos of campus budgeting is more likely to feature retrenchment than growth, and conservation of what is rather than initiation of what may be. Finding new and separate funds to finance innovation is very difficult.

A third financial problem for innovation is that new programs are almost invariably expected to "float on their own bottoms." Definition of such self-support includes generating an operating surplus which must be returned to the core institution. After all, such programs utilize academic space, utilities, library, and a variety of other central administrative services. For "regular" or core programs, such overhead costs are most generally subsidized, either from the core administrative appropriation in the case of a public university or, in the case of an independent college, from endowment earnings, from research grant indirect cost recovery, or from a portion of the tuition revenue.

The requirement to be financially self-supporting is most common in the area of continuing education or extension, by all odds the most innovative segment in higher education. In this area one finds the most dependable and predictable development of new program ideas. But student tuition revenue is practically the only source available to support such innovation. That source, too, is rarely available to continuing education administrators; only the most aggressive and imaginative among them can persuade institutional budget officers and academic vice presidents of the value of a particular new program activity.

Cyril O. Houle, a thoughtful and consistently articulate scholar of adult and continuing education in its many forms, notes the strong link that university extension holds with the larger public community. These interactions force the extension division of a university, to a degree not experienced in "core programs of the institution," to be especially responsive to new clienteles, to emerging curricular needs, and to community organizations. But these programs, almost without exception, are required at least to break even and, preferably, to provide a source of basic institutional funding.[4] How much is left over for novelty and originality? Only the most progressive of senior administrators gives policy and practical support to encourage extension activity.

A fourth problem is the pervasive paradox created by the balance of external and internal funding sources. Just as soon as a program gains the stability accorded by regular budget appropriation, the stimulation for innovation ceases. When a new program becomes sufficiently successful, it may become part of the core institutional program. When this happens, then regular funding provides a level of support which more adequately represents the support-per-student throughout the college. It also means that the population served by the now successful new program has become an accepted part of the central mission of the college.

But when this institutionalization occurs, the innovation itself may be undermined. The very motivations which caused individuals to reach out for separate funding in support of their educational ideas sometimes diminish rapidly. Their interest in creating the new, or in attracting new users, can be co-opted by the need to maintain the now-established. Moreover, as part of the regular budget, a "cap" is sometimes placed on program size, thereby limiting responsiveness to student demand. Now most of the creative or entrepreneurial energy is redirected toward the annual need to enter the budgetary lists, in one arm a lance to pluck off new morsels of budgetary meat, in the other a shield to fend off the lances of competing departments.

It remains a paradox for the financing of innovation that the need to attract new and separate funds for program support both stimulates innovation and entrepreneurship, but the constant uncertainty of external funds makes innovative success highly risky. Conversely, if institutional funds are readily available and ensured into the future, the entrepreneurial capacity to innovate is often lost.

A fifth problem in the financing of innovation is that a new idea sometimes gains financial support by claiming that it will reduce costs. Many new programs in the 1970s featured this claim. While in many cases cost reduction has, in fact, been achieved, this expectation has placed an additional, and often unnecessary, burden of proof on the innovation.

An interesting example which shows how cost factors are affected by large size is gained through an examination of 1986 budget data of the British Open University. During that year BOU served 66,191 undergraduate students, a level essentially stable for the preceding five years. In addition, 1,028 students were matriculated for higher degrees, and non-credit continuing education served about 17,000 persons. In 1986, BOU awarded degrees to 6,391 graduates, bringing its cumulative alumni body to 82,426. These students were served by a full-time staff (faculty, administrators, and support) numbering 2,733 and a part-time staff of 5,083.

Clearly the cost of such a number of staff and students is not inconsequential. But it is remarkable how inexpensive BOU actually is when compared to traditional institutions. The total BOU operating budget in 1986 was £83,417,000, of which £60,000,000 was a direct government grant through the University Awards Council, another £18,791,000 came in student fees, and £5,000 was miscellaneous income. The operating cost comes to approximately £1,260 per student. Since the majority of students are one-half time, the cost per FTE student was about £2,500 (approximately U.S. $4,000).

Comparing BOU and ESC costs to those of an American institution is a perilous exercise. For one thing, there are "invisible" costs, such as library acquisitions and usage, student health care facilities, student housing, 24-hour security, and building and ground maintenance, which are not generally reflected in BOU or ESC costs, although cooperating colleges and universities may bear a marginal additional cost if they serve external students. In some cases, of course, BOU and ESC contract with these institutions for certain services. Given this important exception, however, 1986 data for Empire State College appears to be remarkably close to that of BOU. The total operating (non-capital) budget was $12,696,000. This budget supported 3,791 FTE students at a cost of $3,349 per student. At ESC and BOU, the overall annual cost per student is significantly less than the cost of educating a traditional residential student. Nonetheless, costs are not minor and serve to illustrate the lack of wisdom in promising that an innovation will provide a particularly inexpensive education while encouraging high standards of academic quality.

What remains true both of BOU and ESC (and of some other similar activities) is that they represent, to some extent, an incremental use of established resources in higher education. Both use other university staff and services (in addition to their own) in providing the range of services to their students. This *collaborative* approach to providing educational resources to students is not usually reported and, to my knowledge, never calculated in overall cost-per-student. On the other hand, if one takes a macroeconomic view, such resource sharing increases the efficiency of educational plant and people supported by a state or system.

With these problems and observations in mind, I suggest here some guidelines about financing innovation for the practitioner:

1. DO seek extramural funding from foundations, corporations, unions, and government to help you initiate and develop a new program. Because program development costs would otherwise need to be amortized through an unacceptably high student tuition fee, upfront assistance with these costs can be very important to later success.

There are other good reasons to seek external support. An external grant can significantly improve your credibility in the inevitable budgetary competition within a university. Significant external endorsement, expressed through solid financial backing, is an irreplaceable asset. Moreover, the process of writing a grant proposal will force you to be clear about the purposes of the new program and to define with some precision the likely costs of developing and operating it. Finally, granting agencies can sometimes share ideas with you, helping to broaden the purpose and appeal of the proposal.

2. DO share the external grant proposal widely within the university, and solicit suggestions from administrators *and* faculty. This process may help you to write a clearer proposal, and it can demystify your program for significant others. They may not help you very much, but their increased understanding will be important later.

3. DO build as much "program development" cost and as little "operating" cost as possible into the proposal. The start-up of any new program is costly in terms of human time, trial and error. Assume from the outset that it will take longer than you estimate to get started and to build a paying clientele in the educational marketplace.

4. DO apply for your institution's own funds for innovation. Some colleges do provide internally generated funds systematically for program renewal and innovation. Just as it is common to make available travel and research grants to individual faculty with new and promising projects, so a few institutions provide funds, usually in the form of released time, to support program innovation. Others even set aside a small percentage of the total budget each year for the purpose of reallocation in support of promising new programs. Although this is often a politically difficult process, a systematic and fair program of this kind will usually gain collegewide faculty approval, at least in principle. If only 1 percent or 2 percent of a budget is shifted each year, within a decade significant change can occur. The most recent widely found example is the dramatic shift of faculty positions away from established departments in the arts and sciences to departments of business.

5. DO be realistic and cautious in promising that the innovation will bring significant cost savings to an institution. Few new programs meet the goals established for them at the outset, and failure to fulfill such promises will be held against you later.

6. DO plan to fund the ongoing operating costs of your new program from regular sources, such as tuition revenues or public FTE appropriations, at the earliest possible date.

7. DO set the fees charged to students or to their sponsoring organization at a level which adequately recognizes the full real costs of the program, including such institution-wide costs as facilities, utilities, library, administration, and, if not covered by an external grant initially, the amortization of program development costs. Failure to take these real costs into account at the beginning can seldom be rectified at a later date. A marginally funded program leads to problems of marginal quality. From the outset you will be required to use scanty staff and severely curtail program content and richness. If you cannot charge the customer a price which reflects the true cost, reconsider whether or not the program should be offered.

8. DO include, when possible, the enrollments of the new program within the budgeted FTE enrollment, if you are in a public institution. This will assist the institution in meeting its required enrollment goals and will help to ensure that the public subsidy normally available to core programs is at least partially available to support new programs. But because existing university enrollments may already meet the budgeted goal, it may not be possible at the outset to fund the new program from general university funds. If this is the case, try to negotiate a schedule for transition to regular funding in the future.

9. DO try to find an optimum balance between regular program budget support and marginal external revenue. Since all public institutions function under a funding and enrollment cap of one sort or another, it may ultimately be necessary to maintain your new program on "soft" or unbudgeted revenue from grants, contracts, or student fees. Except in the most generous of external contracts, however, these off-budget revenue sources will not meet the true cost of education. Finding a combination of external and internal funding will provide for program stability and quality, on the one hand, and for program flexibility, experimentation, and growth, on the other. Given the paradox described earlier, it is the least perilous course between endless entrepreneurship and stifling security.

10. DO urge that the university administration set aside reserve funds from any surplus operating income that you generate so as to support the capital development of new program ideas. Without such capital investment, especially in a time when significant grants from foundations are increasingly difficult to achieve, innovation will wither.

The capacity to attract or generate new funds is essential to successful innovation. Although program success is contingent upon many factors, including academic excellence, continued demand for services, and collegial political acceptance or tolerance, most innovation collapses from budgetary inadequacy. Attention to these guidelines can make a difference.

NOTES

1. Peter F. Drucker, *Innovation and Entrepreneurship: Practices and Principles* (New York: Harper & Row, 1985), p. 161.
2. As quoted from a speech by Frank Newman at a joint session of AASCU and NA-SULGC, November 10, 1986, Phoenix, AZ.
3. As an example of the scale of this increase, State University of New York added 3,666 faculty and staff positions in 1965, 3,663 in 1966, and 2,508 in 1967. Proportionately that scale of increase was duplicated across the nation.
4. Cyril O. Houle, *The External Degree* (San Francisco: Jossey-Bass, 1973).

Chapter 13

Innovation: Leadership and Management

Throughout this volume educational leaders have been identified with particular innovative achievements. Without strong leadership, few new ideas are converted to experimental programs, and virtually none last or become institutionalized. Most critical to creators of new enterprises in higher education is dealing with the large number of overlapping authorities or even the near absence of defined responsibility to make decisions.

Any reforms in higher education which focus upon the changing needs of the widely diverse populations will sooner or later run into the established controls of the college or university (i.e., the academic department, the collegewide curriculum committee, specialized and regional accreditation bodies). Since many of the issues which underlie innovation cannot fail to confront these stabilizing if sometimes cautious structures, questions of implementation are not merely academic.

Here are some observations and practical suggestions that grow out of my many years of experience in attempting new things. These may be helpful in planning and carrying out innovation.

THREE PRINCIPLES

Several general principles are important as one approaches the implementation of any program within higher education. First, strategies for implementing any reform hang to a considerable degree upon wider judgments about the sponsors of the reform. Almost nothing of substantial educational reform has originated entirely from *within* the university itself. While the specific plans may emerge from a university committee or an educational entrepreneur, the *impetus* for reform comes almost wholly from without the university,[1] and the means of implementation are themselves propelled by interactions with and resources from the external world. Although those of us who earn our livelihood within the ivy-covered walls would like to believe

150

that we exercise august autonomy in planning and implementing reform, the fact of the matter is more complex. This reality is critical to the question of how one should implement changes in the decades ahead.

The example of the concept of "lifelong learning," a term that entered our lexicon almost a generation ago, is useful.[2] Bringing together a number of usually contending forces in education and government, lifelong learning caught the fancy of the media for a time. There were several concentrated efforts to weld the concept firmly to postsecondary education law. Unfortunately such law was never funded and remains today a wishful title, fully hopeful and totally dead. The concept of lifelong learning failed then, not because it was a bad idea or inherently unworthy. It failed because it was an abstract concept, generated largely from within higher education and lacking sufficient social, political, and economic support to breathe life into the idea. The limited political support which did exist produced legislation, but that support was insufficient to gain needed funding when played against other more compelling political priorities. Today the idea of lifelong learning is emerging once again but from different quarters, and with new alliances outside the university. These new sponsors and supporters change the possibilities as to where implementation can occur, which institutions might be expected to carry the action, which individuals will benefit, and who will pay the bill.

A second principle is that, without clear direction, few new ideas are converted into experimental programs, and virtually none last or become institutionalized. Leadership is essential, and it means more than saying, "Follow me!" Of course the leader must convey to others an intelligent concept or new solution to a problem and give clear direction. But strong leadership must also include skillful management. A leader of innovation must also be a *manager of change*, setting goals, organizing and supervising academic and administrative staff, collecting good information, sniffing changing environmental conditions, making daily judgements and decisions, and, above all, monitoring progress and establishing measures of accountability. The leader's role, paradoxically enough, is to bring innovation into acceptance in the establishment.

The evidence is quite clear. The odds are against translating a good innovative idea into a new operating program. The likelihood of the new program bringing about lasting organizational change is even more remote. Most ideas advanced by thoughtful, creative, and well-meaning people are rejected out-of-hand by the organization to which they are so generously offered. Education, in particular, has always had more than its fair share of unconsummated good creative ideas for innovation and reform. One suspects that some of the early reformers, such as George Ticknor at Harvard, James Marsh at the University of Vermont, or Phillip Lindsley of the University of Nashville, often unsuccessful in gaining acceptance of their interesting educational ideas, may have lacked the essential management skills which were required in order to institutionalize their ideas.

This is worth thinking about. Sometimes an idea is poorly presented, lacking the clarity of expression which might allow for wide understanding; often an idea is so clouded in abstractions that its applicability in solving immediate organizational problems is overlooked; more often, the good idea is born in the midst of struggle and lacks the political polish necessary to persuade skeptics. Whatever the situation, good ideas seldom affect an organization significantly unless they are incorporated as part of a comprehensive management strategy. Systematically applied management can improve the odds for successful organizational change and improvement.

Certainly it is true that ideas can and do succeed as ideas. The political theories of John Stuart Mill, the economic theories of Karl Marx, and the educational ideas of John Dewey were both descriptive and prescriptive and gained many adherents. But such theories do not become reality until they are taken up by some innovating leader who is able to persuade an organization to implement them.

Yet full testing to see whether an idea might become a successful innovation requires embodiment of the idea and its implicit values within a particular educational institution. One can look for a long time at the prevailing mode of teaching and learning at our colleges and universities today before discovering a college or a department that consciously, systematically, or eagerly implements an innovative learning strategy. Relatively few individuals act upon the existing and widely available research about effective teaching and learning. The mere existence of a good idea does not, in itself, bring about organizational change.

Peter F. Drucker, whose concepts of management have been applied not only in the corporate sector but in a variety of other non-profit and voluntary sectors as well, proposes instead a "discipline of innovation." Innovation is not something best left to the dreamers and blue-sky planners, but incorporated as a "new technology" called "entrepreneurial management."[3] The new technology calls for the systematic application of knowledge to human work, a process which ought to be, but seldom is, central to the activity of a university. Innovation is easily misunderstood as a process of interest only to inventors, entrepreneurs, and "idea" people. Limited to those few eccentrics who are usually thought to be unable to implement their creations in a practical manner, innovation is easily relegated to a peripheral, barely tolerated place in an organization. "Entrepreneurs," says Drucker, "see change as the norm and as healthy,"[4] but real organizational innovation involves much more. Drucker calls it "innovative management." Leadership *and* management are seen as two sides of the same activity, both essential to successful innovation.

A third principle is that timing is everything. In his *The Structure of Scientific Revolutions*, Thomas Kuhn describes long periods when there are dominant theories in any given scientific field that seem generally satisfactory to practitioners in those fields.[5] These theories provide a framework within which experimentation can occur. But gradually, through experimentation, evidence is gathered which disconfirms the dominant theories, at least in part. Because it is at variance with received theory, the evidence is ignored at first, or even suppressed. But eventually the weight of it becomes so great that a restructuring of theory is required.

By analogy in higher education, institutional structures might correspond to theory, and student and societal needs to experimental findings. After a period of institutional restructuring, there is a long period in which practitioners in the field believe that all the legitimate needs of students can be and will be accomodated within the system. Only gradually does it begin to dawn on them that there are needs which will never be well accomodated. Pressure for systematic change develops gradually. There is always the danger that if restructuring is delayed too long, existing institutional forms might be abandoned rather than remodeled. In such a circumstance, higher education, like astrology, alchemy, or phrenology in an earlier era, might survive in vestigial form but cease to play the pivotol role it has played in recent decades.[6] There is a right time to introduce change.

The 1960s and 1970s lend credence to this analysis and suggest the importance of the right time for starting an innovation. In 1971, Alan Pifer, with unusual insight, said, "The desire for reform today ... is by no means a monopoly of extremists, know-nothings, and political opportunists. There is a growing body of responsible, well-informed people, both on and off campus, who believe the time has come for substantial changes in higher education. Among these people there is now a questioning of once sacrosanct practices, a new willingness to experiment, a new interest in the needs of students, and a new concern for those who have been denied access to higher education or have not been reached by the conventional system ... It is to the basic nature of the relationship between higher education and society that reform of a fundamental character must be directed."[7]

CHARACTERISTICS OF THE INNOVATIVE MANAGER

For the innovative manager, knowledge of and an appreciation for concepts such as those advanced by Drucker and Kuhn can form a solid basis for understanding the contexts within which his or her work can be promoted. The innovative manager also requires a strong philosophic and conceptual grasp of higher learning. Without such a trenchant understanding of education's purposes, scholarly and academic culture and substance, teaching and learning theory and application, and the social and political environment, the innovator cannot assess value or validity. Andrew White, Charles Eliot, Robert Hutchins, and Walter Perry had this understanding.

The requirement that significant and lasting innovation be built upon a strong conceptual foundation also suggests that innovation seldom appears in a vacuum. Nothing comes from nothing. There is a pattern of genesis, incubation, and diffusion for innovation. There is a linked chain of successful leaders, a clear lineage between those who have been most effective. Important families of such leadership may develop in one institution. Seminal innovators attract creative and energetic individuals to their staff, and, after gaining experience in a kind of mentor relationship, these individuals move on to energize programs elsewhere.

Perhaps the best example of this kind of human idea-chain begins with Alexander Meiklejohn at Wisconsin around 1930, flows to Robert Hutchins at Chicago in the 1940s, then outward to colleges such as St. John's, Shimer, Brooklyn, and Berkeley through leaders who had wrestled deeply with the great books approach. Scott Buchanan worked under Robert Hutchins at Chicago before going to St. John's, and he had been a student in a Meiklejohn seminar at Amherst. Joseph Tussman worked with Hutchins before initiating the Experimental College at Berkeley. Harry Gideonse, an export from the Chicago faculty and president of Brooklyn College from 1939 to 1966, did not bring the great books to New York, but his experience with innovation spawned a number of new and special academic programs for adults, experiments with the core curriculum, exemption from required courses through examination, and in student counseling. Gideonse expressed what innovative leaders required: a president should be "an educator in his own right."[8] Goddard College under its founding president, Royce ("Tim") Pitkin, spawned a lineage of Arthur Chickering (professor at George Mason, VA), F. Thomas Clark (president of Rockland Community College, N.Y.), Jack Lindquist (former president of Goddard, VT), and Douglas Johnstone (dean at Empire State College, N.Y.). The New York Education Department has featured a succession of reformist commissioners, beginning with Algo Henderson (previously president of Antioch and subsequently founder of the Center for Higher Education at Michigan), James Allen, Ewald Nyquist, Gordon Ambach, and Donald Nolan(currently deputy commissioner and, earlier, first director of the Regents College). At this writing, no less than thirteen academics associated in the 1970s with the founding or development of Empire State College have moved to positions of primary leadership at another institution of higher education. Thus a penchant for successful innovation appears to radiate through a chain of reformers, individuals, even disciples, who have been nurtured by an older innovator, have thought deeply and philosophically about the purposes and modes of higher learning, and have made important personal commitments to the social environment within which that learning occurs.

MANAGEMENT PROBLEMS OF INNOVATION

Arthur Levine, until recently president of Bradford College, Massachusetts, defines failure in innovation as a "premature decline in the planned level of impact or influence of an innovation on the host organization. Failure," he says, "results from an innovation's decline in profitability, compatibility, or both."[9] These two measures cover the most observable facets of innovative failure, but they result from causes that need analysis.

The most important of these is the problem of program definition. Some new programs, although based upon highly innovative ideas, are very poorly defined. For example, a number of new programs in the 1970s expressed as their basic academic mission some variation of "individual development and social change." While it is difficult to argue with such a possibly useful purpose, it is not so easy for teachers and students to know what it is they are supposed to do on Monday morning. The problem can be seen in this quotation from the institutional self-study of one innovative college, a college which has since failed:

> The institutionalization of this college's values, attitudes and goals has been a gradual process. Thus although today we consider the College a mature institution, its history and even its present attitudes somewhat resemble those of a "movement" organization. Not bound by a specific ideology, its community is drawn together by similar values and by a shared vision of what institutional education at its best might be.

In other instances, an innovation may be clearly but too narrowly defined. Most frequently, narrowness is the product of a single planner who imposes specific personal values on a new program. Sometimes rigid or narrowly defined innovations are the result of intense internal academic battles over key program principles or values, which, although well-defined and possibly admirable, may turn out to have a limited appeal to students at large. This kind of problem can be found in examples of curricular innovation described in Chapter 3.

Another way in which an innovation may be too narrowly defined is in the use of a single mode of instruction. Such "mono-modal" delivery systems as, for example, New York University's long televised "Sunrise Semester" may regularly attract a modest number of students who find the broadcast video mode manageable and its limitations (in this case schedule) not too restrictive. But an innovation of this kind does not allow the student to have other study options when needed, and so can become unresponsive to student needs. Unfortunately, many of the most interesting innovative programs of recent years, such as the elegant television courses offered by the Public Broadcasting Service (PBS) or the fascinating courses by computer assisted instruction (CAI) offered by Control Data Corporation's "Programmed Logic for Automatic Teaching" (PLATO), suffer from the problem of mono-modality. The result is that these quality innovations with high potential consistently fall short of their goals.

Still another frequently encountered problem is the failure to define and fix academic responsibility. As much as anything, this problem faced the staff of the Consortium of the California State University. As its name might imply, the consortium had no faculty which it could definitely call its own. Decisions about curricula and degree approval were reviewed by the University system senate, a body representing the faculties of the nineteen (at that time) campuses in the California system. Such division of academic authority and judgment placed a very heavy burden on the responsible administrators and may have been an important factor in the termination of the Consortium in 1989.

A serious economic problem can be the high cost of program maintenence. This problem has been especially difficult for distance learning programs which use film or video linked to expensively produced printed materials. Although the initial capital investment is often very high, such costs are frequently met by external grants. But the materials produced by these external grants usually have relatively short shelf life and must be revised or replaced on a regular schedule. Experience thus far shows it to be exceptional for annual operating budgets to assume the burden of such updating. At the British Open University, which had rather extraordinary capital funding for initial course development, the period of time originally planned for course replacement has been stretched out considerably. Moreover, for many courses the use of film has been reduced well below original expectations. Many of the other distance programs which use academic and technical teams for course development have returned to older methods of writing correspondence courses, asking one or two academics to author and edit a course.[10] While some of these courses seem adequate, reduced capital funding for course teams will have some effect on academic quality.

Problems of these kinds pose hurdles which are resistant to facile solution. Yet every successful innovative manager has surmounted these and others, sometimes intuitively, through strategies and principles which ought to be more understandable and therefore replicable. They are strategies which should be understood and acted upon systematically by every member of a program or institutional staff. I now turn to a set of strategies for the successful implementation of new ideas and programs.

STRATEGIES FOR THE INNOVATIVE MANAGER

1. *Frame your innovation clearly.* Successful innovation requires clear definition. Innovation in its natural state is chaotic. Be clear about the idea. An opportunistic adaptation which takes advantage of a short-term fad almost never has a clearly defined idea at its center. If you can't express it, it probably won't work. People have to understand.

2. *Know the meaning of learning.* Take time to understand something about how individuals learn—what works and what does not work with real students. It is surprising how many perfectly plausible proposals are advanced in the absence of such knowledge. Many of the costly failures might have been avoided had this caution been heeded by individuals and corporations active in instructional television and technology.

3. *Time your move carefully.* There are times when the ever-present impulse for modification, change, and innovation is freed from the customary restraints. Just as revolution occurs only in a time of crisis, when normal restraints are absent, so institutional receptivity to change varies from one year to another, from place to place, and even at different phases of the annual academic calendar. If the college agenda is full and key people are diverted in many directions, change will be difficult. If individuals are fresh, as is often the case early in a new term, rather than burdened by an onslaught of student papers and pressing lectures, attitudes may be more receptive. And although the summer recess might seem to provide a good time for uninterrupted consideration of a new program, decisions taken during that period may be viewed as administratively expedient and so resented by those who are not present.

4. *Don't be in a hurry.* Charles Eliot, who, among many things, brought the elective course system to Harvard, took most of the second half of the nineteenth century to bring it off. People need time to assess the advantages and obstacles presented by a new program or approach. Part of a good sense of timing is taking care to allow others the opportunity for reflection, reaction, and response to individual concerns. In the process you will also learn and have time to adapt to needed modifications.

5. *Analyze carefully the ways in which different constituencies will approach the innovation:* will it be welcome or seen as threatening? In communications about the change, emphasize continuity and benefits; de-emphasize the threats, even while acknowledging their reality when raised as a possible objection. Avoid iconoclastic attacks on the established or traditional. Sharp criticism will only make enemies and will not induce the unconverted to accept experimentation.

6. *Focus the discussion on the central purpose of the innovation.* Don't allow the debate to shift to peripheral issues. Use the discussion as a vehicle to educate others about the central issues and purposes, but take pains to avoid preaching. Hold attention to the need of framing innovation clearly.

7. *Select strong leaders who show traits of clarity in understanding and communication, can organize and implement work, have credibility with colleagues, and have previously exhibited pragmatic realism.* Try to build an administrative team that understands the principles of innovative management, and make sure they keep you informed regularly of the plans and efforts under way in their areas of accountability. Otherwise, some of these highly competent and dedicated people will agree with your strategy in principle, speak favorably in your meetings, and then often unintentionally may sabotage the effort in their daily activities. This may result from inexperience or may express passive aggression. Subordinates may be wary about change as it affects their own activities and will try to avoid "rocking the boat." They may underestimate the value of a new idea, citing all of the times "it has been tried before." They may overestimate the level of internal opposition. Changing their perception of the possibilities and style of innovative management as part of a new team is the first necessity.

8. *Acknowledge publicly those who attempt to implement new programs.* Recognize tangibly those who succeed. The corporate practice of awarding salary bonuses for strong performance is not usually exercised so directly in higher education. But to the extent that local practices allow, rewarding individuals is critical for innovative management. Such rewards may be monetary, but time, offered through leaves, re-assignments, and course reductions can sometimes be more valuable. It is also critical that such rewards be consistently offered as an announced institutional practice so as not to be perceived as a system of favoritism.

9. *Keep foremost in mind the importance of faculty.* Finding and keeping qualified and committed persons, as Joseph Tussman cited at Berkeley, is the most difficult aspect of innovation. Avoid above all the anti-faculty/anti-university piety. This is a dead end but a tempting alleyway for budget officers and free-wheeling administrators. David Riesman puts it nicely: Some reformers "try to change the teachers of the students." Others try to "do away with the teachers." Identify those faculty who are opinion leaders, who respond to persuasion, and involve them in the new project.

10. *Take care to involve faculty from a variety of academic departments or disciplines.* It is important not to allow your project to become isolated within a single department, especially if that department is primarily interested in teaching methodology. Every college has a few senior faculty who, more secure than their junior colleagues, may be interested in trying new ideas. Find out who these people are, work with them, and be open to newcomers.

11. *Define an educational niche built on real educational need, and remember that small size can be a real advantage.* One can find numerous examples of academic institutions or programs which have defined an educational niche based upon a single successful innovation. These institutions may continue to serve a modest, narrowly defined clientele over many years, gaining national visibility as a result. Just as single academic departments gain a distinguished reputation for outstanding scholarship, so certain programs which have created distinguished and innovative ways of teaching, and perhaps outstanding graduates, can be widely recognized.

For example, Alverno College in Milwaukee, which shifted its entire curriculum to a competency-based approach to a degree in 1973, is a national leader in this innovative method, yet enrolls only 1,500 students. Although the overall demand is small, sufficient numbers of interested and qualified students can be identified from year to year to support a fully staffed program for this purpose. Gallaudet College in the District of Columbia has gained a special reputation through service to hearing-impaired students. Although the potential student body is large, this college is highly selective in meeting the needs of a specialized clientele. Moreover, it has gained significant extramural financial support from the U.S. Department of Education and elsewhere. Within the United States, there are several such programs, and they appear to flourish so long as the overall size is kept small and academic clarity is maintained.

12. *The innovative manager is also aggressive in considering the impact of new ideas and innovations elsewhere which may affect the appeal or* *established niche of his or her program, as it matures.* In the words of Gerald Grant and David Riesman, "vigilant leadership" is especially important in innovating conditions.[11] Laissez-faire simply will not do. Many of the most creative people have found this out the hard way. Richard N. Foster, using terms more familiar to corporate management, argues that leaders of existing programs or institutions are always at a disadvantage at the encroachment of innovation. Invariably they underestimate the competition, fail to perceive quickly enough the emergence of a new process or technology, believe there will be adequate advance warning of problems, assume they know what the customers really want, and assume they will be able to react quickly if change becomes truly threatening. Foster concludes that the only defense to a surprise attack is realistic and regular assessment of available alternatives, detailed and timely measures of performance, awareness of the limits of an innovative technology, and an understanding that change has predictable cycles of growth and decay.[12]

13. *Finally, know when your leadership role is complete.* If you are temperamentally a "starter," not really sympathetic to the building process, *leave early*; if you can stick to it, think the idea important, have managed with a fair order of success, realize that your innovation is either (1) still vulnerable as innovation—and stay the course; —or (2) has been so overwhelmingly successful that it has become orthodox—and ask yourself whether your job is over!

THREE CODICILS

So much for practical strategies. I turn finally to three codicils worth keeping in mind. The first is that you will be required to exercise significant external activity around what some would call political matters.[13] Matters such as maintaining the confidence of your university or system superiors, and retaining the support of those who provide budget, whether the university fiscal officer, a government examiner, or a corporate training officer, will be absolutely critical. You will need to understand and resolve issues of program accreditation with external agencies in your state and with voluntary regional accrediting associations.[14] You will need to attract allies, friends who believe in the importance of your program. These new constituencies for the university—labor unions, corporations, non-profit and government agencies, all of whom now require education and training—will become important allies to you in explaining, forcefully, the need for your program. They provide the essential external validation without which real change within the university usually does not occur. They can actually help you to reassure your other constituencies, both internal and external, of the program's increasing value and acceptance. And you will need to press the external marketing of the program even as you remain alert to changing environments and other innovations which might render yours obsolete.

Codicil two is that you should be candid about the problems which the innovation may present. Especially important is candor about such tough issues as academic quality control, administrative feasibility, and logistics. Here is where your earlier commitment to measurable accountability will be important. After all, unanticipated problems are certain to develop, and your avoidance or glossing over of these issues will only reinforce doubters and critics. If your innovation requires use of emerging educational technologies, be careful not to promise more than you can deliver. Academics are highly suspicious about electronic gadgetry, which, unfortunately, has the embarassing tendency to malfunction just when your most persistent critic has agreed to try it with her best class. If your innovation rests upon a technology, be certain that it will work routinely and without sophisticated mechanical skills on the part of the user.

With codicil three, I conclude by noting, finally, that success in implementing new programs is not the exclusive license of particular institutions. As with an individual scholar's writing, one can easily become discouraged when grant proposals remain unfunded or carefully wrought writings remain unpublished by juried journals. So members of a faculty or staff will stop offering ideas for change and improvement if they are repeatedly rebuffed by institutional leaders. Innovative management requires that leaders remain open to ideas, offer planned and systemic ways to encourage ideas to be elaborated and tried, take extraordinary measures to minimize bureaucratic blockage and frustration, and find meaningful rewards for those who labor.

Attention to these strategies cannot guarantee the success of a particular innovation, for so much rides on the validity of the idea, the context for its trial, and the vagaries of external conditions and budgets. But, as Peter Drucker tells us, systematic attention to the management of innovation can substantially increase the odds for success. And the leader who combines these principles of innovative management with a profound understanding of American values of egalitarianism, pluralism, and individualism, will have already moved far along the road to success in purposeful innovation.

NOTES

1. Martin Kaplan, "The Wrong Solutin to the Right Problem," in James W. Hall (ed.), with Barbara L. Kevles, *In Opposition to Core Curriculum: Alternative Models for Undergraduate Education* (Westport, CT: Greenwood Press, 1982), pp. 3–12.
2. The term itself is reported to have ben coined by Professor Leon Richardson, dean of University Extension at Berkeley, in 1919.
3. Peter F. Drucker, *Innovation and Entrepreneurship*, pp. 11, 35.
4. Peter F. Drucker, *Ibid*, p. 27.
5. Thomas Kuhn, *The Structure of Scientific Revolutions* (Chicago: University of Chicago Press, 1962).

6. An idea advanced by John H. Jacobson in a memoradum to James Hall, May 19, 1986.

7. Alan Pifer, "The Responsibility for Reform in Higher Education," *1971 Annual Report of the Carnegie Corporation*, pp. 4–5.

8. Murray M. Horowitz, *Brooklyn College: The First Half-Century* (New York: Brooklyn College Press, 1981), pp. 46–50.

9. Arthur Levine, *Why Innovation Fails: The Institutionalization and Failure of Innovation in Higher Education* (Albany, SUNY Press, 1980), pp. 156–157.

10. See Peter Jarvis, "Models of Distance Education," *Bulletin of the International Council For Distance Education*, vol. 11 (May, 1986): 51–58.

11. Gerald Grant and David Riesman, *The Perpetual Dream* (Chicago: University of Chicago Press, 1978), p. 309.

12. Richard N. Foster, *Innovation: The Attacker's Advantage* (McKinsey & Co., 1986), as summarized in *Soundview Executive Book Summaries*, vol. 8, no. 12, part I (December 1986).

13. See also Gerald E. Sroufe, "Navigating the Political Waters of Nontraditional Program Leadership," *Educational Record*, vol. 68, no. 2 (Spring, 1987): 33–35.

14. James W. Hall, "Regional Accreditation and Nontraditional Colleges," *Journal of Higher Education*, vol. 50, no. 2 (March/April 1979): 171–177.

Conclusion

The years immediately before us, I argued earlier, are likely to witness one of the most aggressively innovative periods in American higher learning. I suggested a number of areas which should present the greatest opportunities for change and reform: the uses of educational technology and telecommunications systems, new faculty roles, adult continuing higher education, distance education in its many forms, services to underserved populations, and new approaches to collaboration with external, non-academic organizations.

Because I have been close to some of these new areas for innovation and, of course, intimately involved with Empire State College, my objectivity is somewhat colored. The reader will undoubtedly be able to correct for these excesses. I wrote this book because I believe that programs like the one I've had the privilege of leading can help our country function better as a democracy by enabling more people to gain a higher education.

Yet none of the areas for reform that I have talked about is likely to support significant and lasting innovation unless changes are rooted firmly in those values which have promoted and sustained American higher learning from its earliest days. Lasting and successful innovation must emerge out of real needs in the American social environment. For example, one such widely expressed need is *access* to education. Only needs like this, expressed widely and deeply within the population, can give rise to change, support new models, and provide sustenance for growth and development. We have seen how in the past interaction with and response to such needs and values has lead to sound, significant, and lasting change.

The first chapters traced the development and blooming of the American college and university—the spreading ivy—reminding us that its entire history can be understood as a continual process of outreach, greater inclusiveness, and elaboration of forms and programs. The gloriously pluralistic, if loosely defined, national structure has metamorphosed repeatedly to meet the wide range of individual and communal needs. Whenever a particular institution was unable to alter or adapt, or its leaders were unable to perceive the need for change and response, then new institutions sprang up to meet the need. The spread of denominational colleges, the coming of the land grants, the spawning of community colleges, the recurrent and persistent validity of continuing education, and the rapid recent growth of the corporate sector as an agent of higher learning are all expressions of the power of social need and cultural values to transform the old and to create the new.

Today such transformation should again be high on our agenda. Conditions are changing so dramatically that it is no longer clear whether or not colleges and universities, as they are now constituted, will respond with sufficient speed and clarity. Today our national social environment is lifting up a very different agenda for higher learning. Basic policy questions, like "Who needs to learn?" "When and at what level?" are joined by new ones: "Where should learning occur?" "How effective are our present approaches to learning?" "Could mastery learning change the rate of success?" "How can technological change influence, or even improve, the communication of information?" "How will the costs for these services be met?"

Unfortunately, such serious educational issues as these are almost never debated within the core of an academic institution—its academic departments. At that critical locus of power in the college, an insulated, confident professoriate resists external influences which threaten stability and tradition. Those few who perceive the need for change, or who attempt to alter the system, are denied tenure and promotion or leave the department in the naive expectation that as an administrator they can be more effective. At the institutional core, reform is very difficult, yet the university is now challenged to change more rapidly and more extensively than at any time in its history on this continent.

At the outset I spoke of the sea change in the way that our national life is being undertaken. Consider a few areas for which new solutions will be required. The area of access returns us to the questions of *Who should learn* and *when and where should they learn*? For a long time the great majority of students pursuing tertiary education have done so in ways other than at a four-year, full-time, traditional liberal arts college. As evidenced by the endless fingerstalls over *general* or *core* study in the liberal curriculum, the mythology of higher education in America simply hasn't caught up with this reality. This disjunction misleads current leaders and causes them to be blinded to the urgent needs for more fundamental reforms and new services.

For example, innovation is needed in extending service to underserved, and often underprepared, populations—those millions of people including immigrants from varied cultures, Hispanics, African-Americans, Native Americans, rural whites, the physically impaired. These are people that the nation needs for important social and economic purposes but who currently represent too small a proportion of those who enter and succeed in higher learning. Training, teachers, and technology—these three T's—are areas that could make a difference but will require the most urgent attention and ingenuity of our educational leaders and reformers.

Another example. The baby-boomer generation, the most favored group ever with respect to educational opportunity, remains significantly *undereducated* in terms of the future needs of our society. About 70 percent of this largest school cohort earned a school diploma. Only 50 percent of these graduates made their way to some form of postsecondary, tertiary education.

Finally, barely one half of those who entered college have earned associate or baccalaureate degrees. Thus from start to finish, less than 20 percent of the eligible young people who entered school from this largest single group of Americans hold a college degree. Therefore, even as we plan how to meet the educational needs for the newest college-age generation, it is important to recognize this large group of older, experienced, working, but undereducated people.

As the baby-boomer generation ages, it will experience an increasing need to continue to work, to prolong involvement with the workforce, to defer retirement. Not fully replaceable by the smaller generation of youthful workers, these greying folk will work longer and in better health than their parents. They will work both because they are urgently needed to fill the major employment gaps in the workforce and because they will want to work to meet personal expectations and income needs not covered by a relatively declining Social Security stipend.

Unfortunately for this already productive generation, the workplace is changing so rapidly that their current skills will be outmoded rapidly. In order to continue to work productively and to move forward in level of responsibility, these adult learners will require substantial, repeated, recurrent opportunities for learning and training. Colleges and universities, even while they extend themselves to meet the very demanding educational requirements of a much more diverse and educationally underprepared youthful group, may also need to reach out into the community, the workplace, and the home to provide high-quality, individually tailored, convenient continuing education opportunities for the older generation.

Because this is a sizable constituency, most colleges will want to become more interested in and attentive to the particular learning requirements and styles of older students. Because each adult arrives at the college door at a different stage of preparation for study, educators will need to strengthen educational planning and advisement to determine better the student's interests, needs, and capacities. As educators, we will have to find ways to capture the motivation of a student or to stimulate such motivation if it is weak. In so doing, we will recognize the different and bifurcated schedules of adults and arrange for learning to occur at times and places that are at least feasible, if not always convenient. We will devise new mechanisms to get learning resources—books, texts, references, examinations, and faculty feedback and evaluation—to where the student is located. Finally, we will focus much more consciously upon the purposes of the learning itself and design pedagogies which will nurture and elicit good learning from students.

Reaching outward in this way, although historically very much in the tradition of success for the American university, will require significant innovations in educational delivery. The undergraduate college will act more like today's community college than like the denominational liberal arts college of the past. In many ways, that community model will become the norm for undergraduate and other tertiary education. Although the research university and its graduate curricula will continue to be supported for other essential reasons, teaching will again become front and center in the undergraduate college.

This transformation will be aided by technology. Clearly technological change is going to be the most transitive predicate of change. Chapter 9, on the concept of an electronic university, described many of the capacities of new technology for educational use and reviewed some exemplary programs. Experimentation and demonstration projects now abound in academe. Not surprisingly, they have begun to penetrate the teaching/learning process, albeit timidly. Remarkably, even the immediately applicable possibilities for information transfer are poorly understood and minimally used. The external world's use of such technologies now runs far ahead of the university's use.

How can the university engage with these key domains of technological change: (1) problem solving, (2) information transfer, and (3) direct pedagogic interaction? Problem solving is increasingly used by individual researchers, especially in the areas of math, science, engineering, and a wide variety of design technologies. We assume that, like the important research matters that are solved as an ongoing part of academic research, these applications of technology will increase rapidly and become an important tool for all university research. In this domain, the university already works closely with external organizations in utilizing the most sophisticated software technology. The principal problem for universities has been in gaining sufficient funds to acquire, support, and rapidly update hardware and software.

Information transfer is still in its infancy. Important data bases for research are already maintained by professional organizations, most notably the medical, legal, and scientific fields, and are widely utilized in academic research. But general bibliographic and textual transfer for less specialized users is still largely unavailable. Although the technology now exists for storage and transmission of bibliography and whole texts via telecommunications, most university libraries are barely beyond the electronic card catalogue stage. Although this current level of progress adds convenience for students and faculty, it merely scratches the surface of possibility.

The third area, direct interactive pedagogic uses of technology, remains the uncharted frontier for higher education. Once upon a time, the nation's needs for well-educated people could be satisfied by sending a small proportion of its most academically talented youth (mostly male) away to four years of study. These students learned in an environment that gathered, at one place and at one time, all of the necessary books, facilities, and scholars. Since these valuable resources were limited, it was necessary as well to limit the number of students who might gather in that place at a given time. Scarcity provided an easy rationale for the university, secure behind its ivory towers, to relegate to a lower academic priority and status those who—because of conditions of age, academic preparation, physical handicap, work obligation, family responsibility, distance, or requirements for mobility—needed to study part-time, or in the evening, or at off-campus locations.

Today we know that meeting the workforce requirements of the nation, the needs of underserved populations, and that tapping the talents of the vast numbers of potential students who cannot come onto the campus regularly will require the university to reach out as never before, to find new ways to educate, to retrain and upgrade, and promote lifelong learning. Much of this will necessarily take place beyond the campus—in the community, the corporation, the union hall, the government agency, the home. But technology offers the promise to overcome scarcity, to open the boundaries of space, time, and cost that previously limited participation in higher education. Only through instructional use of technology can the university begin to contemplate such radically redefined services.

And as technology makes the *locus* of study less confined, more extended, the possibility of learning on a "global" campus becomes increasingly feasible. Even as I am writing, walls are literally tumbling down in many areas of the world. As new opportunity becomes possible, the need for increased access to education at every level will become urgent. Already the British and Dutch Open Universities have joined a European federation of distance learning institutions in anticipation of an integrated Europe in 1992. Because the costs of a technological infrastructure will exceed the fiscal capabilities of a single university, regional consortia and partnerships with state governments will be required. Such major investments, already begun or contemplated in many states, are necessary *before* widespread educational use is affordable. Fiber optic backbones, once in place, can transmit rapidly the necessary bibliographies, data bases, and texts needed for advanced learning at any location. But it will require a public and private investment beyond anything yet accomplished.

Can American higher education embrace and adapt such changes? Certainly it has over its three centuries, with extraordinary vigor and responsiveness. But the university's continued success in meeting the urgent demands of society will require substantial change, and soon. The history of educational institutions also tells us that rapid response has almost always required new structures. Such structures have not usually supplanted the old but, in the pluralistic tradition of America, have supplemented, gradually modified, or even enveloped the old. Such new structures are in the process of developing even now, but, not surprisingly, they are not generally recognized within academe. Partly this is so because it is difficult to think exogenously from within an existing college. For example, privatization of education has occurred rapidly, with corporate colleges[1] assuming roles once thought proper only at a non-profit institution. Reigning assumptions about behavior and practice are difficult to overcome, and budgets are always inadequate to purchase change (see Chapters 12 and 13).

Yet money *is* made available for those services that our society concludes are essential. Union contracts include newly negotiated major funds for members to upgrade their skills through tuition reimbursement. Government and industry are combining to fund basic literacy programs in cities where skilled employees are unavailable. Specific job-training courses attract combined funding strategies as well. Even already costly elementary and secondary ed-ucation may be accorded new funds when American society is convinced that a higher expectation for student performance is the only way for this nation to maintain its modernity. So new educational structures continue to appear and gain financial support, and gradually they become part of the rich fabric that is our national tapestry of education.

As the university enters these new collaborations and reaches out to meet expanding societal expectations, inevitably the question is raised whether the price of democratic access is lowered academic standards and quality. So often, throughout our history, the claim from those who have resisted the university's centrifugal desire to reach out and extend has been that, inevitably, quality would be lowered. Even so, outreach and extension have gone forward. Has quality been lowered? I would offer several observations in response to that important question.

At the apex of the American institutional pyramid, there is little doubt that the scholarly peaks of excellence achieved in some American colleges and universities are equal to or surpass those of any university in the world. Certainly the many undergraduates and graduate students who come to the United States to study attest to this fact. Yet most American colleges are not especially selective in admissions, and few are staffed with faculties banked with Nobel Laureates and widely published scholars. As reformers within these institutions attempt new approaches to outreach, they are obliged to answer the question of quality.

The most visible area for this debate is within the "traditional" curricu-lum. As new students, especially those with different cultural backgrounds, express interest in modified curricula, are standards of expectation necessar-ily lowered? For example, currently there is a recognition around the edges of the academic circle that the old measuring sticks for excellence which judged the visions and voices of white male writers may be less appropri-ate for the expressions of women and people of color. Does the inclusion of Womens' Studies dilute the curriculum by turning attention from classical texts? Does the new social history, which focuses less on documents and writ-ten texts and more on material artifacts of culture, weaken academic study? I think not. Rather, they challenge us to rethink what constitutes excellence. Measures of symmetry, climax, and denoument may be valued differently than fluidity and circularity. Indeed, as we reshape, for example, the core texts for American literature, it may be necessary to study less of Nathaniel Hawthorne and to include more of Charlotte Perkins Gilman. But while the content of what we require to be known will shift, surely we can still demand that our students think (reason, logic, synthesis) and communicate (debate, exercise human understanding and sensitivity, and apply knowledge) in the best possible way—excellently.[2]

Pluralism implies multiple indices of excellence. I put myself on the side of those who argue that the measure of the quality of an educational insti-tution must necessarily be what it makes possible for its students. Pluralism in America is the acceptance, the functional validity, not of a single mark of academic excellence but of many marks toward which individuals of differing talents and motivations might aspire. In these terms, the excellence of Oberlin College for one student might be matched functionally by the excellence of Rockland County Community College for another. Evidence of comparability is difficult to assemble but an important area for serious thinking.

Our nation requires high competence. Equally important, it requires wide aspiration toward that competence. A system that sets high, but attainable, goals and then gives students the opportunity, the support, and the individual flexibility to achieve them in a variety of ways cannot be considered inferior. In the final analysis, education *is* about the quality of the society itself.

How do we know when innovation succeeds? An earlier chapter presented a case study of how two experiments, the British Open University and Empire State College, became institutionalized. Does the fact of institutionalization mean that an innovation is successful? In another chapter I offered counsel to administrators and faculty about how to create, develop, and manage an innovative program. Does the implementation of an innovation, after facing and resolving all of the daunting conceptual, political, budgetary, and staffing problems, represent success?

A higher test of success would be whether or not the innovation *changed* higher education. Did the impact reach beyond the place and the moment of its own penumbra and lead others to new ways of teaching and learning? Did it offer new or better opportunity for substantial numbers of students? By this measure, a reliable evaluation of success may take decades to achieve. Yet in retrospect we can see the major American innovations that have been widely replicated: the land grant concept, the community college, the concept of financial aid based upon family income, the "open" university, and the wide acceptance of part-time students. These are aspects of American higher learning which are recognized throughout the world.

What is the effect of national economic conditions on educational experimentation? As a general observation, our history suggests that it is in periods of economic expansion that colleges and universities have been most willing to accept change. In periods of economic difficulty, perhaps when change is most needed, higher education becomes more defensive, less willing to support untested ventures.

Economic expansion produces the strong impetus for university outreach and extension, as corporations, unions, and government agencies seek expanded education and training for their employees. Conversely, we observe periodic upswings in the enrollment of non-traditional students *as the economy begins to soften*. So far it is not clear whether or not this indicates an increased level of personal anxiety among workers and potential job seekers. But in the years ahead, successful innovation will require a strong, expanding economy.

And when is an innovation no longer that? Certainly we no longer think of the Carnegie credit unit as an innovation. Nor would we today regard the community college as new. Continuing adult education, serving largely part-time commuting students, has been the most widely developed and replicated change within the American university since its first appearance just before this century began. Although vital continuing education programs continue to create new and adventuresome programs, isn't it time to agree that such university services are now in the mainstream of university activity? It may be that so long as an institution or program reaches out, responds to new challenges and needs, and is amenable to internal change, its innovative character is maintained.

Throughout I have stressed the positive role of individualism, pluralism, and egalitarianism as prodders of educational innovation in the past. But, under changing circumstances, even these underlying values may be, in themselves, insufficient. A much more difficult matter is whether or not these dominant American values will be as appropriate to a more complex world in the future. These values have their downside as well. Pluralism, as I have already suggested, is being replaced by multiculturalism, a more actively positive value in an increasingly complex world. Individualism has been critiqued recently by those committed to general education who argue that common learning and values which stress community and mutual interdependence are now needed in our curricula. Finally, egalitarian values in education are challenged by a world in which high competence and intense competition increasingly reward meritocracy and power.

But even with these reservations, I believe that the American values of egalitarianism, individualism, and pluralism, when pursued vigorously by creative leaders and visionary educators, have within them the capacity to awaken us from our national educational malaise and to carry forward what has been, and must yet again become, arguably the finest educational system in the world. If that happens, America will continue to lead the world in economic, humane, and spiritual strength into the next century. I am persuaded that *innovative* is not only the most consistent but the most necessary descriptor of American higher education. In that sense, the spreading ivy seems inevitable.

NOTES

1. Nell P. Eurich, *Corporate Classrooms: The Learning Business* (Princeton, N.J.: The Carnegie Foundation for the Advancement of Teaching, 1985).
2. A number of volumes are available that touch on this fundamental topic. One suggested is Leonard Freedman, *Quality in Continuing Education: Principles, Practices, and Standards for Colleges and Universities* (San Francisco: Jossey-Bass, 1987).

Index

P

Palmer, George Herbert, 78
Parker, Bernard, 95
Part-time students, 28, 69, 124, 169
   attrition rate of, 78
   categories of, 73
   financing problems of, 77
   growth in, 73–74
   needs and wants of, 75, 80
   services to, 74–75
Part-time teachers, 77
Peace Corps, 100
Perry, Lord Walter, 129, 134, 153
Peters, Thomas, 127
Philanthropy, private, 143–44
Physically handicapped students, 31,
   139
Pifer, Alan, 33, 85, 90, 153
Pitkin, Royce S. (Tim), 91, 121,
   154
PLATO (Programmed Logic for
   Automatic Teaching), 155
Plessey v. Ferguson, 53, 63
Pluralism, 11–13, 16, 23, 32, 60, 88,
   167, 169
   and adult students, 78
   resistance to, 65–66
Preceptorial teaching, 118
Princeton University, 118, 119
Prior learning, credit for, 93, 97. *See
   also* Experiential learning
Private two-year colleges, 52. *See also*
   Community colleges
Problem-solution-centered approach, 77
Professional schools, 10, 24, 72, 75,
   101
Program on Non-Collegiate Sponsored
   Instruction (PONSI), 84–85
Project LEARN, 79
Public Broadcasting Service, (PBS), 76,
   155
Pulling, Bruce, 114

Q

Queens College, 57

R

Radicalism, 32, 41, 44
Ramapo College, 41, 43
Read, Sr. Joel, 87
Reed College, 41
Regents College, 67, 86, 87, 107
Regents External Degree Program. *See*
   Regents College
Regulation, 12, 42, 65
Remedial courses, 54, 124
Report on Higher Education, 33. *See
   also* Newman Report
Residential colleges, 26, 32, 44, 52, 74,
   83, 108
Rhodes, Frank, 106
Riesman, David, 33, 37, 43, 46, 53, 87,
   121, 122, 125, 127, 158, 159
Rockefeller, John D., 3, 24
Rockefeller, Nelson, 129, 130, 131
Rockland County Community College,
   98, 154, 168
Rogers, Carl, 41, 42
Roger Williams College, 91
Roosevelt University, 72
Rosovsky, Henry, 119
Rudolph, Frederick, 19
Rush, Benjamin, 18

S

St. John's College, 40, 42, 154
Sangamon State University, 41
Santiago, Isaura, 64
Sarah Lawrence College, 96
School and Business Alliance, 57
School of Extended Learning (Central
   Michigan University), 80
Schwartz, Jacob, 105
SEEK (Search for Education, Elevation
   and Knowledge) program, 54
Self-support, 145
Separate but equal education, 53, 63
Separatism, 11
Servicemen's Adjustment Act of 1944
   and 1945, 49. *See also* G.I. Bill
Serviceman's Opportunity College, 85